Robert Hooke
and the
English Renaissance

A conjectural likeness of Robert Hooke, based on descriptions by John Aubrey and Richard Waller. (Drawing by Rachel Chapman.)

Robert Hooke
and the
English Renaissance

edited by

Paul Kent and Allan Chapman

GRACEWING

First published in 2005

Gracewing
2 Southern Avenue, Leominster
Herefordshire HR6 0QF

ISBN 0 85244 587 3

Typesetting by
Action Publishing Technology Ltd, Gloucester GL1 5SR

Printed in England by
Antony Rowe Ltd, Chippenham, Wiltshire

Contents

List of Illustrations   vii
Contributors   ix
Preface, *Sir Arnold Wolfendale F.R.S.*   xi
Acknowledgements   xii
The late Professor Edmund C. Hambly: an Appreciation   xiii

1   Robert Hooke: London's Leonardo   1
Edmund C. Hambly

2   Robert Hooke: the man and his ideas   8
Allan Chapman

3   Hooke's early life at Oxford   39
Paul W. Kent

4   Hooke and the Royal Society   65
Sir John Enderby F.R.S.

5   Hooke's concepts of the Earth in space   75
Ellen Tan Drake

6   Hooke's telescopic observations of Solar System bodies   95
Allan Chapman

7   The impact of Hooke's *Micrographia* and its influence
on microscopy   124
Gerard L'E. Turner

8   Springs, and Hooke's mechanical genius   146
     Allan A. Mills

9   The civic virtue of Robert Hooke   161
     Michael A. R. Cooper

     Index   187

Illustrations

Frontispiece   Robert Hooke
1.1   The dome of St Paul's cathedral   5
2.1   Freshwater Church, Isle of Wight, in 2003   10
2.2   Westminster School in the eighteenth century   13
3.1   A plan of the defensive earthworks built around Oxford   43
3.2   Christ Church, Oxford, in Commonwealth times   44
3.3   Thomas Willis, Hooke's teacher at Christ Church   48
3.4   Beam Hall, Oxford   50
3.5   Honourable Robert Boyle   55
3.6   Deep Hall, Oxford   56
3.7   Christ Church, Oxford, in 1673   59
3.8   Wadham College, Oxford   61
5.1   The relationships among continental drift, polar wandering
and biogeography   87
6.1   Hooke's drawing of his 60-foot telescope   99
6.2   Hooke's observations of Mars, Jupiter and Saturn   102
6.3   The lunar crater Hipparchus   107
6.4   Hooke's observations of the comet of 1677   110
7.1   Hooke's microscope   126
7.2   The trade card of John Yarwell   128
7.3   The syllabus devised by William Whiston   130
7.4   Hooke: 'Of a Flea'   131
7.5   Hooke: 'Of a Louse'   132
7.6   Hooke: 'Of the Eyes and Head of a drone-Fly'   133
7.7   Hooke: 'Of the Point of a sharp small Needle'   135
7.8   Adams: foot and head of a fly   138
7.9   Adams: flea and louse   139
7.10 Adams: infusoria   140

7.11	Ledermüller: sting of a bee and point of a needle	141
7.12	Wood: *Common Objects of the Microscope*	142
7.13	Daguerreotype photomicrographic plates made by J. B. L. Foucault	143
8.1	Hooke: investigation of a helical spring	148
8.2	Hooke: application of a spiral spring	149
8.3	Diagrammatic graph of stress *versus* strain for a typical spring steel wire	151
8.4	The basic constant-tension spring	154
8.5	The basic constant-tension spring used as a book-end	156
8.6	One of a range of constant-tension springs manufactured by Spiroflex Ltd	156
8.7	Principle of the constant-force retraction spring	157
8.8	Constant-tension motor, type A	158
8.9	Constant-tension motor, type B	158
9.1	John Wilkins as Bishop of Chester	163
9.2	John Wilkins' *Mathematicall Magick*	165
9.3	Measurements made by Boyle and Hooke of levels of mercury	169
9.4	Published data from the J-tube experiments which led to Boyle's Law	170
9.5	One of Hooke's certificates for ground compulsorily purchased	174
9.6	Survey lines used for mapping the rebuilt City of London	180
9.7	An English semicircle and tripod	181
9.8	Detail of Ogilby and Morgan's map of the rebuilt City of London	183

Contributors

Sir Arnold Wolfendale F.R.S.	Former Astronomer Royal; Emeritus Professor of Physics, Durham University
Edmund C. Hambly	Former President of the Institution of Civil Engineers and of the Royal Academy of Engineering; Visiting Professor, Oxford University
Allan Chapman	Visiting Professor, Gresham College, London; Author and Scientific Historian; Member of Wadham College and the Faculty of Modern History, Oxford University
Paul W. Kent	Emeritus Student of Christ Church, Oxford; formerly Dr Lee's Reader in Chemistry
Sir John Enderby F.R.S.	Physical Secretary of the Royal Society; H. O. Wills Professor of Physics, Bristol University
Ellen Tan Drake	Scientific Historian, College of Oceanic and Atmospheric Sciences, Oregon State University, USA
Gerard L'E. Turner	Visiting Professor, Imperial College, London; Research Assistant in the Museum of the History of Science, Oxford University

Allan A. Mills	Honorary Fellow, Department of Physics and Astronomy, University of Leicester
Michael A. R. Cooper	Emeritus Professor of Engineering Surveying, City University, London

Preface

A senior diplomat once remarked to me that our subjects differed markedly, in that mine dealt with inanimate matter and was practiced by demure and straightforward individuals, whereas his own was the reverse. It would be undiplomatic to say 'what nonsense', but it would also be true! Every scientist is, of course, prone to personal whims and ambitions to some extent, but pride of place must surely be given to Robert Hooke, whose death 300 years ago we commemorate. He was one of the most complicated scientists of the century – and also one of the most gifted and inventive.

Hooke is often referred to as an 'inventor', and it is true that he did invent mechanisms in horology, the spring balance and so on; but he was primarily a scientist. Indeed, the 'inventor' of 300 years ago was essentially what we would now term a scientist. Nevertheless, his discoveries did tend to have rather immediate practical application, and it was perhaps this feeling that his early work did not gain him recognition in these rapidly advancing technical fields which caused his considerable prickliness with respect to the work of others, such as Newton and Huygens. Perceived lack of priority made him ultra-secretive in his work, and this hindered rather than helped him in his quest for adequate reference – and deference.

Notwithstanding Hooke's lack of personal skills, his contribution to inventiveness, or science – call it what you will – were legion, and his reputation is assured. The present volume contains papers by both scientists and historians, and their story illustrates the many contributions and some of the excitement that arose from his evident lack of diplomacy.

Sir Arnold Wolfendale F.R.S.
14th Astronomer Royal

Acknowledgements

The renewed interest nationwide in the life and works of Robert Hooke in 2003, the tercentenary of his death, found its expression in several ways. A memorial service at Willen Church (the church which he built), near Newport Pagnell, Buckinghamshire, on the anniversary date was followed by a notable conference of scientists and historians at the premises of the Royal Society in London, then by a public symposium at Oxford, organised by Christ Church.

This volume, offered as a postlude to those commemorations, seeks to review some of the aspects of the personality and scientific inventiveness of this remarkable pioneer in his late Renaissance setting.

The editors express their deep gratitude to all those who have contributed to the pages that follow, and to the learned bodies that have lent their support and interest, especially the Royal Society, the Royal Academy of Engineering, the Royal Astronomical Society and the Linnean Society, as well as others who wish to remain anonymous.

We acknowledge with thanks those who have granted permission to reproduce illustrations or text from documents in their possession, particularly Mrs Rachel Chapman, the executors of the late Professor E. C. Hambly, the executors of the late P. S. Spokes, the Governing Body of Christ Church, the Governing Body of Westminster School, and English Heritage (National Monuments Records).

We are deeply indebted to the many friends who have generously provided suggestions, help and advice, including Dr J. F. A. Mason, Professor Roger Davies, Sir Henry Harris, Professor Robert Fox, Mr E. Smith, Dr R. Whittington, Mr Kenneth Kennedy, Mrs Judith Curthoys, Mrs Anne Spokes Symonds, Mr Peter Hingley, Mr Kevin Kilburn and Dr M. Grossel.

We are also especially grateful to those who have contributed to the technical production of the work: Jennifer Smith, Margaret Molloy, Tina Hill and Robert A. Marriott.

The late Professor Edmund C. Hambly: an Appreciation

The year 2003 brought the tercentenary of the death of Robert Hooke, marked by commemorations in London, Oxford and others places in the UK. This national commemoration of the achievements of Robert Hooke – the outstandingly inventive scientist whose memory has for so long remained in the shadows – owes much to the continuing interest and lifelong enthusiasm of the late Professor Hambly.

Edmund Cadbury Hambly was educated at Eton and Trinity College, Cambridge, where he studied for the Mechanical Engineering Tripos. His early research gained him a Fellowship at Emmanuel College, from which he moved into engineering consultancy, finally with his own practice.

Distinguished contributions to advanced civil undertakings, offshore projects and risk assessment analysis accorded him a world-wide reputation, and he became President of the Institution of Civil Engineers and a leading member of the Royal Academy of Engineering.

Throughout his outstanding career he made notable contributions to the educational world, especially in introducing engineering to young people. His numerous publications are held in high regard, and from 1989 to 1992 he served as a Visiting Professor of Industrial Design at Oxford. Professor Hambly had a lifelong interest in Hooke, and used his influence in the attempt to reinstate Hooke's memory, to which this volume is the latest contribution.

Chapter 1

Robert Hooke: London's Leonardo

Edmund C. Hambly

Robert Hooke (1635–1703) was an all-round genius like Leonardo da Vinci. As a scientist he had a profound understanding of microscopy, cell biology, evolution, respiration, combustion, crystallography, the vibratory nature of heat, the wave behaviour of light, the laws of motion, the kinetic behaviour of gases, astronomy, and so on. As an engineer and inventor his contributions included the anchor escapement and balance spring in clocks, the spring balance, spring suspension for vehicles, the universal joint, helical gears, the automatic gear cutting machine, the milometer, the spirit level, the photocopier, the camera iris, the octant ... He reckoned he made more than 1,000 inventions and discoveries. Few people realise how many times a day they use them. The modern motor car would not exist without them. In addition to all this, Hooke was a talented architect who spent the busiest part of his life working alongside Christopher Wren, rebuilding London after the Great Fire.

Hooke was recognised as a genius by his contemporaries. John Aubrey wrote of him:

> Mr Robert Boyle recommended Mr Robert Hooke to be Curator of the Experiments of the Royal Society, wherein he did admirable good worke to the Commonwealth of Learning in recommending the fittest person in the world to them ... He is certainly the greatest Mechanick this day in the world.

After a meeting of the Royal Society, on combustion, in February 1665, Samuel Pepys made the following note in his Diary:

> Above all, Mr Boyle today was at the meeting, and above him Mr Hooke, who is the most, and promises the least, of any man in the world that I ever saw.

In August 1665, John Evelyn recorded in his Diary:

> The 7th, I returned home, calling at Woodcot and Durdans by the way, where I found Dr Wilkins, Sir William Petty and Mr Hooke contriving chariots, new rigs for ships, a wheel for one to run races in, and other mechanical inventions: and perhaps, for parts and ingenuity, three such persons together were not to be found elsewhere in Europe.

Robert Hooke, the son of a curate, grew up on the Isle of Wight. His father died when he was thirteen, and he went to London to work as an apprentice to Peter Lely the Court painter. But Hooke found he was not learning much, and so he lodged his inheritance of £100 with Dr Busby, the famous headmaster of Westminster School. There he made rapid progress, mastering the first six books of Euclid in a week! From Westminster School he went to Christ Church College, Oxford, where he had a place as a servitor – a student who earned his keep as a servant to another wealthier student. At Oxford he met the famous group of scientists who went on to found the Royal Society, including John Wilkins, Christopher Wren and Robert Boyle. Hooke became an assistant to Boyle, and designed the air pump with which Boyle derived Boyle's Law concerning the compressibility of gases. Today we experience Boyle's Law for ourselves every time we use a bicycle pump, which is a development of Hooke's air pump. While at Oxford Hooke started his long line of inventions relating to clocks. In this work he leap-frogged with Christiaan Huygens in new ideas, and he invented the new mechanisms for Thomas Tompion's famous clocks.

In 1662 Robert Hooke became Curator of Experiments to the new Royal Society. It held meetings at Gresham College every two weeks or so, and Hooke was required to demonstrate a number of new experiments at each meeting. Many of his demonstrations are reported in his outstanding book *Micrographia*, which at first sight appears to be about the world Hooke saw under the microscope. However, the most fascinating and awe-inspiring parts are his speculations and deductions about the nature of materials and phenomena that could not be seen. He observed coloured interference patterns and rings in thin layers of mica and soap bubbles, and from these he deduced that light had a wave behaviour which could be compared with waves on a pond. He theorised on the structure of ice and quartz crystals by comparing their shapes with the regular packing of lead shot.

One of the most famous illustrations in *Micrographia* is of sections of cork, from which Hooke deduced the cellular structure of plants. Other beautiful illustrations are of minute animals. It is probable that Jonathon Swift's inspiration for *Gulliver's Travels* developed from Hooke's frightening drawings of the eyes of a fly as large as a melon, a flea as large as a cat, and a louse as large as a dog. Hooke was fascinated and delighted by the animals he illustrated, and he speculated on the reasons for their forms in the most endearing style. For example, he wrote of the 'Book-worm':

> When I consider what a heap of sawdust or chips this little creature conveys into its intrals, I cannot chuse but remember and admire the excellent contrivance of Nature, in placing in Animals such a fire, as is continually nourished and supply'd by the materials convey'd into the stomach, and fomented by the bellows of the lungs.

This not only provides an indication of Hooke's admiration for the Creator, but also illustrates his understanding of how respiration is a process of combustion which takes something out of the air.

The Great Fire of London of 1666 presented Robert Hooke with his greatest challenge, as it did also to Christopher Wren. The Fire destroyed more than 13,000 buildings over 400 acres between the Tower of London and the Temple. Within two weeks of the Fire, both men had produced plans for the reconstruction. The City Corporation was so impressed with Robert Hooke that they appointed him Surveyor and one of their three Commissioners for the rebuilding. The King appointed Christopher Wren one of his three Commissioners. Wren and Hooke worked tirelessly together, as a sort of partnership, supervising the construction of all types of works from sewers and water supplies to pavements, bridges, buildings, churches and spires. Robert Hooke's most famous commissions as an architect included the Bethlehem Royal Hospital, known as 'Bedlam', and the Royal College of Physicians, which was thought so fine that a French guide-book of the period recommended that tourists pay someone threepence to be shown around. Hooke, unlike Wren, designed many private houses, and he had a most impressive clientele which included Lord Burlington and Lord Montague. He designed Ragley Hall, near Stratford upon Avon, for Lord Conway (the Hall was later altered, and opened to the public), and Ramsbury Manor for Sir William Jones. As a result of this work Hooke became a wealthy man. In the 1670s he was earning around £500 per year – today eqivalent to several hundred thousand pounds.

Hooke helped Wren with many of his City churches, including St Paul's cathedral. Of these, the greatest monument to Hooke's work is the dome of St Paul's, since he devised the method of design. His Diary entry of 5 June 1675 notes of Christopher Wren: 'He was making up of my principle about arches and altered his module by it'.

The dome of St Paul's is a masterpiece of structural engineering. It is like an egg-shell in comparison with Brunelleschi's fine dome for the Duomo in Florence. Hooke knew that a masonry structure could transmit only compression forces and not bending or tension forces. He also realised that the distribution of forces around a dome depended on its shape and spread of weight. Hooke had the extraordinary idea of making a model upside down out of a flexible material, like chain-mail, which could only hang in pure tension (without bending or compression forces). By adding links and weights in the right places he could produce the desired shape, and then the dome could be built the right way of up with exactly the same shape and distribution of weight. To understand why Hooke's method produced precisely the right shape for the shell dome, imagine that the perfected chain-mail model is dipped in plaster which is allowed to set. When turned the other way up, all the tension forces reverse to become pure compressions with a distribution ideal for masonry.

Charles II took a keen interest in Hooke's work and encouraged him to undertake research for the practical problems of shipping and navigation. Hooke invented the octant in which the image of the Sun, or other heavenly body, is superimposed with an adjustable mirror on the image of the horizon. Charles appointed Hooke as one of the Commissioners for setting up the Royal Observatory at Greenwich, and Hooke designed many of the instruments.

Hooke continued his work as scientist and Professor of Geometry at Gresham College simultaneously with his work as Surveyor. He lectured regularly, and during the 1670s he published several famous lectures, including his explanation of flames and his theory of springs. The latter is fundamental to the modern computer-aided design of skyscrapers and off-shore platforms. In 1705, after Hooke's death, more of his lectures were published, including some on navigation, lights, comets and earthquakes. In one he explained, from his study of fossils:

> [There] have been many other Species of Creatures in former Ages, of which we can find none at present; and that 'tis not unlikely also but there may be divers new kinds now, which have not been from the beginning.

When considering how hard and long Darwin had to work for the acceptance of the theory of evolution, it can be understood why

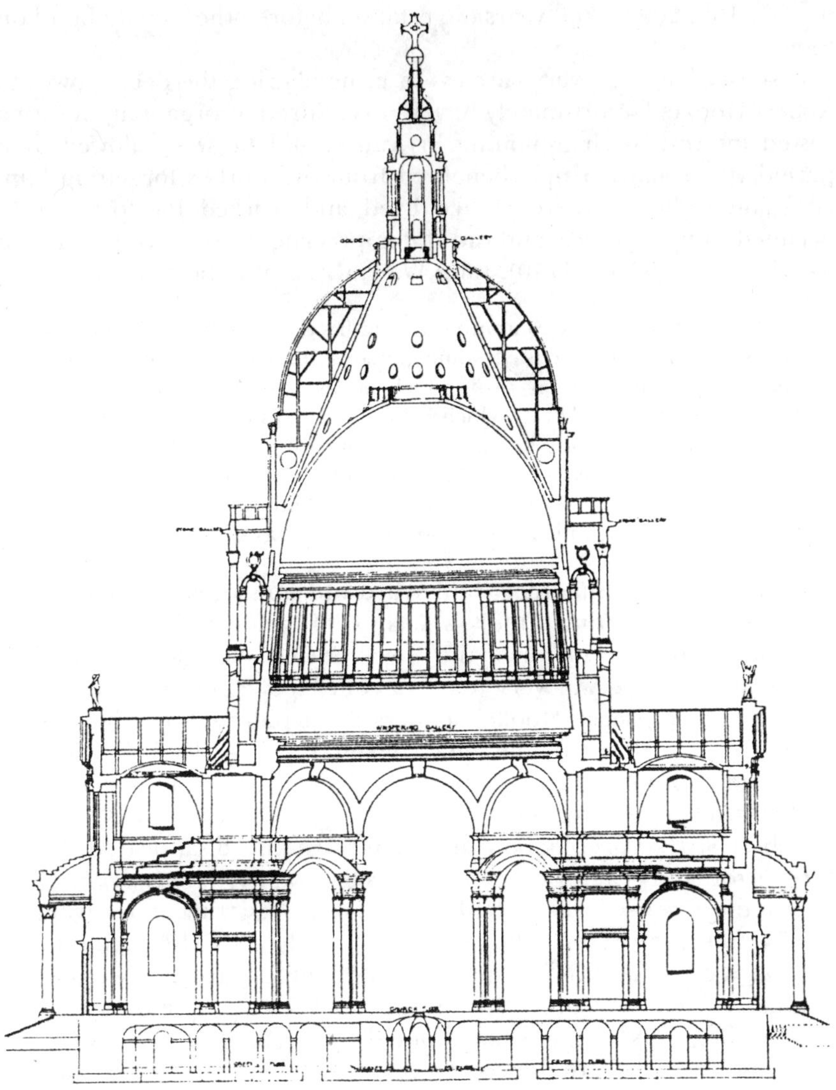

Fig. 1.1. The dome of St Paul's cathedral, constructed by Wren on Hooke's principles of the catenary curve.

Hooke's passing lectures were overlooked. Robert Hooke has been criticised by some for not staying long enough with his different subjects after his breathtaking advances. However, it seems wrong to criticise him for moving too fast for others to keep up. Many of his ideas needed 100, 200 or 300 years of gestation before others could build on them.

Posterity has been very careless in remembering the debt it owes to Robert Hooke. Unfortunately he left no children or organisation with a vested interest in championing his cause, and he was followed by a period when many people benefited from the world's forgetting him. Gresham College, where Hooke lived and worked for forty years, declined in importance, and did not appreciate its asset. In his *Lives of the Gresham Professors* (1740), John Ward wrote of Robert Hooke:

> For at first he was very communicative of his discoveries and inventions, till, as he was wont to say, some persons improving upon his hints published them for their own, which at last rendered him close and reserved even to a faùlt; by which means many things are lost; which he affirmed he know. But he seems, in some instances at least, to have carried those pretensions too far; particularly in his claim to several things in the theory of Sir Isaac Newton's 'Philosophiae naturalis principia mathematica', which that illustrious writer has shown to be his own.

One can only presume that John Ward did not study for himself the documents supporting Hooke's claims of prior publication. Isaac Newton became President of the Royal Society after Robert Hooke's death, and Newton was very touchy about Hooke and his work. Little was done to preserve Hooke's papers from pilfering and his instruments from breakage. By the time Newton died in 1727, Robert Hooke was largely forgotten, and his portrait, which hung in the apartments of the Royal Society, was lost.

Robert Hooke's reputation in architecture also disappeared. When Wren's son and grandson wrote Wren's biography, *Parentalia*, in 1750, they indicated that Hooke had been Wren's assistant and attributed Hooke's works to Wren. The Monument, in the City of London, today has a sign crediting Wren, whereas it was built for the City by Hooke to Hooke's design (now in British Museum). Wren's proposal (now in All Souls College, Oxford) was not adopted.

Accepted 'truths' are difficult to correct. Robert Hooke's genius has been well publicised over the years. Thomas Young, in his famous 'Course of Lectures' at the Royal Institution in 1802, made many references to the work of Hooke; and today, many University text-books on geology, cell biology, and so on, mention Hooke's signpost contributions to those subjects. Hooke's books are being published more and more frequently, particularly overseas, and his profound comments and endearing style are available for us all to share. Before long Robert Hooke will be reinstated in popular history, and an institution somewhere will find a vested interest in re-establishing his reputation. Why not the City University and Gresham College?

(Copyright estate of E. C. Hambly. A radio version entitled 'Robert Hooke: London's Leonardo' was broadcast as a Christmas Lecture on BBC Radio 4 on 3 January 1987. Reprinted by permission.)

Chapter 2

Robert Hooke: the man and his ideas

Allan Chapman

Robert Hooke is in many ways a paradoxical figure. While the main events of his life are recorded in detail and, like a modern scientist, he recognised the importance of putting his researches into the public domain by publication, there are nonetheless many aspects of his inner life and motivation outside science about which we know virtually nothing. This becomes even more surprising when one remembers that Hooke kept a detailed Diary between 1672 and 1680 and a less detailed one between 1688 and 1693, for while the earlier Diary in particular gives an almost hour-by-hour account of his professional life, its asides upon the wider world are irritatingly thin on the ground.[1] Unlike the famous Diary of his friend and Royal Society Fellow, Samuel Pepys, Hooke's Diary is almost devoid of introspection and self-examination, and one is obliged to attempt to reconstruct his inner mental life from occasional snippets of comment and from his deeds and conduct.

Getting to know Hooke the man, as opposed to Hooke the scientist, therefore, is an adventure replete with gaps and pitfalls for the historian and biographer. It is nonetheless an essential adventure if one wishes to understand the whole man, and place him in a wider social and intellectual context.

The basic facts of his origin are well known, and over the last twenty years or so have been richly supplemented by local historians working on the records of his native Isle of Wight. Robert Hooke was born on 18 July 1635 at Freshwater, Isle of Wight, the son of the Revd John Hooke and his second wife Cecellie, née Gyles or Giles. Whether or not his father was an Islander is not clear, but as Robert subsequently told his biographer friend, John Aubrey, he was supposedly descended from the family of Hooke (near modern Basingstoke) in Hampshire. His mother Cecellie, however, seems to have been descended from an Isle of Wight mercantile family from Brading – where John Hooke, serving as curate, married her as his second wife in 1622 – and as Robert's subsequent Diary and later lawsuits record the comings and goings of several Giles and Gyles characters, one can only assume that his in-laws were all too well aware of the importance of their connection with their famous uncle.[2]

Robert was the youngest of John and Cecellie Hooke's four recorded children. Exactly how old his parents were upon marriage is not clear, but as Robert was the child of a second marriage, and as his mother outlived her husband by seventeen years, one assumes that Cecellie was considerably younger than John.[3] And while the records of both Oxford and Cambridge Universities mention the matriculation of a couple of John Hookes of the right generation around 1600, neither of them was from Hampshire or the Isle of Wight.[4] But as Robert later told his friends John Aubrey and Richard Waller, who wrote down the first brief biographical accounts of Hooke, he had been a sickly child. The Revd John Hooke, therefore, despaired of subjecting him to the rigours of a poor boy's place at a good school, and seems to have educated him at home until John's death in 1648.

Even so, these formative first thirteen years of his life at Freshwater seem to have sparked the young Robert's imagination. He displayed a genius for making clocks and working models – including a model ship with firing guns – and for drawing. Indeed, his untutored draughtsmanship so impressed the visiting artist John Hoskyns that he suggested that the boy should be trained formally in art.[5]

One also wonders – and this is one of those possible formative influences for which there is no written record – how far the western tip of the Isle of Wight itself, where Freshwater is located, helped to colour Robert's wider creative imagination. The Isle of Wight is not only the frequent butt of violent storms and weather systems roaring in from the Atlantic, but is also a place of wonderfully changing light. Storms, scudding clouds, spectacular sunsets, and man's struggle with nature in the shape of the great men-o'-war battling with the elements to put in and out of Portsmouth, or even a packet boat fighting its way across the Solent, must all have been part of his juvenile experience. Nature, indeed, was full of grand and wonderful forces, and one can speculate how much his adult interests in light, colour, and optics, and in pressure, force, and rebound, and the possibility of understanding them by means of instruments and ingenious devices, had their origins in his Freshwater childhood.

Then add to these the spectacular geology of the Island with its occasionally collapsing cliffs, its rich beds of shells and fossils well above the present sea-level, and the constant evidence of the erosive power of the sea. Could these local conditions have lain at the heart of Hooke's interest in scientific geology? We certainly know that when the 30-year-old Robert revisited the Island after the death of his mother in 1665, he made detailed surveys of the high shell- and fossil-bearing strata around Freshwater. This is known because he said as much in an 'Earthquake Discourse' delivered to the Royal Society in either 1666 or 1667.[6]

We do not know the cause of Cecellie Hooke's death, but considering the fact that she married in 1622, she was probably in her early to mid-sixties at least: a good age for the seventeenth century, indeed, when many people failed to reach forty. The cause of John Hooke's death is not known, nor what age he was in 1648, but 'for three or four Years before his Death [he had] been much afflicted with a Cough, a Palsy, Jaundice and Dropsy'.[7] A cough, palsy (paralysis) and dropsy (oedema) could very well point to a degenerative cardiovascular condition, and to what would now be called congestive heart failure; and as these are conditions of ageing, it is not unlikely that John Hooke was relatively elderly at the time of his death. And as we shall see at the end of this chapter, Robert himself displayed similar symptoms, including what could well have been kidney complications, in the last few years of his own life, which ended in his sixty-eighth year. John Aubrey, however, stated that the Revd John Hooke commited suicide by 'suspending himself', though in this respect, as in others, the author of *Brief Lives*

Fig. 2.1. Freshwater Church, Isle of Wight, in 2003.
(Photograph by M. C. Grossel.)

was clearly confusing his facts.[8] The Revd John Hooke left a will which was proved soon after his death, and moreover was buried in consecrated ground – neither of which would have been probable in the case of a suicide.[9] On the other hand, Robert's elder brother John, who seems to have been inept with money and whose Newport, Isle of Wight, business failed, certainly hanged himself in 1678.[10]

From Freshwater to Oxford and London

In the present context, this part of Hooke's life can be passed over relatively quickly, as it is dealt with in detail in Chapter 3. One might, however, add a few observations that may help to amplify our understanding of his circumstances.

Exactly when and under whose auspices the 13-year-old Robert Hooke left the Isle of Wight for London, following the funeral of his father on 17 October 1648, we have no record; but as the Revd John Hooke seems to have been of Royalist Anglican allegiance in the revolution and civil wars then engulfing Britain, and as the absentee Rector of Freshwater, the Revd Cardell Goodman, was also a Royalist Anglican, it is possible that the Goodman family might have assisted their deceased curate's talented son to get on in the world.[11] Some substantiation of this possibility might derive from another garbled tale – no doubt oral in origin – which Richard Waller subsequently wrote down in his life of Hooke. This story recounted that Robert Hooke first entered Christ Church, Oxford, as Servitor to Mr Goodman, although the Registers of Oxford University show no-one by the name of Goodman resident in the University between 1653 and 1662, when Hooke was there.[12] Is it possible, therefore, that, instead of accompanying a Goodman student up to Oxford, and receiving in turn a free education in the role of Servitor, the orphaned Robert Hooke was quite simply the recipient of Goodman family patronage?

On the other hand, we must not fall into the trap of believing that Robert had been left in poverty when his father died. While the recent discovery of the Revd John Hooke's will in Isle of Wight records shows that Robert was not left the £100 mentioned by Aubrey, but only £40, plus £10 from his late grandmother's estate, and some possessions (his elder brother John received £60, making up the £100 mentioned by Aubrey), this was still a far from contemptible sum in 1648.[13] Nor did it include two sums of £30 each to sisters Anne and Katherine, further sums held in trust by John for the four children from their material grandmother, Ann Giles, and sums and items of unspecified value left to the widowed Cecellie. And by way of perspective, one should remember that when Robert was appointed Gresham Professor of Geometry – a prestigious City of London chair – in 1665, his annual salary stood at £50, at a time, moreover, when an Oxford college Fellowship paid its holder £20 a year.[14]

The Revd John Hooke, therefore, was not an especially poor man, and to see him as such would be to distort the values and priorities of that age. And by way of providing a further perspective on the value of money in seventeenth-century England, it should be noted that in the 1670s Robert Hooke was paying only £4 – the going rate – to his own servants for a whole year's work![15] So while Hooke no doubt needed contacts to take him up to and settle him in London, he still had something in the region of £20,000–30,000 in modern purchasing power behind him. Not a fortune, it is true, but still a respectable way up from indigence.[16]

Perhaps acting on the suggestion of John Hoskyns, Hooke entered the London studios of Peter (later Sir Peter) Lely, with a view to an apprenticeship, 'but Mr Hooke quickly perceived what was to be donne, so, thought he, why cannot I doe this by my selfe and keep my hundred pounds?'[17] This was an astute decision for a lad of thirteen or fourteen to make, and was perhaps the first recorded instance of that financial shrewdness which was to be a constant feature in Hooke's life, and by which, no doubt, he accumulated the hefty fortune which he left in 1703.

On leaving Lely's studio, Hooke managed to enrol himself into Westminster School, where he seems to have been boarded in the house of the Head Master, the Revd Dr Richard Busby (though, as Aubrey reminds us, he was not a King's Scholar, or its Commonwealth equivalent). At Westminster his mathematical, technological, and linguistic ingenuity seems to have impressed Busby, and a friendship was formed between Head Master and boy which was to continue into Hooke's adult life. His Diary of 1688–93 often records visits to and dinners with Dr Busby.[18]

Infuriatingly for us, Hooke left no record of his Westminster years; but it is hard to imagine that the unfolding of momentous revolutionary political events within a five-minute walk from the School gates did not leave their impression upon him. Was he, for instance, already in London on 30 January 1649, when Charles I's head was struck off just a short walk up the road in Whitehall?[19] What were his reactions to the escalating political turmoil as Presbyterians, Independents, and religious fanatics fought it out in the Parliament House which stood around the corner past the Abbey, in their several attempts to found a Commonwealth of Saints in Republican England? And what were the teenage Hooke's views on the growing power of General Oliver

Fig. 2.2. Westminster School in the eighteenth century.

Cromwell, the man who could be King? As a Westminster boy, Hooke could not have flown a kite or slipped out of school to treat himself to a custard tart in a local cookshop without seeing soldiers, politicians, street-preachers, mobs, and the great Lord Oliver himself passing by the School gates. Indeed, he was living in a place in which the greatest trauma in British constitutional and social history was unfolding. Yet he tells us nothing.

It is unlikely, however, that his entry into Christ Church, Oxford, on some unrecorded date in 1653, was made without assistance from some friends on the Isle of Wight. There was, of course, the Revd Cardell Goodman, himself an old Christ Church man who in 1651 had been deprived of his Freshwater rectory because of his detestation of the new Puritan régime. Cardell Goodman was clearly a family friend – described in John Hooke's will as 'my worthy and well beloved friend' – and was charged in that same will with 'overseeing' its just execution.[20] And could this duty of care also have included Robert's future education? Again, we have no idea whether the Revd Dr Samuel Fell – evicted from the Deanery of Christ Church for his High Church Royalist loyalties in 1647 – might also have helped Hooke, for he too had been Rector of Freshwater (1615–1621), and could well have known the young John Hooke. Alternatively, Robert Hooke might have arrived in Oxford on the strength of some connection with the young Thomas Newham Esq., the only Islander to come up to Christ Church who was a contemporary of Robert.[21]

But as is noted in the succeeding chapter, Robert Hooke's genius was recognised in Oxford by the Revd Drs John Wilkins and Seth Ward, the young Dr Christopher Wren, Dr Thomas Willis, the Hon. Robert Boyle, and several others, who gave him what we would now call post-graduate contract work by employing him as assistant and co-worker in a variety of experimental pursuits that included the design of flying machines, the discovery of the properties of air, and the investigation of human and animal physiology.

When, at the Restoration of the Monarchy in 1660, these men moved their main base of operation from Oxford to London to form the Royal Society, they were keen to secure Hooke's continuing services (as described in Chapter 4). Consequently, in November 1662 he was appointed Curator of Experiments to the newly-chartered Royal Society, though it was Boyle who continued to pay him and provide him with accommodation in Pall Mall until the Society was able to 'get Stock' enough to pay him a salary of £30 per annum. Thus Robert Hooke became the first Englishman to become a formally salaried research scientist.[22] In 1663 Hooke's friends were able to secure the bestowal of his Oxford M.A. degree, seemingly without examination, by Lord Clarendon, Chancellor of Oxford University. It could be argued, indeed, that the circumstances surrounding the granting of Hooke's M.A. degree provide a clear indication of the high and valued standing which he had come to enjoy in the estimation of some of the cleverest and best-connected men in the land. In 1663 he was also elected to Fellowship of the Royal Society, and when in 1665 the Mercers' Company and the City of London jointly elected him to the vacant Professorship of Geometry at Gresham College, London, the crowning accolade of academic respectability had been accorded him.[23] His professorial appointment gave the 30-year-old bachelor Hooke a spacious set of rooms and the use of stables and out-buildings in Gresham College, next door to where the Royal Society met, although he was obliged to remain unmarried. In these rooms he was to live, work, and finally, on 3 March 1703, draw his last breath.

Hooke's scientific ideas

Robert Hooke was undoubtedly one of the greatest, most original and most ingenious experimental scientists that have ever lived. But he did not invent the concept of experimentation, as a controlled technique whereby one might ask carefully thought-out questions of nature. The experimental study of geomagnetism – whereby the properties and coordinates of the Earth's magnetic field first came to be clearly understood – had been firmly established by William Gilbert in *De Magnete* (1600), while Sir Francis Bacon's writings up to 1620 had laid down the rules of experimentation and urged 'natural philosophers' to bring about 'the Advancement of Learning' by their careful application. Bacon and Gilbert had deeply influenced those men who became Hooke's Oxford mentors, and Dr John Wilkins had argued in works such as *Mathematical Magick* (1648) that the application of ingenious machines could transform the human condition.

Yet why should such new ideas about the natural world and how to study it have taken on such a relevance and an urgency by the seventeenth century? This took place, I would argue, because of the way in which a succession of new and relatively chance discoveries had fundamentally challenged the science of Aristotle, Galen, Ptolemy, and other classical writers whose works had come to constitute the scientific 'orthodoxy' of the Medieval and Renaissance universities. Yet the post-1492 Columban voyages suddenly revealed new continents and oceans unknown to earlier geographers, while the researches of anatomists like Vesalius and Harvey and astronomers such as Copernicus, Tycho Brahe, and Galileo transformed mankind's understanding about the nature both of living things and of the Cosmos. The image of Columbus using a ship – which one might consider as a type of scientific research tool – to take human understanding beyond the logical systems and philosophies of Aristotle and the 'School men' was a powerful one in the seventeenth century, and both Bacon and Hooke refer to Columbus, Magellan and Drake as heralds of the newly-perceived fact-driven, experiential, form of knowledge. It was an approach to knowledge, moreover, that had become instinctively suspicious of what they called authority, or the pronouncements of the ancients, so that it was not for nothing that the Royal Society chose as its motto *Nullius In Verba* – a contraction of the Horatian 'nullius addictus iurare in verba magistri' (*Epistles* 1.1.14), 'not bound to swear allegiance to any master'[24] – a Latin maxim of great potency to independent-minded scientists such as Hooke and the early Fellows of the Royal Society, for whom Horace, Virgil and the other classical Latin authors would have constituted their educational mother's milk!

At Oxford, the young Hooke – already a competent linguist – would have become familiar with all of these ideas, ancient and modern, along with those of the contemporary French philosopher René Descartes, who regarded motion as the key to all things, which motion was transmitted by successive impacts throughout the length and breadth of Creation.[25] According to Descartes' system, everything –

from the propagation of light from the stars, to the circulation of the blood around living bodies – was the product of mechanical actions, collisions, and impacts. Hooke's own ideas on physics would owe much to Descartes, though as a self-conscious Baconian he recognised the central importance of experimental proof and testing, if scientific explanations aspired to be more than just elegant philosophical theories.[26]

Many of the physical scientists of the mid-seventeenth century regarded themselves as mechanists or mechanical philosophers, for in envisaging the whole of nature as a great machine, or as something analogous to clockwork, one could attempt to explain all manner of phenomena which had once been attributed to occult agencies. By 1660 natural forces were not seen as acting through some mysterious 'action at a distance', but as the results of numerous mechanical impacts, in much the same way as the fingers which moved across a clock face did so because of complex pressures relayed through the clock's gear-teeth. Far from being regarded as atheistical in its implication, this mechanism was seen, especially by English scientists, as elegantly reconcilable with Christianity, in so far as God was seen as the 'Celestial Clockmaker' whose cosmic machine was open to study and reasoned inquiry by man. Robert Boyle developed his own theory of chemical atomism in accordance with the above principles, viewing atoms not as the random, blindly-moving particles conceived by ancient atomists like Lucretius, but as physical building blocks that the hand of God directed into beautiful and useful natural structures.[27]

Robert Hooke's entire approach to nature hinged on the concept of mechanical action, and virtually all of his great research publications – from his ideas about crystal formation, in *Micrographia* (1665), to his attempts to explain combustion, the brightness of comets, the action of the air and blood in living bodies, and even the nature of gravity itself – presuppose a mechanical, particulate, impact-driven Universe. Indeed, it was the very job of the research scientist (or natural philosopher) to unravel and demonstrate these impacts and thereby to advance learning.[28]

It is evident that by 1665 a mature physical system was already present in Hooke's thought, in accordance with which he would conduct his researches over the next thirty-odd years. The following are some of the key components of Hooke's system:

1   Motion is fundamental to all things. Nature is never still: even the continents themselves are being slowly eroded and changed, and the Earth's poles are 'wandering' over time (Chapter 5). Even dead things may move within themselves, as witnessed, so Hooke argues,

by the faint glow emitted by rotting fish or rotten wood when viewed in the dark.[29] Even this decomposing motion produces friction, and friction produces light.

2   The wave-form is the universally observed path followed by things in motion. For examples, one need only look at the tides of the ocean, the waves generated by a stone falling into water, the sonorous booms produced by explosions, earthquakes and echoes, and the original vibration and induced sympathetic vibrations created between the bowed and tuned strings of musical instruments. Most of all, light itself seems to be a sinusoidal vibration, as Hooke tried to demonstrate by means of experiments. As one side of the geometrical wave crest strikes the retina of the eye, so, he argued, on the strength of his experiments, it creates the impression of redness, whereas the opposite crest generates an impression of blueness. The other colours, the yellows, greens, and oranges, result when those parts of the curved wave line which connect the two peaks impact on the retina.[30]

3   Even gravity itself acts through a mechanical wave form.[31]

4   All motions, wave-forms, and forces diminish and grow weaker with distance. Sounds fade, lights dim, and ripples smooth out with their distance from the radiant point. This they do, moreover, not in a random way, but in accordance with a precise mathematical ratio that is a function of the distance which the wave has travelled from the impact point, which in turn is governed by the mechanical strength of the original disturbance. Hooke came to realise that in the case of gravity (and probably with the other forms of natural forces as well) this motion changes in accordance with the inverse proportion of the distance.[32]

5   The ceaseless motions inherent within nature and their wave forms also predicate the existence of a mechanical action and reaction principle that lies implicit within nature. This principle is manifested in the flux and reflux of the winds and tides and in the properties of springs of all kinds. It was a concept intimately bound up with Hooke's idea of vibration constituting the primary agent whereby power, weight, or force (he had no precise concept of what we now call energy) was transmitted throughout the whole of nature. Hooke's famous Law of Spring of 1678 – namely, that power released by a spring is directly proportional to the force needed to tension it – was his most exact quantification of this principle[33] (as is more fully explored in Chapter 8).

6   Not only is the whole of nature bound together by a great set of mathematical and geometrical laws and proportions, but these forces can be comprehended and even modelled by the human

intellect. Consequently, experiment becomes much more than a simple business of ingenious trial and error. It becomes, rather, a structured scientific method whereby we can, as it were, dismantle the parts of the accessible Creation and learn how God put it together in the first place.

Central to the above, however, were the techniques by which these experiments were performed. Very prominent in the mind of Hooke – as it had been for Bacon sixty years earlier – was that awareness of how 'the moderns' (those men mentioned above) had, in the last 100 years or so, raced beyond the boundaries of natural knowledge fixed by the ancients: men who had sailed through and beyond those metaphorical 'Pillars of Hercules' depicted on the frontispiece of *Novum Organum* (1620) and had discovered new continents and oceans unknown to Ptolemy and Strabo. To Columbus, Drake, and the great geographical discoverers, Hooke added Galileo, Kepler, Harvey, Torricelli, and those other early seventeenth-century figures who had sailed out into new waters of astronomy, medicine and experimental physics.

Yet what the ship, the telescope, controlled medical studies, the thermometer and the barometer all shared in common was their power to extend and make more precise human senses and understanding. Just as Drake's *Golden Hind* bore him into new oceans and brought him new experiences that would have been impossible for a European with only a rowing boat, so Galileo's telescope had revealed celestial phenomena otherwise invisible to the naked eye. Therefore, were not ships, telescopes, and other instruments 'artificial organs' that strengthened the human senses?[34] And if that was so, then should we not strive to invent more 'artificial organs' to see yet deeper into nature before going on to use the fruits of these discoveries to frame more 'ingenious experiments' and carry our researches for ever deeper into nature?

This was Robert Hooke's vision of science. It was an instrument- and technology-based vision, which saw research as continuously progressive by its very nature, and also capable of yielding a practical increase that could 'relieve man's estate' in its ever-growing bounty of discoveries and useful devices. Indeed, Hooke's science, while practical in its investigative techniques, was deeply visionary in its underlying assumptions; and that scientific vision, moreover, was even hinted by him as possessing a clear Christian redemptive power as well, for 'as at first, mankind fell by tasting of the forbidden Tree of Knowledge, so we, their Posterity, may be in part restor'd by the same way, not only of beholding and contemplating, but of tasting too those fruits of Natural Knowledge, that were never yet forbidden.'[35]

Had not Adam and Eve brought about the fall of the human race by eating of the Tree of Knowledge in the Garden of Eden against the express instruction of God, and thereby coming to know the nature of good and evil? Yet why should not we moderns, as Adam and Eve's descendants, taste of that new natural knowledge which God had never forbidden, yet which our ignorance had hitherto hidden from us?

In Hooke's mind the practical, the transcendent, the useful and the reverential all coalesced into one single and harmonious body of understanding.

Robert Hooke in his world

Not only has history so long neglected the significance of Robert Hooke's contributions to science – sometimes, indeed, depicting him as little more than an ingenious mechanic who was foolish enough to cross Newton – but there was even a stage when it was fashionable in scholarly circles to downplay his social status as well. After all, had not Waller presented a rather sad picture of the elderly and ailing Hooke, with his reclusive melancholy, uncut hair, and untidiness?[36] And were there not several famous quarrels in Hooke's career – especially those fought out with Henry Oldenburg and Sir Isaac Newton? Therefore, could not one imagine Hooke as some kind of social inferior, uncomfortable and resentful in the presence of the well-born Fellows of the Royal Society, and preferring the company of tradesmen and dressing like an artisan? Sadly, this depiction has become an enduring one in certain quarters, and has coloured many people's mental image of Hooke, especially when that image is compared with that of the grand and courtly Newton (who was, let us not forget, a Lincolnshire farmer's son) as immortalised on the canvases of Sir Godfrey Kneller.[37] Yet such a historical construction not only does Hooke's memory and reputation a monumental disservice, but, more importantly, the image of the man which it conjures up is flatly contradicted by the historical record.

For one thing, what was Hooke's actual status in seventeenth-century society? Well, let us remember that Robert Hooke was born the son of a comfortably-off clergyman and went to Westminster School and Christ Church, Oxford, where his burgeoning genius was recognised and encouraged by some of the most original intellects of the age. Through their influence, moreover, he received his M.A. degree without examination, and became a Fellow of the Royal Society at the age of twenty-eight.[38]

How, therefore, can one cast Robert Hooke in the guise of a social inferior treated like a minion by the magisterial figures of science? It is true that, as a salaried assistant to Willis and Boyle, and as paid

Curator of Experiments of the Royal Society he was referred to as a 'servant' in the respect that he worked for his living. But the seventeenth-century 'servant' is closer to our modern equivalent of 'employee' or even 'Civil Servant'; it did not signify a domestic menial. After all, as salaried Clerk of the Acts to the Navy, Samuel Pepys fully accepted that he was a 'servant' of the Admiralty; but no historian ever speaks of Pepys as a figure of low or doubtful status, in spite of the fact that Pepys, the son of a working London tailor, came from lower down in society than Hooke the clergyman's son![39]

In fact, Robert Hooke came from what might be called the minor gentry or rural middle class, and his subsequent education and social standing in London by the time he was thirty – as Gresham Professor, F.R.S., and M.A. – gave him the undisputed status of a gentleman. While he may not have had the ancestral wealth or connections of a Boyle, a Wren, or a John Evelyn, the fact that he dined at these men's tables, socialised with them in the same coffee houses, and publicly acknowledged them as his friends, made his status as a gentleman unassailable. Nor must we forget that his appointment as Gresham Professor in 1665 indicated the nature of his standing in the eyes of the City of London and its great Livery Companies. For instance, Sir John Lawrence, F.R.S., Lord Mayor of London in 1665,[40] became a great admirer and friend of Hooke's, and during his Diary-keeping years in the 1670s Hooke made many references to being in his company on social occasions. And after the Great Fire of 1666, when Christopher Wren was appointed Surveyor of the King's Buildings, Hooke was elected to the equivalent Surveyorship to the City of London – a post, indeed, of high standing in the City, from which Hooke made a fortune of several thousand pounds. Professor Michael Cooper has undoubtedly done the ground-breaking research into Hooke's work as a City Surveyor[41] (Chapter 9).

By his mid-sixties, however, Robert Hooke had become worn down by ceaseless work, illness, and a sense of intellectual betrayal in the way that the Royal Society had backed Sir Isaac Newton's claims for the discovery of universal gravitation, rather than his own. And it was this, I would argue, that gave him the meagre, suspicious, melancholy and reclusive aspect mentioned by Waller.

The younger Hooke, however, is a very different figure. In his late thirties and early forties, by contrast, during the years that he kept his Diary, he comes across as a highly convivial figure: a great diner-out, a clubman, a man who spent his money on good clothes and fashionable periwigs, and who enjoyed a very wide circle of friends which included clever artisans at one end and Royal physicians, Lord Mayors, and bishops at the other. Yet while Hooke was a gentleman, with gentlemanly tastes, he was certainly no snob, and obviously had the ability to relate to anyone who had something ingenious or novel to say, irrespective of that person's social place. One suspects that it was Hooke's social openness and willingness to learn from and cooperate with bricklayers, glaziers, mechanics and craftsmen such as Thomas Tompion that has led some people to see him as a mechanical.[42]

On the other hand, his preferred company was quite decidedly male, and one suspects that he may have felt a little out of place in the company of women of his own and of his friends' social standing. His Diary, for instance, records, in 1678, a rather wounding encounter with Boyle's sister, Lady Ranelagh, where her 'scolding' made him sulk,[43] though we do not know who said what, and are left to wonder whether he was inclined to 'put his foot in it' when in the social company of ladies. This tendency could also explain why, even before his appointment as a bachelor Professor in Gresham College, he seems never to have made any attempts to marry an heiress. After all, such a strategy would have been entirely in keeping with the career strategy of a well-educated and well-connected man of such conspicuous promise but who lacked broad acres of his own. Yet there is no evidence for any serious matrimonial strategies, or even of serious sweethearts, among women of his own class. But we must not read too much into his 'scolding' encounter with Lady Ranelagh. After all, by that time he had known her for more than a decade, and had probably even lodged in her Pall Mall house in the early 1660s, when he was employed as Boyle's 'operator' in London and Oxford.[44] He was certainly undertaking architectural commissions for Lady Ranelagh, as his Diary records, and their contretemps may well have related to one of those irritations which many clients feel when urging on a building project. Hooke's Diary, however, does record dining in the company of other ladies, such as Wren's first and second wives, Mrs Elizabeth Tillotson, the Archbishop of Canterbury's wife, and the risqué Abigail Williams, Viscount Brouncker's live-in mistress, without adverse comment. On the other hand, these ladies appear in the Diary as little more than names, and their conversations are not recorded.[45]

In spite of his possible shyness with ladies, Robert Hooke was certainly attracted to women, and some of the most lurid passages in his Diary describe encounters with his female servants and dependents, though for a man of Hooke's sickly constitution, even these incidents were not without risk, as indicated in the 1672 Diary entry which recorded 'Played with Nell. ♓ Hurt Small of back.'[46] However, within the social conventions of the day, where it seems to have been tacitly assumed that working-class girls were fair game, especially for their employers, Hooke's relations with Nell Young, Bridget Taylor,

Doll Lord, Bette Orchard, and others – and one presumes that there must have been plenty of others before 1672, for he was thirty-eight years old when his Diary record began – were not without genuine affection, as Hooke was a naturally kind and generous man.[47] He seems, for instance, to have enjoyed a post-sexual friendship of sorts with Nell Young for years after she left his service to get married, as he found her work, and she occasionally called to see him in Gresham College.[48]

One woman with whom Robert Hooke seems to have had a somewhat obsessive relationship, however, was his niece, Grace Hooke, the daughter of his suicidal brother John. Grace left the Isle of Wight firstly to go to school in London, and at the age of around twelve went to live with her uncle Robert at Gresham College. Grace was clearly an extremely attractive and vivacious girl for whom, it was hoped, her influential uncle would secure a good City marriage.[49] But this did not work out, and as she grew into early womanhood, Hooke seems to have developed an obsessive and unhealthy attachment to her, bought her expensive gifts, and clearly resented the considerable number of young men who flirted with and paid court to the rather wayward and beautiful Grace. Then, in October 1676, when she was still only sixteen, Hooke and Grace ended up in bed together, as signified in the Diary by the cryptic '♓Grace' and 'Gr.♓' and their variants.[50] The astrological symbol for the zodiacal constellation Pisces was Hooke's usual way of indicating a sexual encounter in his Diary.

According to Robert's Diary, however, Grace seems to have visited family on the Isle of Wight quite regularly, and on the night before her departure for one of these visits, on 10 August 1677, Robert had ended his Diary entry for the day with 'Grace♓'.

Back on the Isle of Wight, Grace seems to have entered into a liaison with the Island's 55-year-old bachelor Governor and philanderer, Sir Robert Holmes, to whom an illegitimate daughter, Mary Holmes, was born in 1678.[51] Though Holmes acknowledged his paternity of Mary, the name of her mother is not known, and some scholars have suggested that Grace Hooke could well have been she.[52] Indeed, if this was the case – and there is no direct documentary evidence that it is – then the shame of his daughter's pregnancy could well have been a contributory cause of Grace's father John Hooke's suicide in February 1678.[53] Monica Mears has even further suggested that if Grace was perhaps the mother of Mary Holmes, then her uncle Robert, and not Holmes, could well have been the father, as Robert Hooke records sleeping with Grace on 10 August 1677.[54] No matter what happened to Grace on the Isle of Wight during the winter of 1677–78, with the exception of a bout of measles,[55] she was certainly sufficiently recovered to return to London alone on 9 June 1678, when Robert Hooke recorded her arrival back in Gresham College.[56]

Arguing against the likelihood that Grace Hooke gave birth to a child on the Isle of Wight in the spring of 1678, however, is a total absence of any reference to the fact in Hooke's detailed Diary. As references to the sending and receipt of letters in his Diary show, Hooke was certainly in regular contact with friends and family on the Island – including Grace herself – especially in the wake of his brother John's suicide in February 1678. Indeed, had his clearly beloved Grace really been pregnant, it is difficult to imagine that the slightest hint of his concern for her condition would not have entered his very private Diary – a Diary that was so private, moreover, that he plainly felt safe to record in it acts of 'playing', 'wrastling', fornication, adultery, and incest.

Nearly a decade later, at the beginning of the year 1687, while still living in Gresham College, the 26-year-old Grace suddenly died of a fever, and thereby plunged her uncle into an inconsolable grief.[57] It was this grief, coinciding exactly with the publication of Newton's *Principia Mathematica*, and with Hooke's bitter sense of intellectual rejection by the Royal Society, which now sang the praises of Newton and chose to ignore his own prior fundamental published researches into gravity, that precipitated one of the turning points of Hooke's life. His great scientific creativity – with the possible exception of his continuing 'Discourses of Earthquakes'[58] – was over, and friends like Aubrey and Waller increasingly noted, in their own writings, Hooke's declining health and ever-closer brushes with death. Before examining Hooke's illnesses and death, however, attention must be paid to what we can piece together about his religious and moral beliefs.

Religious and moral beliefs

One might reasonably argue that any man who took regular sexual advantages of his servant girls and committed incest with his own niece – irrespective of the individual women's willingness or otherwise to participate – had no religious or moral scruples worth the name. One wonders, however, before dismissing him out of hand, how far the taking of such advantages was reckoned less reprehensible in the world of seventeenth-century gentlemen who did not live in family environments than it would be today, especially if the liaisons did not result in pregnancies, did not include explicit physical cruelty, and involved a certain amount of genuine affection. Nowhere in the extensive record do we find any reference to Hooke as a cruel man. Cantankerous he may well have been on occasions when he perceived that fellow gentlemen were not giving him his due, but to ordinary folk, and especially to his domestic establishment in Gresham – several of whom were Islanders – he often seems touchingly kind and generous. Let us not forget, however, that seventeenth-century England was a much harsher, sterner, and more hierarchical place than it is today, and that what to us may appear an abuse of privilege and rank would probably have been accepted more naturally by a gentleman – and, perhaps, even by the women themselves – living in Charles II's London.

I would suggest that it is to this natural kindliness and generosity that one should look when trying to fathom Hooke's religious and moral views. According to his long-standing friend John Aubrey F.R.S., he was 'a person of great vertue [*sic*] and goodnes[s]',[59] while in 1677 Charles II told Hooke to his face that he thought he 'was a very able and honest man'.[60] And even the Diary itself – so thin when it comes to capturing the inner Hooke – does contain its occasional revelations, such as when, on the last day of 1676, he recorded 'Much love to all my friends I owe'.[61] Not the remark of a selfish or ungenerous man, one might suggest! But while he was undoubtedly astute financially and knew how to drive good bargains, there seem to have been no accusations of corruption with regard to his work as Surveyor, which was quite an achievement in that peculatory age. Indeed, only one criticism of the financial accuracy (rather than probity) of his dealings seems to have left its written record as far as his work as City Surveyor and architect was concerned. The incident took place in 1691 when Hooke, under the Will of Alderman Aske, supplied designs for an almshouse at Hoxton, London, and because the eventual cost exceeded Hooke's written estimate, accusations were made. But Hooke was quick to defend himself on two grounds which, among other things, gives an insight into his contracting system. Firstly, he said the expenditure shot over estimate because his plans were modified by Aske's trustees after submission, and without his being requested to readjust costs; while secondly, the trustees had not engaged the reliable building contractors that he had recommended.[62] Was this an early example of trustees engaging cheaper, 'cowboy', builders rather than the more expensive reliable tradesmen, only to complain after having their fingers burnt? According to Aubrey, moreover, Hooke suffered a life-threatening illness in the early months of 1691, and one also wonders how far his consequent unavailability may have been a contributory factor.[63]

Quite apart from any architectural or building practices, what the Aske's Hospital business indicates is Robert Hooke's great concern for his good name and reputation. He was a man of integrity whose word could be relied upon, and was clearly proud of that standing.

Reaching to the heart of his specifically religious beliefs, as opposed to his sense of honour and goodness, however, is a less straightforward business. It is true that, as indicated above, he came from a Royalist Anglican background on the Isle of Wight, and worked and perhaps lived in Willis's house in Oxford at a time when illegal Anglican worship was being conducted there in the 1650s; yet his eight-year Diary is almost totally silent on the subject of religious observance. His Sundays were spent in coffee houses, with scientific cronies, and on at least one occasion, in bed with Grace. In that church-going age, Hooke scarcely ever seems to have set foot in a church for purposes of worship – unless one assumes that he simply did not record his church-going, which seems unlikely, especially when considering the detail with which he recorded the rest of his daily comings and goings between 1672 and 1680. And when he did go to church, he seems to have done so as part of a group of other Royal Society Fellows, as when on a Sunday in May 1673 'I Received the Sacrament at St. Peters Poor with Dr. Pope, Dr. Croon, Sir James Oxendine' and several others.[64] Then again, on a Tuesday in March 1678 he 'walkd with Dean of Canterbury [John Tillotson] to St. Laurence Church and with Dr. Whitchcot ... missed Sir Chr. Wren';[65] but whether or not this was to partake in an act of worship, attend a meeting, or inspect the fabric, is not clear. What is also possible, however, is that these acts of church-going were public declarations of his Protestantism and loyalty in the wake of the recent Test Act, which piece of legislation was intended to isolate and expose Roman Catholics in public life.[66]

Hooke's Diary is bereft of references to religious conversations or any specific religious studies, prayers, or exercises, yet his biographer Waller makes very clear that 'He always exprest a great Veneration for the eternal and immense Cause of all Beings, as may be seen in very many Passages in his Writings, and seldom receiv'd any remarkable Benefit from God without thankfully acknowledging the Mercy.' Waller also tells us that Hooke acknowledged God's 'Omnipotent Providence, as many places in his Diary testify', which is entirely true.[67] The Diary may not have discussed religion, but it does record many brief expressions of thanks to God. Hooke was also 'a frequent studier of the Holy Scriptures in the Originals',[68] by which one presumes the Hebrew, Greek, and Latin which he would have acquired at Westminster, though whether this intense Bible study was a daily exercise simply not noted in his Diary, or was a habit of his post-Diary old age, and after surviving the life-threatening illness of 1691, we do not know. His Diary does, however, make brief allusion to conversations with Sir Christopher Wren about a new French Bible and the 'Alexandrian Bible of Tecla' in 1678, though these references are, annoyingly, supplied without any wider context.[69]

One of Hooke's most explicit expressions of thanks for Divine Providence came on his 61st birthday, 18 July 1696, when he at last received a decision in his favour at the end of a tortuous Chancery lawsuit, though his thanks are prefaced by an adaptation of a pagan Roman prayer to the Great Being: 'D.O.M.S.H.L.G.I.S.S., Deo Opt.[imo] Max.[imo] Summus Honor [Laus] Gloria in Secula Secularum Amen [To the best and most high God be the greatest honour, praise, and glory for ever and ever, Amen]. I was Born on this Day of July 1635, and God has given me a new Birth, may I never forget his Mercies to me: whilst he gives me Breath may I praise him.'[70] I find there are no grounds, however, on which to agree with those who have recently tried to argue that this sixty-first birthday exclamation is an indication that Hooke had become a 'born again' Christian. Although the idea of being 'born again' in the Holy Spirit has a Gospel precedent going back to the conversation that took place between Christ and Nicodemus in John III:4, and many of the religious groups of the Civil War and Cromwellian period spoke of their own spiritual rebirths, such use of language is quite at odds with what we know about Robert Hooke's mental and spiritual perspective. He had no love of emotional or ecstatic religion of any kind, nor is there any record that he was ever involved in such worship after 1696. However, what *does* seem to have taken place in the early 1690s – possibly after his serious illness of early 1691 – is that he began to attend church, for many Sunday entries in his Diary by March 1693 begin 'M. [mane, 'morning'?] St. Helens', 'M. St. Peters', 'M. Westminster'. St Helen's, Bishopsgate, standing just across the road from Gresham College, was his local parish church, where Grace was buried, while St Peter's was only a short walk away.[71]

In spite of the possible ambivalence of Hooke's religious beliefs, it must be remembered that no-one, it appears, ever attempted defamation of Hooke's character by the application of one or both of the two great insult words of the seventeenth century: no-one seems to have called him either a papist or an atheist. On the other hand, why should they? We must not forget that Hooke moved in well-connected clerical circles. Bishop Wilkins was a well-known anti-fanatic and a staunch Protestant Broad Churchman, while Archbishop John Tillotson was an inclusive Protestant, famed for his diatribes against Roman Catholicism; and it was Tillotson, who ascended to the Arch-Episcopate via the Deaneries of Canterbury and St Paul's, London, under which titles Hooke referred to him, who conferred the Lambeth degree of Doctor of Medicine upon Hooke in 1691.[72]

It seems possible that the mature Hooke may have been something of a Deist: a man who believed in and revered the Great Creator God, but who may have been quietly sceptical on such points as the Incarnation, the Resurrection, and the Sacraments. But very importantly, he seems to have kept his inner thoughts to himself, and probably steered clear of religious questions even when drinking coffee with friends who were deans and bishops. And since he displayed no Catholic leanings nor apparently had any Catholic friendships (with the possible exception of Richard Townley in Lancashire), his beliefs posed no political threat to the state. While high-profile Roman Catholic sympathisers could suddenly end up in the Tower, especially after the ultra-Protestant Test Act of 1672, silent, conformist Deists were not seen as a danger to the State – especially if they were considered to be men of virtuous moral character (which we know Hooke was not) and friends with the Archbishop of Canterbury (which Hooke was). One suspects, however, that the undisclosed privacy of Robert Hooke's personal beliefs on matters of religion was best summed up by Waller when he said: 'If he was particular in some Matters, let us leave him to the searcher of Hearts.'[73]

Hooke's health and medical ideas

The first entry in Hooke's Diary, 1 August 1672, began with a description of one of his procedures of self-medication: 'Drank [steel] and [mercury]. At Wapping with governors. Took beet, slept not well.' The following eight years of his daily personal record contain much of the same, as he was purged, bled, took powerful vomits, induced sweats, and consumed a bewildering array of nauseous substances in his search for his health. Of course, nearly everything that he took was intended to be purgative in some way, be it to rid his head of aches and noises or his 'gutts of slime', for seventeenth-century doctors regarded illness as occasioned by some kind of obstruction of the body's natural vital processes that had to be somehow released. People have sometimes laughed at the seeming irrationality and apparent absurdity of Hooke's self-medication, but to do so presumes a Whig view of the history of medicine. Seventeenth-century doctors envisaged the disease process in fundamentally different terms than we do today – not in terms of germs, faulty cell replication or complex organic chemical reactions, but of a natural pathway becoming blocked by something that was deemed malefic and which needed to be shifted. Seen from this point of view, Hooke's medical procedures begin to make sense.

Yet what was actually wrong with Hooke? While his Diary contains a bewildering set of references to symptoms, we can pick out his dominant tendencies. In his late thirties Hooke suffered from headaches, nausea, breathlessness, noises in the head, fainting fits, chronic insomnia, blurred vision, and constipation. On the other hand, he does not seem to have suffered any life-threatening or seriously disabling illnesses until 1691 and thereafter.[74] How far these symptoms were psychosomatic, hereditary, personality-related (he was clearly sustainedly and unrelievedly manic), life-style-related or deep-seated physiological it is hard to be sure. Nor can we tell to what extent decades of powerful self-medication, often with toxic substances, undermined his constitution and helped contribute to the deepening debility of his final years.

Perhaps an initial clue might be found in Waller's statement that the 16-year-old Hooke became 'very crooked' and thin 'by frequent practicing, turning with a Turn-Lath[e]',[75] by which Waller probably refers to the hunched-up position required for working the lathe's treadle at the same time as turning the tool upon the work. But as a growing person would not have become permanently deformed by what could only have been a hobby activity for a Westminster School boy, it must be considered whether his spinal deformity came from another source. If so, a possible candidate could have been tuberculosis of the spine, and perhaps that condition which would receive its classical clinical description in the eighteenth century from the surgeon Perceval Pott. 'Pott's Disease' manifested itself in the tubercular softening of the spinal vertebrae, causing the backbone to twist and produce a major permanent deformity. Pott's Disease, moreover, can in certain and relatively rare cases cease its ravages after a while, and allow the person to grow up to be an otherwise healthy hunchback.[76]

No skeletal or histological remains come down to us from Hooke, and we cannot be certain. Even so, it is not impossible that Hooke had a long-term systemic tubercular problem which not only deformed his youthful spine but also undermined his general constitution. Tuberculosis, after all, was rife in seventeenth-century Europe, especially in the cities, and it could be that a young lad from the relatively healthy isolation of the Isle of Wight might have had little resistance to the disease on arriving in London.

On the other hand, there is no evidence that Robert Hooke ever suffered from the tuberculous abscesses which often accompanied Pott's Disease, and which in the great majority of cases led to paralysis, severe disablement, and early death.[77] Perhaps a more probable explanation of Hooke's 'awry' appearance – one more appropriate for a man who lived into his sixty-eighth year after the apparent onset of the deformity at sixteen – is that he suffered from either a lateral displacement of the spine, scoliosis; an exaggerated frontwise or backwise curvature, kyphosis; or a combination of both, kyphoscoliosis. Scoliosis can have a hereditary element, and often becomes more pronounced during the rapid growth spurts of the teenage years, leaving the adult victim looking short in stature, especially with relation to leg and arm length.[78]

The adult Robert Hooke was, according to his obituarist, abstemious in his food and alcohol intake. But he does seem to have been a coffee habitué, and in his Diary he makes reference to visiting nearly seventy separate coffee houses as well as taverns that sold alcoholic drinks, some of which, such as Childs, Garaways and Jonathans, were his regular haunts.[79] The coffee, tea, and 'chocolat' drunk in these establishments must also be reckoned as additional to those quantities consumed at home in Gresham College and at the private dinner-tables of friends such as Boyle, Wren and Sir John Lawrence. All in all, therefore, one might suggest that by the midnight or later bed-times of most days, there was perhaps sufficient caffeine and theobromine in his bloodstream to give him a headache, impair his vision, make his hands shake, or render him sleepless until dawn – all of which conditions he complained of in various Diary passages over the years.[80]

Last years and death

Considering the damage to his constitution caused by caffeine, theo-bromine, metallic 'elixiers', toxic purges and vomits, and an almost complete absence of proper rest, Hooke did extremely well to live into his sixty-eighth year. It has already been shown, however, that the year 1687 was something of a turning-point in his life, where his anger over the Newton controversy and the death of his beloved Grace brought about long-standing changes in his attitudes to life and to people in general, and almost certainly plunged him into a depressive state that would remain, on and off, to his death. One wonders whether his 'skin and bone' emaciation, referred to by Waller, had something to do with this depressive state, in which he used coffee and tea as stimulants and ate little food. There could also have been an hereditary component at work as far as depression was concerned: his father John Hooke had been 'melancholic', and his elder brother had committed suicide.

Then, in late 1690 or early 1691, he suffered from that unspecified illness which in April 1691 John Aubrey said had caused him, and other friends, to despair for Hooke's life. He recovered, but in 1697 a syndrome of problems began to develop that were to dog him and become worse over the remaining six years of his life. These included swollen and blackened legs (though his body was but 'skin and bone'), general oedema, breathlessness, and progressive blindness. Things were made no better when, in a faint, he fell downstairs and badly bruised his head, shoulders and ribs. And as always, there was insomnia. In spite of this appalling collection of symptoms, Hooke remained intellectually active, and in December 1702 (by which time his eyesight had become so poor that he could not write) dictated an account of an instrument intended to measure the apparent solar diameter to a new level of accuracy, though it was not a success.

Robert Hooke died in his Gresham College rooms on 3 March 1703, and several days later was buried with considerable pomp at his local parish church of St Helen's, Bishopsgate, in the City of London, with the Royal Society turning out in force to form the cortège.[81]

What, therefore, killed Robert Hooke? Though it is difficult for a modern physician to untangle the symptoms recorded by a colleague of three centuries ago, because disease concepts were so different then, and early-eighteenth-century doctors placed stress on different factors from their modern counterparts, I have shown Waller's detailed account of Hooke's last illness to several modern diagnosticians, who have all, interestingly enough, drawn some matching conclusions.[82]

Atherosclerosis, it was suggested, as a progressive disease of the arteries, could have led to hypertension, oedema, blackening of the feet and breaking of the swollen skin, fainting and light-headedness, and even retinal blindness. Also present was probably kidney failure, and perhaps diabetes too. The oedema, fainting and breathlessness, in particular, being aspects of the systemic cardio-vascular condition of atherosclerosis, could well have resulted in chronic cardiac failure, the ultimate deterioration of which was most likely the actual cause of death. Indeed, this syndrome of diseases would have produced symptoms not unlike those of palsy, cough, jaundice and dropsy, which killed the Revd John Hooke, as previously mentioned. Whether this came about because of heredity or because of the long-term effects of the superabundance of salt and saturated fats used in seventeenth-century food preservation and cooking, not to mention, in Robert Hooke's case, forty years of high caffeine intake and several decades' usage of metallic purges, vomits and 'elixiers' damaging his kidneys, it is impossible to know.

Conclusion

Robert Hooke was one of the most remarkable Englishmen of his day. Inspired, no doubt, by the physical characteristics, climate and geology of the Isle of Wight, and possessing a genius that was recognised and encouraged early, he moved with remarkable facility in the world of gentlemen of experiment. In spite of his absence of private means,

Hooke was undisputedly a gentleman in his education, culture and conduct; yet his career was only possible because he was seemingly happy to live a bachelor life devoted entirely to learning, with no apparent interest in any domesticity that went beyond the figures who passed through his Gresham College rooms. Hooke was also proud of his achievements, and was fully cognisant of what he had achieved for the world of learning in general, and for the success of the Royal Society in particular; and when he felt betrayed, especially after 1687, it is evident that a fundamental change took place in him, dampening his old conviviality and turning him into the 'Melancholy and Cynical' figure mentioned by Waller.

Upon his death in 1703, Robert Hooke left well over £10,000 in money and in properties – a gentleman of ample estate. It seems, according to Waller, that he had intended to use at least some of this money to help endow the Royal Society; but he never finalised his plans or completed his will, and he died intestate.[83]

The tragedy is that following his death, Hooke's reputation as a pioneering and outstandingly original scientist faded away, and he was largely forgotten in the ascendancy of the Newtonian approach to science. Indeed, this sidelining even extended, inadvertently, to his architecture, where many of Hooke's best buildings came to be popularly misattributed to his friend Sir Christopher Wren. And when, in 1758, Edmond Stone published his translated and considerably amplified edition of Nicholas Bion's treatise on scientific and mathematical instruments, references to Hooke were surprisingly few.[84] Nevertheless, in spite of this neglect, he had never been entirely forgotten at Christ Church, his old College in Oxford, and on four occasions in 1815, 1911, 1937 and 2003, the Gaudy Oration was delivered in his honour, this Commemorative Oration being an annual speech given by a B.A. of the College on the day of Encaenia.[85]

However, the tide of scholarly opinion began to turn in Robert Hooke's favour following the acquisition of his manuscript Diary by the Guildhall Library, London, in the 1890s. This manuscript was carefully transcribed and edited by Henry W. Robinson and Walter Adams and by Robert T. Gunther, who published their respective volumes for the 1672–80 and 1688–93 diaries in the mid-1930s.[86] Then it suddenly became clear that Robert Hooke was far more than an obscure seventeenth-century virtuoso who happened to be good with his hands and who had been unlucky enough to cross Newton. Hooke began gradually to claw his way back into the wider consciousness of scholars and historians of science. In 1956, Margaret Espinasse wrote an excellent first biography of Hooke,[87] and from the 1960s onwards, and largely following the Royal Society's celebration of its own tercentenary, increasingly serious attention has been paid to him.[88] Then, in 2003, in the year marking the 300th anniversary of his death, several Hooke biographies and scholarly studies appeared in print, and two major commemorative conferences were held – one at the Royal Society in July, and the other at Oxford, organised by Christ Church, the following October.[89]

And so it is hoped that, in the wake of this burgeoning new interest, the life, contributions and significance of Dr Robert Hooke, F.R.S., M.D., M.A. will come to be better understood and appreciated, and placed within the wider context of our knowledge of that scientific Renaissance which took place in seventeenth-century England.

Notes and references

1 Henry W. Robinson and Walter Adams (eds.), *The Diary of Robert Hooke, M.A., M.D., F.R.S., 1672–80 (transcribed from the original ... in Guildhall Library)* (Taylor and Francis, London, 1935, reprinted 1968). Also Robert T. Gunther, 'The Diary of Robert Hooke: Part I, November 1688 to March 1690 and December 1692 to August 1693', in *Early Science in Oxford*, **10** (Oxford, 1935), pp. 1–265.

2 John Aubrey, 'Robert Hooke', in *Brief Lives*, edited from original manuscripts by Oliver Lawson Dick (Secker and Warburg, London, 1949, 1975), pp. 164–7. I am indebted to Rob Martin and his colleagues at the Isle of Wight History Centre for the information, from Island archives, on their website, which includes several pages on the Hooke family:
http://freespace.virgin.net/roger.hewitt/iwias/home.htm
'The Hooke Family Tree (including the Giles family tree)',
http://freespace.virgin.net/ric.martin/vectis/hookeweb/tree.htm

3 Isle of Wight History Centre website (ref. 2):
'The Scientist, The Grocer, The Governor, and Grace'
http://freespace.virgin.net/ric.martin/vectis/hookeweb/sggg.htm
'John Hooke and Freshwater Parish'
http://freespace.virgin.net/ric.martin/vectis/hookeweb/par.htm

4 Joseph Foster, *Alumni Oxonienses. The Members of the University of Oxford, 1500–1714*, **2** (Oxford, 1891); (1) John Hooke, Warwickshire 'cler. fil.', Trinity College, matriculated 14 March 1599/1600, aged sixteen; (2) John Hooke, Bramshot, Hampshire, Armigeri 1622/23, aged seventeen. John Venn and J. A. Venn, *Alumni Cantabrigiensis*, Part I (Cambridge University Press, 1922), p. 402: John Hooke, Matriculated Sizar, Emmanuel College, Easter 1602.

5 Aubrey, 'Robert Hooke' (ref. 2), p. 164.

6 Hooke went to the Isle of Wight in the autumn of 1665, as he informed Boyle in advance: Hooke to Boyle, 26 September 1665, in Michael Hunter, Antonio Clericuzio and Lawrence M. Principe (eds.), *The Correspondence of Robert Boyle*, **2** (Pickering and Chatto, London, 2001), pp. 537–8. In an undated 'Earthquake Discourse' which was part of a series given to the

Royal Society before September 1668, he spoke of geologising by the south coast of England 'this last summer': Richard Waller (ed.), *The Posthumous Works of Robert Hooke, M.D., F.R.S.* (London, 1705), p. 292; reprinted with introduction and commentary by Ellen Tan Drake, *Restless Genius. Robert Hooke and his Earthly Thoughts* (Oxford University Press, 1996), p. 272.

7 Waller, 'The Life of Dr Robert Hooke', in *Posthumous Works* (ref. 6), p. ii.

8 Aubrey, 'Robert Hooke' (ref. 2), p. 164.

9 Hideto Nakajima, 'Robert Hooke's family and his youth: some new evidences from the Will of the Rev John Hooke', *Notes and Records of the Royal Society*, **48**(1) (1994), 11–16, esp. 15.

10 Robert heard the 'Fatall news of Brother John Hooke's death' on 1 March 1678. *Diary ... 1678–80* (ref. 1), 1 March 1678. The Isle of Wight History Centre website includes extensive citations from Newport civic documents pertaining to John Hooke:
'The Life of John Hooke'
http://freespace.virgin.net/ric.martin/vectis/hookeweb/john.htm
'Newport Corporation and the Suicide of John Hooke'
http://freespace.virgin.net/ric.martin/vectis/hookeweb/corp.htm

11 Cardell Goodman, one of his 'worthy and well beloved friends', was appointed by the Revd John Hooke as one of the 'Overseers' of his Will in 1648: see Nakajima, 'Robert Hooke's family ...' (ref. 9), 15. Cardell Goodman matriculated simultaneously at Christ Church, Oxford, and Emmanuel College, Cambridge, on 28 January 1625/26: Foster, *Alumni Oxoniensis* (ref. 4), p. 582, and Venn, *Alumni Cantabrigiensis* (ref. 4), 235. He became Rector of Freshwater in 1641, and was deprived of his living in 1651.

12 *Posthumous Works* (ref. 7), p. iii, for Goodman. Foster, *Alumni Oxoniensis* (ref. 4), mentions no Goodman for the 1650s. The Christ Church Alumni Office has also searched its databases, but has found no person of that name for the 1650s.

13 Aubrey, 'Robert Hooke' (ref. 2), p. 164. For John Hooke's Will, see Nakajima, 'Robert Hooke's family ...' (ref. 9), 14–15.

14 In addition to his £50 p.a. Gresham professorial salary, Hooke received £30 p.a. as Curator of Experiments of the Royal Society: Thomas Birch, *History of the Royal Society of London* (London, 1756–57), 11 January 1665, p. 4. Fellows of Wadham College in 1620 statutorily received £20 p.a., with occasional reduction when necessary: Thomas G. Jackson, *Wadham College, Oxford* (Clarendon Press, Oxford, 1893), p. 58.

15 Hooke, *Diary ... 1672–80* (ref. 1): '3 April 74, £3 p.a. for Bette'; '30 Sept. 74, £4 for Mary'.

16 It is very difficult to give an exact modern equivalent for a seventeenth-century sum of money. In March 1998 the Bank of England issued *Equivalent Contemporary Values of the Pound: A Historical Series, 1270 to 1998*, in which one Pound Sterling in 1640 stood at £76.57 in 1998, making Hooke's total £50 legacy a mere £3,828.50 today. A more realistic measure of value can be gauged – albeit very roughly – from the incomes of certain professional groups such as Oxford College Fellows or London professors.

Today, £30,000, rather than £3,828.50, is closer to a modest professional salary.

17 Aubrey, 'Robert Hooke' (ref. 2), p. 164.

18 Hooke, *Diary ... 1672–80* (ref. 1) contains many references to Dr Busby, sometimes with relation to architectural commissions. The 'Diary ...' 1688–93 (ref. 1) does likewise: on 31 October 1689, Hooke also recorded 'Westminster Scollers dind at the Colledge [Gresham]', which clearly shows his continued connection with his old school.

19 It is not known where Hooke was living on 30 January when Charles I was executed, but the Westminster boys were kept locked in the School to prevent their witnessing the event. Samuel Pepys, however, was somehow able to excuse himself from St Paul's School, for he was an eyewitness: Claire Tomalin, *Samuel Pepys: The Unequalled Self* (2002; Penguin, 2003), p. 34.

20 Nakajima, 'Robert Hooke's family ...' (ref. 9), 15–16.

21 I am indebted to Judith Curthoys, Archivist of Christ Church, for material supplied from the College's database of members, 1525–1660. Thomas Newnham appeared, at an unrecorded age, in 1656.

22 Hooke was still using Boyle's Pall Mall address when he wrote his letters to Boyle in July 1663: *The Correspondence of Robert Boyle*, **2** (ref. 6), Hooke to Boyle, 3 July 1663, pp. 96–8. For Hooke's salary discussions at the Royal Society, see Birch, *History of the Royal Society of London* (ref. 14), **1**, 2 November 1664, p. 479, 23 November 1664, p. 496, **2**, 11 January 1665, p. 4, and others.

23 Anthony Wood, 'Robert Hooke', in *Athenae Oxonienses*, **2** (second edition, Oxford, 1721), pp. 1039–40.

24 I am indebted to Professor Sir Henry Harris, of Christ Church, Oxford, for informing me of the full citation of the passage from Horace's *Epistles*, from which the contracted *Nullius In Verba* was used by the Royal Society for its motto.

25 While at Oxford, Hooke was instructed in Descartes' philosophy by Boyle: Wood, *Athenae Oxonienses* (ref. 23), p. 1039.

26 Hooke set out this experimental agenda with great force and clarity in the 28–page 'Preface' to *Micrographia, or Some Physiological Descriptions of Minute Bodies Made by Magnifying Glasses with Observations and Inquiries Thereupon* (London, 1665).

27 Lucretius, *De Rerum Natura* (*c.*40 B.C.), Book I, discusses atoms. Robert Boyle, *The Origins of Formes and Qualities* (Oxford, 1666), discusses Boyle's views on atoms.

28 Hooke, *Micrographia* (ref. 26), p. 85.

29 Hooke, *Micrographia* (ref. 26), p. 55.

30 Hooke, *Micrographia* (ref. 26), p. 67.

31 Hooke, 'Of Comets and Gravity' (undated, early 1680s), in *Posthumous Works* (ref. 6), pp. 184–5.

32 Hooke had probably come to this conclusion by the early 1660s, but his definitive statement of the fact was in *An Attempt to Prove the Motion of the Earth from Observations* (London, 1674), p. 27. Hooke's claim was also advanced by Aubrey in 'Robert Hooke' (ref. 2), pp. 166–7.

33 Hooke, *Lectures de Potentia Restitutiva, or, Of Springs, Explaining the Power of Springing Bodies, to which are added Some Collections* (John Martyn, London, 1678), p. 5; facsimile in Robert T. Gunther (ed.), 'The Cutlerian Lectures of Robert Hooke', *Early Science in Oxford*, **8** (Oxford, 1931).

34 Hooke, *Micrographia* (ref. 26), 'Preface', unpaginated, sig. aa recto. The empirical discovery metaphor of the great ocean voyages of Columbus, Drake and Magellan had been emphasised in the writings of Sir Francis Bacon in *Novum Organum* (1620), Aphorism XCII, and *The New Atlantis* (*c*.1617, published 1627).

35 Hooke, *Micrographia* (ref. 26), 'Preface', sig. bb recto and verso.

36 Waller, 'The Life of Dr Robert Hooke', in *Posthumous Works* (ref. 6), p. xxvii.

37 These portraits are published in most major biographies of Newton: see R. S. Westfall, *Never at Rest: A Biography of Isaac Newton* (Cambridge University Press, 1980).

38 Wood, *Athenae Oxonienses*, **2** (ref. 23), pp. 1039–40.

39 Tomalin, *Samuel Pepys* (ref. 19), Chapter 1.

40 Sir John Lawrence (or Laurence), F.R.S., was one of the great dignitaries of the Restoration City; see *Diary ... 1672–80* (ref. 1), 7 September 1672, 25 April 1673, 15 May 1673, 10 January 1674, 24 February 1674, and others, for social and business relations with Lawrence.

41 Michael A. R. Cooper, *'A More Beautiful City'. Robert Hooke and the Rebuilding of London after the Great Fire* (Sutton, Stroud, 2003); also Cooper, 'Hooke's Career', in J. A. Bennett, M. A. R. Cooper, M. Hunter and L. Jardine, *London's Leonardo: The Life and Work of Robert Hooke* (Oxford University Press, 2003), pp. 1–61, p. 61 for Cooper's estimate of Hooke's earnings.

42 The index to the *Diary ... 1672–80* (ref. 1) contains many social references to Tompion. On 2 June 1676 Tompion was even included in a group of friends – mainly Fellows of the Royal Society – who went to see Shadwell's play *The Virtuoso*.

43 *Diary ... 1672–80* (ref. 1), 20 June 1678.

44 See ref. 22 for references to Hooke living with Boyle in Pall Mall in the early 1660s.

45 *Diary ... 1672–80* (ref. 1), 16 August 1677, 2 July 1679 and 18 October 1679 for Lady Wren; 25 November 1674 for Irish ladies at the Boyles' house; 12 September 1678 for Abigail Williams.

46 *Diary ... 1672–80* (ref. 1), 28 October 1672. Hooke used the astrological symbol for Pisces ♓ to note a sexual encounter.

47 Hooke never records whipping or similar physical cruelty being inflicted upon his servants, as was common at that time, though he clearly expected sexual favours.

48 On 22 April 1676, for instance, Hooke did 'Eat eggs and drank wormwood beer at Nell's', *Diary ... 1672–80* (ref. 1). In 'Diary ...' 1688–93 (ref. 1) there are several references to friendly visits by the *c*.40-year-old Nell Young, and even her children, to Hooke in Gresham College. Some contained a work component, such as stitching, and others not: 4 April 1689, 6 October 1689, 12 March 1693, 2 April 1693, 13 April 1693 and 21 May 1693.

49 Things seemed to be going well for a marriage to the son of Sir Thomas Bloodworth, a former Lord Mayor, but the match never came off: *Diary . . . 1672–80* (ref. 1), 13 September 1672, and various entries in July and August 1673.

50 *Diary . . . 1672–80* (ref. 1), 16 October 1676, 11 November 1676, and others.

51 Robert Ollard, *Man of War: Sir Robert Holmes and the Restoration Navy* (1969; Phoenix, London, 2001), p. 188.

52 Rob Martin, 'The Scientist, The Grocer, The Governor, And Grace', Isle of Wight History Centre (2000): http://freespace.virgin.net/ric.martin/vectis/hookeweb/sggg.htm.

53 See ref. 10; also Martin, 'The Scientist . . .' (ref. 52).

54 *Diary . . . 1672–80* (ref. 1), 10 August 1677; also Monica Mears, 'Grace Hooke'. I am indebted to Monica Mears of Willen, near Newport Pagnell, Buckinghamshire, for the typescript of her unpublished article, which is undoubtedly the most thorough biography of Grace Hooke to have been produced.

55 *Diary . . . 1672–80* (ref. 1), 26 February 1678, for Grace's measles.

56 *Diary . . . 1672–80* (ref. 1), 9 June 1678.

57 Waller, 'The Life of Dr Robert Hooke', in *Posthumous Works* (ref. 6), p. xxiv.

58 The 'Discourses of Earthquakes' were published in 1705 in *Posthumous Works* (ref. 6), pp. 279–450, and are reprinted with definitive scholarly commentary by Ellen Tan Drake in *Restless Genius* (ref. 6).

59 Aubrey, 'Robert Hooke' (ref. 2), p. 165.

60 *Diary . . . 1672–80* (ref. 1), 27 February 1677.

61 *Diary . . . 1672–80* (ref. 1), 31 December 1676.

62 Waller, 'The Life of Dr Robert Hooke', in *Posthumous Works* (ref. 6), p. xxv.

63 John Aubrey to Anthony Wood, 21 April 1691, printed in Maurice Balme, *Two Antiquaries: A Selection of the Correspondence of John Aubrey and Anthony Wood* (Durham Academic Press, Edinburgh, Cambridge, Durham, U.S.A., 2001), p. 133.

64 *Diary . . . 1672–80* (ref. 1), 4 May 1673.

65 *Diary . . . 1672–80* (ref. 1), 12 March 1678.

66 The Test Acts of 1672 and 1678 were pieces of legislation drafted by an ultra-Protestant Parliament, and were designed to exclude Roman Catholics from all public offices, civil and military. The focus of the Test Acts was James, Duke of York – Charles II's brother, and the future short-reigned James II – who had converted to Roman Catholicism and, it was feared, was trying to pack the British establishment with his co-religionists, with the suspected intention of returning England to Rome, overturning the Reformation, and making England an absolute monarchy, like Catholic France and Spain. The Acts set out key qualifications for all public office holders, such as swearing allegiance to the 39 Articles of the Church of England, abjuring the Roman Catholic Mass, and publicly taking the Anglican Communion, all of which would have been impossible for Roman Catholics on grounds of conscience.

67 Waller, 'The Life of Dr Robert Hooke', in *Posthumous Works* (ref. 6), pp. xxv and xxviii, for religious observations.

68 Waller, 'The Life of Dr Robert Hooke', in *Posthumous Works* (ref. 6), p. xxviii.

69 *Diary ... 1672–80* (ref. 1), 17 September 1678.

70 Waller, 'The Life of Dr Robert Hooke', in *Posthumous Works* (ref. 6), p. xxv.

71 'Diary ...' 1688–93 (ref. 1): several Sunday Church references after the end of 1691 – 19 March 1693, 9 April 1693, and others.

72 Waller, 'The Life of Dr Robert Hooke', in *Posthumous Works* (ref. 6), p. xxv.

73 Waller, 'The Life of Dr Robert Hooke', in *Posthumous Works* (ref. 6), p. xxviii.

74 Aubrey to Wood (ref. 63).

75 Waller, 'The Life of Dr Robert Hooke', in *Posthumous Works* (ref. 6), p. xxvi.

76 Pott's Disease – tuberculosis of the spine – is discussed in Thomas Dormandy, *The White Death: A History of Tuberculosis* (Hambledon Press, London, 1999), pp. 2, 74; also J. Walton, J. A. Barondess and S. Lock, 'Pott's Disease', in *The Oxford Medical Companion* (Oxford University Press, 1994), p. 785.

77 Dormandy, *White Death* (ref. 76), p. 24, mentions that 'self-limitation' – the disease suddenly switching itself off, leaving the victim permanently affected – 'was the exception rather than the rule'.

78 I am indebted to Dr Richard Whittington, an experienced physician and retired Coroner to the City of Birmingham, for this suggested non-tubercular cause of Hooke's reported spinal deformity.

79 *Diary ... 1672–80* (ref. 1), pp. 463–70, for a list of coffee houses mentioned.

80 In the *Diary ... 1672–80* (ref. 1), there are many references to coffee, and also insomnia. On 25 October 1673, however, Hooke experienced what might strike us as contradictory symptoms: 'Slept well after 2 dishes of Coffee – hand shook.'

81 Waller, 'The Life of Dr Robert Hooke', in *Posthumous Works* (ref. 6), pp. xxvi–xxvii, for all the above references to Hooke's last illness, death, and Waller's assessment.

82 These include Dr Richard Whittington (see ref. 78), Dr John Lester, a very experienced retired General Practitioner of Walsall, and the late Professor John Potter, of Oxford.

83 Waller, 'The Life of Dr Robert Hooke', in *Posthumous Works* (ref. 6), p. xxvii, for the intentions of Hooke's bequest. However, as Professor Lisa Jardine has shown in *The Curious Life of Robert Hooke: The Man who Measured London* (Harper Collins, London, 2003), pp. 316–7, Hooke left a draft Will, but as it was incomplete and unsigned, it had no legal authority. The Probate Inventory, dated 22 April 2003, valued his estate, excluding Isle of Wight holdings, at £9,850 14s 8d. This Probate Record, discovered by Frank Kelsall in the Public Record Office, is reproduced in 'Hooke's possessions at his Death: a hitherto Unknown Inventory', in Michael Hunter and Simon Schaffer, *Robert Hooke: New Studies* (Boydell Press, Woodbridge, 1989), pp. 287–94.

84 Nicholas Bion, *The Construction and Principal Uses of Mathematical Instruments*, translated by Edmund Stone, with Stone's 'Supplement' (London, 1758), pp. 263–325.

85 The Gaudy Orators who spoke on Hooke were T. V. Short, 1815; W. A. Akers, 1911; G. J. Whitrow, 1937; and T. Rogers, 2003. I am indebted to Dr Paul W. Kent for kindly tracing these speeches in Christ Church archives.

86 Robinson and Adams, and Gunther (ref. 1).

87 Margaret Espinasse, *Robert Hooke: New Studies* (London, 1956).

88 E. N. Da C. Andrade, 'Robert Hooke', *Notes and Records of the Royal Society*, **15** (1960), 137–45. Hunter and Schaffer, *Robert Hooke* (ref. 83).

89 The Royal Society and Gresham College conference was held during 6–10 July 2003, and the Christ Church, Oxford, conference was held in the Examination Schools, Oxford, on 2 October 2003.

Chapter 3

Hooke's early life at Oxford

Paul W. Kent

Robert Hooke spent a relatively short period of his life in Oxford, but those years (1653–61) were to be deeply formative in the career of one who would become one of Britain's most inventive scientists.[1]

As a lowly but exceptionally talented youth he benefited less from formal teaching than from the interactive learning with like-minded contemporaries of outstanding ability, such as Christopher Wren and John Locke, gathered informally round a notable tutor of anatomy and chemistry, Thomas Willis. All benefited further from close association with older colleagues – a group of more senior and experienced scholars assembled by John Wilkins, Warden of Wadham, amongst whom were John Wallis and Thomas Spratt (mathematicians), Seth Ward (astronomer) and Robert Boyle (chemist). The bringing together of groups of talented individuals has occurred periodically throughout Oxford's history, and has often proved to be impressively conducive to originality.

Boyhood days

Hooke's early years were lived mostly in times of trouble and turmoil then pervading Britain. He was barely seven when the Civil War began (1642) and the ensuing years of conflict led to the overthrow of the Royalist cause (1647) and the execution of Charles I (1649). With the King out of the way in England, Cromwell sought to govern at first through various adaptations of Parliament. These finally failing (1654), real authority lay with the Army and with Cromwell as Lord Protector

– a ruler with near absolute power.[2] In other parts of the British Isles, this situation not being accepted, a second phase of Civil War in the 1650s erupted into violent campaigns to subdue the Welsh, Irish and Scots. Ultimately the country settled under an uneasy military dictatorship. In Europe the overthrow of a Royal House, the execution of a crowned monarch, and the outstanding military success by a hitherto unknown leader, provoked a mixture of surprise, alarm and respect.

In 1647–48 the Civil War came close to Hooke's home at Freshwater, Isle of Wight, where his father was curate. Charles I – by then in the hands of the Parliamentarians – was held under open arrest at nearby Carisbrooke Castle (pending Cromwell's decision on the next step). The twelve-year-old Hooke must have been well aware of the distinguished neighbour. As a rather sickly boy, he nevertheless began to show his talents to learn and to invent ingenious toys as well as to show his skill at drawing. His life, however, changed when his father died in 1648, bequeathing to him his books and a small legacy (£40). Hooke then went to London to further his education, and for a short time worked in the studio of (Sir) Peter Lely before anrolling at Westminster School.

Commonwealth times

The Parliamentarians' political control, with their influence extending into the nation's cultural life and into everyday affairs, was nowhere better seen than in Oxford. Up to 1646 Oxford had been the King's capital city, his residence, and a military stronghold. The staunchly Royalist sympathies of the City and University were furthered even more by the activities of the University's printers, from whom emerged a flow of publications in the Royalist cause. The fall of the City to Parliamentary forces (1646) nevertheless allowed honourable terms to the Royalist forces to march out 'drums beating and flags flying'.

Cromwell and his party lost little time in making their presence felt. The Covenant already in force in Scotland (1644) was to be imposed on England, abolishing the Church of England, its bishops and parish clergy, its cathedrals and its organisational framework.[3] The Directory – a Parliamentary-approved manual of public worship enjoining extemporary prayer and extensive sermonising – replaced (1645) the Book of Common Prayer, which was totally proscribed. By law, all Englishmen over the age of eighteen were thus required to subscribe on oath to the Covenant.

Cromwell set about reorganising the University, allowing himself to be made Chancellor (but putting his functions into the hands of five

Commissioners) and conferring honorary degrees on some of his leading officers.[4] The business of reorganisation fell to Parliamentary Visitors[5] charged with the task of testing the loyalty to Parliament of senior members and office holders. Over a period of about four years (1647–51) the Visitors summoned individuals before them, inquisitorially probing their attitude to Parliamentary authority. A large number of individuals at all levels refused to submit, and were summarily dismissed from their positions.[6]

Christ Church as the Cathedral of Oxford and a Royalist stronghold was especially vulnerable, since on 30 April 1649 all Cathedral chapters in England and Wales were declared dissolved and their lands and property forfeit.[7] At Durham, for example, every official was dismissed, and the immense Cathedral with its surrounding buildings including the Castle (the bishop's residence) left empty and open to ruin. Christ Church was treated as an exception; existing canons, like Heads of Houses were ejected but replaced by Parliament's own men, a mixture of Presbyterians and Independents. Only one – John Wall – was allowed to remain in office throughout the Commonwealth and to survive into the reign of Charles II.

Samuel Fell, the Dean (1636–47) and Vice-Chancellor (1645–47), declining even to appear before the Visitors, was imprisoned from September until November 1647, and when released was deprived of all his offices.[8] He went to live in his sole parish remaining to him: Sunningwell, near Oxford, where he died in 1649 on hearing of the King's execution.[9]

Samuel Fell was replaced as Dean by a Presbyterian, Edward Reynolds, said to be a reputable scholar, who from 1649 until 1651 was Vice-Chancellor. Far-reaching changes were made in the University as well as in Christ Church, making for stern discipline, strict order, plain living, earnest study and obsessive religion. Levity and traditional recreations were set aside. A rare pleasurable innovation at this time was the coming of coffee to Oxford which was sold to the public at 'The Angel' in the High Street.

In 1651 Reynolds refused to take the Independent Engagement (to agree to the Independent's dogma), and was replaced in the Deanery by John Owen, who remained in office until 1659. Owen, an Independent, appears to have had a tolerant personality. He published serious works on religious subjects, was held in high regard by some of the Puritan following,[10] and made a significant contribution to the theory of toleration in matters considered not prelatical or papist. His liking for sartorial elegance was a matter of comment.

Throughout the Commonwealth the University and Christ Church existed under an uneasy régime of Presbyterian and Independent rule.

Those deposed earlier – such as Richard Allstree, John Dolben and John Fell (son of Samuel Fell) – went to live elsewhere in the City but remained resolutely loyal to the Church of England, maintaining its liturgy first in Canterbury College and then in Beam Hall, Thomas Willis's house in St John's Street (now Merton Street), where Robert Hooke went to live.[11]

The effect of the changes resulted in the loss of experienced personnel[12] to serve Colleges and University, declining financial resources, and creeping poverty – a trend which worsened as the Commonwealth years went by.

Oxford City in Hooke's day

The City of Oxford to which Robert Hooke first came in 1653 was still in its essentially mediaeval form, with many citizens living in cramped conditions within the confines of the ancient walls. The East Gate spanned the High Street, North Gate the Cornmarket Street, and the West Gate adjoined the Castle, still an important defensive structure. To the south, Friar Bacon's Bridge (Folly Bridge) and the river gave protection from that direction. During the siege of Oxford in the 1640s the defences of the City, inadequate as they were, had again assumed importance. To strengthen the position, Royalist forces in the City constructed a system of bulwarks[13] to protect the approaches using stone and other materials from abandoned monastic institutions such as Osney and Rewley Abbeys. These defences extended as far north as St Giles' Church, and encompassed colleges such as St Johns, Balliol, Trinity, and the newly founded (1612) Wadham College which lay outside the old walls[14] (Figure 3.1). Magdalen Bridge was breached and converted into a drawbridge.

The result produced (temporarily) an enlarged and protected area for the City, permitting greater space for movement and storage. Through these years, chronic problems arose in maintaining adequate supplies, not only of munitions, but of food, fuel and essential commodities. This situation was further aggravated when, in October 1644, fire broke out in Thames Street (now George Street), devastating property in Cornmarket and New Inn Hall Street, and quickly reaching Carfax and Butchers Row (Queen Street). From there the flames crossed over to Pennyfarthing Street and St Ebbes, causing further devastation. It is estimated that approximately a quarter of the old City was destroyed.

The normal population of ordinary residents was less than 10,000, but between 1642 and 1646, with the King residing in Christ Church

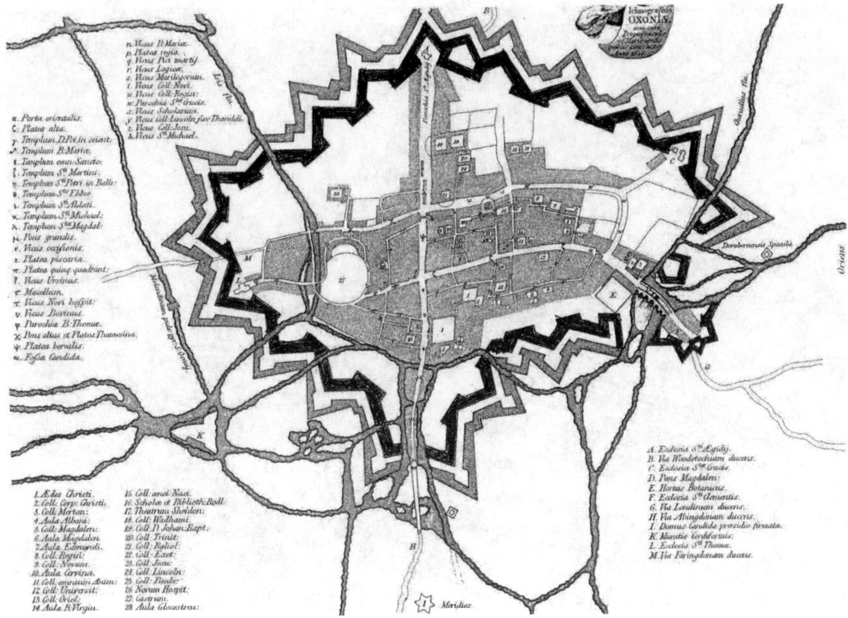

Fig. 3.1. A plan (1648) of the defensive earthworks built around Oxford by
Charles I after 1642.

and the Queen in Merton, together with a sizable entourage, and the
encamped troops and undergraduates enrolled as militia, the City was
grossly over-extended. In these circumstances some citizens took
refuge in temporary make-shift shelters on open ground nearby. Even
after the Royalist withdrawal, the occupation by Parliamentary troops
and their accompanying personnel maintained this civic predicament.

Poor hygiene, overcrowding and dubious water supplies inevitably
contributed to the production of a grossly unhealthy environment.
From 1643, camp-fever was rife in both armies for several years, and
there were serious epidemics of plague in 1654, 1656 and 1658.[15]
During these times, John Wilkins and some of his scientific group occasionally went to live outside Oxford, and possibly took Hooke with
them.

Further problems arose from rising crime. Not all Royalist troops
withdrew at the capitulation, and destitute stragglers, with other
deserters, resorted to robbery and theft, although they received short
shrift from the Puritan rulers.

The behaviour of the occupying Parliamentary forces occasioned
concern, though Cromwell took steps to ensure that the Bodleian
Library was not pillaged, and other leading figures (Wilkins and

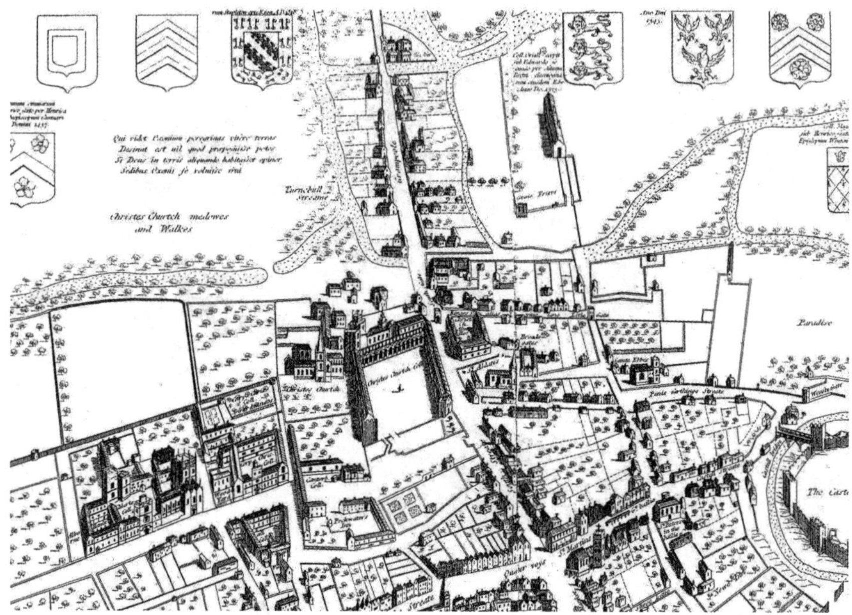

Fig. 3.2. Christ Church, Oxford, and adjacent colleges in Commonwealth times, as Hooke knew them. Here, Tom Quad (Christ Church) is not yet complete. (From Agas, 1578.)

Fairfax) sought to suppress ignorant wanton damage. Nevertheless, windows, statues, decorative works of art considered idolatrous, prelatical or papist, fell to the iconoclastic fervour.

At Christ Church, the Van Linge painted glass windows in the Cathedral, installed earlier in the century, were considered 'anti-Christian, diabolical and popish' and were largely destroyed.[16] Even Wilkinson, one of the newly intruded Commonwealth canons, took a leading part in their destruction. John Evelyn, visiting in 1654, commented on the windows of the Cathedral as 'much damaged'.[17]

One window, depicting Bishop King, the first and only Bishop of Osney, was removed by his relatives and hidden until the Restoration, when it was reinstated to its present position. The Cathedral's silver-mounted Book of Common Prayer and the Bible, presented in 1638 by Canon Henry King, were taken into safe keeping in 1647 (some say wrapped and buried in the college grounds) to be recovered by Canon Gardiner and returned for use in 1660.[18]

The buildings, for the most part, were as Wolsey had left them, with Tom Quad only part finished (Figure 3.2). The adjoining old Peckwater Inn and Canterbury College which Christ Church now possessed provided additional, if poor, accommodation. Dean Samuel

Fell had built the exquisite fan-vaulted stairway to the Hall (about 1640), and had commenced work on the building of canons' residences in the empty north side of Tom Quad. His successor, Dean Reynolds, immediately dismantled the part-built structures and demolished the timber frameworks for use as firewood, as might be expected in view of the shortage of fuel.

Undergraduate life in Commonwealth years

The way of life at Christ Church under Puritan rule was very different for those with long memories[19] who could remember more relaxed years. The Directory – the approved manual – was now in full use in the Cathedral. Daily prayers were between 5 a.m. and 6 a.m. and at 5 p.m., and on Sundays there were services morning and evening. The Church of England chaplains continued in office, and though contemptuous of their new masters, were permitted to excuse themselves from services. On Thursdays, the University Sermon was preached at Christ Church at 4 p.m., and was followed by religious exercises for members of the college. Stern discipline imposed the attendance of all members of the House at these prayers, weekdays and Sundays alike. Tutors were required to urge their pupils to private prayer and to reflect on their devotions. On Sunday evenings between 6 p.m. and 9 p.m., undergraduates and B.A.s were required to gather and give accounts of the sermons they had heard that day.

Discipline was rigorously imposed on all aspects of everyday life. In an edict on dress and likewise, it was ordered:

> That the Dean and Sub-dean and Censors do take special care to reform all scandalous fashions of long and powered hair, and habits contrary to the statutes of the University and that decency and modesty which is necessary for young students.

Also,

> That some order be taken to punish the abuse of swearing, viz., that for the first and second time he that sweareth be fined 12d. for every oath; and when convicted the third time shall be proceeded against as a scandalous person.

In 1653 a further edict sought to regulate what was considered to be extravagant habits by junior members. The Chapter took action:

> For the repressing the immoderate expences of youth in the College, that

> no gentleman commoner shall battel in the buttery above 5 shillings weekly; no under commoner above 4 shillings weekly; no scholar of the House above 3 shillings weekly; and the butler is hereby required to give notice to the Dean or Sub-dean at the end of the week of such as shall exceed this allowance.

In 1656, the use of Latin was strictly enjoined on the following terms:

> Whereas by several orders both of the Committee of Parliament and the Visitors of this University all scholars and students are commanded to use the Latin tongue whensoever they discourse and speak together in the Hall at dinner and supper and all other meetings there; it is this day ordered by the said Dean and Chapter that the said Orders be (and are hereby) revived and reinforced, with strict injunction that they be observed accordingly by all of this College herein concerned, giving them further notice that whosoever shall be found faulty herein shall be proceeded against by them as contemners of wholesome discipline and public authority.

Not surprisingly, undergraduates were not all excited by this gloomy and restrictive régime. One, it is reported, on 17 September 1653 incurred the wrath of the Chapter for being 'in a tippling house in the city of Oxon on the Lords Day' and then for 'traducing the government of the House publicly in the Hall'. He was severely admonished and placed under sentence of further proceedings. Earlier, in 1650, Henry Stubbe, a 19–year old Westminster student, had fallen foul of the Censor and fared worse: 'After abusing the Censor Morum, Will Segary that noted disciplinarian, duly whipped Stubbe in the Hall' ('Public Refectory').[20]

Hooke in Oxford

Little of this would have surprised Hooke when at the age of eighteen (1653) he came to work and study in Oxford, though it seems probable that as a servitor living out of College he escaped the full rigour – unlike his friends John Locke and Christopher Wren, who were fully matriculated undergraduates and under College discipline. By 1653 Wren had taken his M.A., and after becoming a Fellow of All Souls (1657) he thus had the advantage of seniority. At Westminster School,[21] Hooke, Locke and Wren had been taught by that remarkable Headmaster, Richard Busby, and Hooke actually resided in his house.[22] Under Busby's punishing régime, few sat comfortably at his feet, though Hooke appears to have had much regard for him. On

Busby's retirement many years later, Hooke designed a church for him at Willen, near Newport Pagnell, Buckinghamshire.

Hooke already had numerous friends at Christ Church when he was admitted. The formal connection between the University and Westminster School established by Elizabeth I, provided for up to four boys each year to be elected as scholars of Christ Church (and four more as scholars of Trinity College, Cambridge).[23] Hooke, however, was not amongst those elected in 1653,[24] and he entered Christ Church as a servitor (or chorister, or possibly both), initially to a Mr Goodman.[25]

Servitors were a particular category, existing until the mid-nineteenth century, of junior members who were remunerated for performing some service in colleges such as serving at meal times or acting as a personal servant to a wealthy undergraduate, but were allowed to proceed to degrees. They took their meals apart from undergraduates, and wore distinctive attire.[26] If Hooke had been a chorister it was unlikely that it would have been in the conventional manner in view of the nature of cathedral worship then prevailing, though he may have been given the emoluments of a chorister. A Chapter order of the early Commonwealth years required 'that the Orgain's in the Quire of this church be taken down' – no doubt a disappointment for young Hooke, who was a competent organist. He was well prepared for University studies in numerous other respects, as he was fluent in Latin, had a good command of Greek, knew some Hebrew, was talented in mathematics, and had considerable ability as a draughtsman. He is said to have mastered the first six books of Euclid in a week, and to have learnt to play the organ (perhaps the one in Busby's house) in twenty lessons.[27]

His friend and contemporary John Locke (1632–1704), who was also elected to Christ Church from Westminster and matriculated in the previous year,[28] followed the usual path to the B.A. (1655/56) and M.A. (1658), studying works of Greek and Latin authors, and poets, philosophy and logic (including mathematics). Another slightly older friend, Christopher Wren (1632–1722/23),[29] who entered Wadham (1647) from Westminster School at the tender age of fourteen and graduated B.A. (1650/51) and M.A. (1653), followed the similar course of studies as did Richard Lower (1631–1691), who also came to Christ Church (1649) from Westminster, graduated B.A. (1653), M.A. (1655), B.M. and D.M. (1660), and became F.R.S. (1667) and F.R.C.P. (1665).

For Hooke, as a servitor, life was different in that he does not appear to have taken the usual B.A., but went (1654) to live in Thomas Willis's household as his assistant. In this regard Hooke could have a much more free-ranging space for learning than could many of his friends. Willis (1621–1675)[30] (Figure 3.3) was an outstanding teacher and researcher in anatomy and chemistry at Christ Church. He was a man

Fig. 3.3. Thomas Willis, Hooke's teacher at Christ Church. (From an engraving in the Hope Collection.)

of local origin, his family having farmed at North Hinksey, and they were devoted Royalists (both his parents died of camp-fever at Oxford in 1643). Willis himself, in his early days (1639), had been a servitor to one of the Canons of Christ Church, and it can be presumed that he might be particularly sympathetic to the young Hooke, who was similarly placed. His house – Beam Hall (Figure 3.4), in St John's Street (now Merton Street) opposite Merton College – was a substantial stone building with principal rooms having early seventeenth-century wood panelling, and was probably considerably more comfortable than many other houses in Oxford. Here Willis, with John Fell (later Dean), John Dolben and Richard Allstree – friends who had been displaced from Christ Church – continued to maintain the services of the Church of England, despite their illegality. The intruded Dean Owen seems to have turned a blind eye to such irregularity going on under his nose. The young Hooke, in this avowedly Royalist surrounding, kept a low profile. Little has been reported about him at this time, even by the loquacious Anthony Wood, the diarist and antiquarian, who lived nearby at his parental home in Merton Street.

Hooke as assistant to Thomas Willis

In his scientific studies, Willis and those about him had adopted the new-fashioned Baconian ideas. Francis Bacon[31] (1561–1626, born three years before Galileo) published his chief work, *Novum Organum*, in 1620, just a year before Willis's birth. This book challenged the old Greek philosophy, advancing the concept that new knowledge about the natural world could be obtained by experimental enquiry. This revolutionary way of thinking made an immediate impact on many philosophers of the day, including those in Oxford, who described themselves as Natural Philosophers.

Willis was an experimentalist,[32] though his chemical ideas were those of iatrochemistry, which considered earth, fire and air to be essential elements with salt, sulphur and mercury as principles. Such was the rudimentary state of this branch of science, to be radically changed by Robert Boyle just a few years ahead. Willis carried out analyses of animal and vegetable matter, and investigated combustion and the properties of aureus fulminans (gold fulminate); and fermentation as a process of change also occupied his attention. Though Willis did not contribute to outstanding chemical advances, he was the first to identify the disorder known as diabetes mellitus. Even at this stage chemistry was held generally in high regard as a useful art in which traditional skills were the basis of the technologies of the day such as

Fig. 3.4. Beam Hall, St John's Street (now Merton Street), Oxford; Willis's home, where Hooke lodged. (*Top*) exterior, 1958. (Photograph by P. S. Spokes.) (*Bottom*) interior, 1938. (Crown copyright National Monuments Records.)

glass-making, brewing, tanning, dyeing, smelting, and sundry herbal remedies.

To anatomy, however, Willis made notable contributions, particularly in tracing the nervous system and in investigating the structure of the brain, immortalising his name in the Circle of Willis – a unique structure which he observed and characterised in the base of that organ. Willis's dissecting investigations were assisted by the young scientists around him: Hooke, Wren, Locke and Lower. Richard Lower was particularly skilful in helping Willis with his investigations for his celebrated publication *Cerebri Anatome* which appeared (1664) after the Restoration. Lower was one of the first to achieve transfusion of blood from one animal to another, to recognise the changes in blood as it circulated through the lungs, and to accurately dissect the heart.

John Locke was dissatisfied with the philosophy as then taught, and participation in Willis's work aroused in him much interest which he came to regard as training for a medical career.[33] After graduation (B.A. 1655/56, and M.A. 1658) he pursued this end seriously, and eventually had a small but successful medical practice, acquiring public recognition for his treatment of the Earl of Shaftesbury for an infected cyst. Later (1663) he incorporated (M.A.) at Cambridge, and received the degree of B.M. at Oxford (1674/75).

Christopher Wren joined in the experimental work of this group with enthusiasm, and gained much from the anatomical studies. He made useful contributions to the study of blood transfusions, skin grafting, and injections into the bloodstream of living animals, and played a special role in the group due to his brilliant talent for drawing. The accurate recording of dissections was crucial, and would provide the illustrations for Willis's *Cerebri Anatome*; and similarly, in later years he provided illustrations of Hooke's work in the latter's *Micrographia*.

Apart from these enthusiastic young people, others such as John Mayow, Thomas Millington and Robert Boyle also came to gather round Willis and benefit from the experimental observations and interchange of ideas. Boyle devised the valuable technique of using spirit (alcohol) to preserve anatomical specimens. Moreover, the group's social relationship extended beyond the confines of academic study, and they managed to enjoy convivial times together. Anthony Wood, who lived nearby, noted the occasion when he 'drank with Richard Lower, a half-pint of sack at the Meeriemaid Tavern, $4^{1}/_{2}$d'. They seem to have been particularly partial to this hostelry, which is frequently mentioned, amongst others, in Wood's Diary.

The young Hooke, approaching twenty years of age, was thus launched on his apprentice style of studying, and was expanding his interests as he was drawn into the Wilkins group at Wadham College. In the Commonwealth days, Wadham – founded in 1612 – was one of the newest Colleges, only a few years older than Pembroke, founded in 1624 from the earlier Broadgates Hall, with Dr Thomas Clayton, Regius Professor of Medicine, as its first Master. In the manner of new institutions, these seemed more open and receptive to fresh ideas and new ways.

Hooke and the Wadham group

At Wadham College, a talented group of older experienced scientists gathered for regular weekly meetings around the Warden, the Revd John Wilkins, to discuss the New Philosophy, their experimental findings, and proposed explorations. John Wilkins (1614–1672)[34] had a compelling desire to encourage the growth of science – a desire which he had gained in London some years earlier from informal meetings, at the Bull's Head in Cheapside, with friends such as Wallis, Goddard and Petty. Wilkins was the Oxford-born son of a local goldsmith, was educated at Magdalen Hall (B.A. 1631 and M.A. 1634), and was chaplain first to Lord Saye and Sele and then to Prince Charles Louis (Prince Elector Palatine, the nephew of Charles I). During the Civil War his allegiance shifted to the parliamentary side, though he sat lightly with respect to the Presbyterian or Independent parties. Enjoying Cromwell's favour he was intruded as Warden of Wadham (1648) by the Parliamentary Visitors, and set about satisfying his ambitions for the sciences.

As Wilkins was installed as Warden of Wadham, William Harvey – the discoverer of the circulation of the blood – was ejected (1646) as Warden of Merton when Oxford fell to the Parliamentarians.[35] Harvey had been physician to Charles I, and had arrived with him in Oxford after the Battle of Edgehill in 1642.

In 1648 Wilkins published an influential and widely read book, *Mathematicall Magick*[36] (dedicated to Prince Charles Louis), dealing with the basic principles of levers, pulleys, gears and spirals, and speculating about flying 'automata' and possible voyages to the Moon. It was – and still is – a masterpiece of descriptive writing about mathematical subjects, and had a stimulating influence on the young Hooke.

Wilkins' ingenious and inventive mind was in close accord with Hooke's needs. Wilkins had already written *The Discovery of a World in the Moon* (1638), followed by *Mercury, or the Secret Messenger* (1641) – a cryptographical study. In his garden he established a transparent apiary for the observation of bees, and devised a hollow statue from which a voice was contrived to emerge. He also invented the way-wiser, a wind gun, and numerous other devices.

Wilkins' group, as it expanded, included his old friends from London – Wallis, Goddard and Petty, who had moved to Oxford. William Petty (1623–1687) was an outstanding practitioner of clinical medicine who joined the Oxford scene in 1651 as assistant to Thomas Clayton, Professor of Anatomy (son of the first Master of Pembroke, and later a cantankerous Warden of Merton College), and lived in Wilkins' lodgings. In 1652 he left Oxford to become physician to Cromwell's army in Ireland when Lambert, Fleetwood and Henry Cromwell followed as Viceroys. His influence on Hooke was probably more by repute than by personal contact, his chief friend being John Locke.

One having more direct influence on Hooke was Seth Ward (1617–1688/89), who came from Cambridge (Sidney Sussex 1632, B.A. 1636/37 and M.A. 1640) having refused to submit to the Covenant nevertheless incorporated at Wadham College in 1649 (D.D. 1654). From 1649 until 1661 he was Savilian Professor of Astronomy and briefly (1659–60) President of Trinity College, Oxford. Ward made substantial contributions to astronomy, and imparted his ideas to Hooke.

Also imported from Cambridge was John Wallis (1616–1703), one of the foremost pre-Newtonian mathematicians of the day,[37] incorporated at Exeter College (M.A.) and appointed Savilian Professor of Geometry by the Parliamentary Visitors in 1649. Originally at Cambridge he was one of the Emmanuel Puritans (1632, B.A. 1637 and M.A. 1640), and had acquired a considerable reputation from his brilliant skill in the decipherment of Charles I's incriminating correspondence following the Battle of Naseby (1645). In 1655 he published his decisive and influential book *Arithmetica Infinitorum* – which, it is said, the young Isaac Newton read with delight, and was so stimulated that he was led to formulate the binomial theorem. Wallis was relatively wealthy, and like Robert Boyle and, in the following century, Joseph Banks, could be considered to be a patron of the sciences who used private means to further his own academic interests as well as those of others. Wallis's contribution to Oxford science and mathematics was immense, due not only to his outstanding ability but also the prodigious length of time for which he productively held the Savilian chair until his death in 1703. In his lifetime he overlapped with Robert Boyle and Isaac Newton, and played a major role in the affairs of the Royal Society. Having known Hooke from his earliest days in Oxford, it is very probable that Hooke's mathematical and later architectural design skill owed much to the influence of Wallis.

Christopher Wren – elected a Fellow of All Souls College in 1657 – found, amongst his slightly more senior colleagues, Thomas Sydenham (1624–1689), who had previously studied medicine as a member of Magdalen Hall (B.A. 1643 and B.M. 1648). Sydenham was another outstanding physician of his day. His interests in discriminating between different diseases, and his methods of clinical treatment of ague, gout and smallpox, placed him in the first rank of English physicians, and he was known as 'the English Hippocrates'.

Hooke, Boyle and their colleagues

About the time of Hooke's arrival, John Wilkins took a step which transformed the little scientific community when in 1653 he invited Robert Boyle[38, 39] (Figure 3.5) to join it in Oxford. At the time, Boyle was trying to carry out experiments in Dublin, but was encountering difficulties. Now aged twenty-seven, he accepted Wilkins' invitation, and the following year took up residence in Deep Hall in High Street (Figure 3.6), opposite All Souls, near the apothecaries' shops where necessary materials could be obtained, and near the coffee houses. Boyle was a man of means, and not a member of the University, though he was awarded a D.M. in 1665. In 1656 Hooke (aged twenty-one) went to live in Boyle's house, possibly as a paid assistant, and there their outstanding collaboration began.

Boyle already had prior ideas about the weight and properties of air, but it was at Oxford that experimental data were obtained. There being no laboratory or specific location for experimentation, investigations nearly always took place in the studies or private houses of investigators. The construction of the air pump, even with Hooke's ingenuity, was not a simple matter yielding to instant success, and even as late as 1659 Boyle commented that he had 'not yet brought the engine to work as it should'.[40]

Hooke's quick and enquiring mind tended to lead him simultaneously in numerous directions – an attitude of mind that would affect him throughout his life. With the Wilkins group he was experimenting with various methods of flight, and about this time (1658) was concerned with his ideas for escapement and balance spring mechanisms for the watch – ideas with which Christiaan Huygens was also engaged. The results of the investigations of the whole group in Oxford were at this stage regarded more for internal discussion and assessment than for publication. Diffusion in the wider world would await the Restoration.

Despite the uncertainty of the times and the imposition of

Fig. 3.5. Hon. Robert Boyle (1627–1691), with whom Hooke lived and worked. (Engraving after the marble bust in the Royal Garden at Richmond.)

Fig. 3.6. Deep Hall, High Street, Oxford; Robert Boyle's residence.

Puritanical rule, the Oxford scientists were allowed to meet and pursue their researches in relative peace. Wilkins' personality was a notable factor as a broad-minded man of vision and discretion as well as a gifted leader. Added to this, he assiduously avoided religious controversy and secured his social position by marrying Cromwell's sister.

Personal circumstances in the group, however, were changing. In 1657 Willis married John Fell's sister, and in the same year Christopher Wren left Oxford to become Professor of Astronomy at Gresham College – a position which he held until 1661 when he returned to All Souls as Savilian Professor of Astronomy.

In 1659 Boyle added further interest to the Oxford group by bringing Peter Stahl, the notable chemist, from Strasbourg. Stahl initially had rooms in University College, but taught small groups of students in premises nearby. According to Anthony Wood, these lectures attracted large numbers, including Christopher Wren, (Sir) Joseph Williamson, John Locke, Nathaniel Crew, John Wallis, Richard Lower, Viscount Brouncker, George Bathurst, and Wood himself. In 1663 Stahl built a 'elaboratory' in the Ram Inn – an old hostel in High Street – where he continued to give instruction until 1664, when he was called to London to be 'operator' for the Royal Society. Stahl's chemistry was centred on the changes involved in the combination of substances, and invoked the concept of phlogiston as a causative agent – a theory which largely side-tracked the subject until resolved by the quantitative experiments by Lavoisier and Priestley.

Hooke himself finally matriculated at Christ Church on 31 July 1658, though the reasons for this long delay are uncertain. It is possible that he was simply impecunious, though the 'gap years' suited him well in academic terms and in the width of opportunities which they presented.

In what was to be a last attempt to support higher education, Oliver Cromwell – despite all the complexities of his tortured personality – gave effect to a bid to found a new University College at Durham.[41] In May 1657, Letters Patent were issued instituting a corporate body consisting of a Provost, two Senior Fellows, twelve Junior Fellows, twenty-four Scholars and three Exhibitioners, some of whom were from the free school in the (Durham) College. The first Provost was to be Philip Hunton, M.A., a graduate from Wadham College, then incumbent of Westbury, Wiltshire. Fellows, Professors, tutors and schoolmasters were named – men of academic accomplishment, and some of them connected with Wilkins' group of scientists. Mathematics was to be taught by Robert Wood, Fellow of Lincoln College. The disused Cathedral and its premises were to be the College (the south Close there still carries that name).

This scheme was not universally popular, and was vigorously

opposed by the Quakers. Even George Fox spoke out against it. Had Durham College continued it is reasonable to suppose that it would have attracted many more of the leading figures from Wilkins' group.

The days of the Commonwealth were manifestly coming to a close as the whole edifice began to crumble under a load of debt, lack of management and political uncertainty in a nation weary of military administration. The decisive stroke came when Cromwell died on 3 September 1658, to be succeeded by his son Richard.

1660 and the Restoration years

In 1660 the Restoration brought rejoicing and relief to many in the University and the City, though both faced another period of upheaval as had occurred some twelve years previously. Royal commissioners, appointed to assess the claims of those ejected from their positions by the Parliamentary Visitors, were not slow to begin their work.[42] At Christ Church, Dean Reynolds and the intruded Canons were expelled, former Canons were restored, and new appointments were made. The new Dean was the witty and accomplished George Morley, appointed in July 1660, and shortly afterwards made Bishop of Worcester. John Fell, John Dolben and Richard Allstree, who had loyally maintained Anglican position throughout the Commonwealth, were duly rewarded with Canonries. The new Chapter[43] had the following composition:

Jasper Mayne, replacing H. Wilkinson
John Fell, then Sebastian Smith, replacing R. Button
Richard Gardiner, restored, replacing Christopher Rogers
John Dolben, replacing J. Paynter
William Creed, replacing H. Cornish
Edward Pocock, restored, replacing John Milles
Richard Allstree, replacing H. Longley
John Wall, appointed 1632, and survived throughout

Robert Sanderson was also restored, but was almost immediately created Bishop of Lincoln. The appointment of John Fell as the new Dean, at the age of thirty-five, was of commanding importance for the College and University, as he was a man of gifted intellect, a capable administrator, and was closely attuned to the needs of the time. The College, like most in Oxford, was in a pitiful state. During the Commonwealth years, buildings had fallen into decay, some had been demolished, and virtually no new buildings had been erected. Rents had not been collected from the neglected estates, and the finances neared destitution. In the face of this challenging situation, John Fell was installed on 30 November 1660.

In the Cathedral, the Book of Common Prayer was restored (the Solemn Covenant and Oaths to subscribe to it were abolished by Parliament, the Covenant itself being burnt publicly in London by the common hangman). Surplices were again worn, the organ (not totally destroyed) was repaired and played again, and a second organ was bought to speed the reintroduction of the customary Anglican worship.[44] Fell himself lived in the Priory House as his Deanery whilst he resumed his father's task of the building of the north side of Tom Quad to house Canons, as well as the extensions to complete the west and east sides (Figure 3.7).

The University fared well with Fell as Vice Chancellor – not least in his concern to establish a University press, for which he designed the renowned Fell type fonts. The press, however, had to acquire permanent premises, but this was not achieved until 1669 when the Sheldonian Theatre was completed.

According to Wood, printing for the University was carried out until then on private presses such as that of Peter Lichfield in Castle Street. This had implications for the Oxford scientists, since up to the Restoration few of their ideas and results of their investigations had been published, though preparations to do so must have been well in hand. Consequently, this all changed dramatically after 1659 as important publications began to appear. In that year, Willis published his

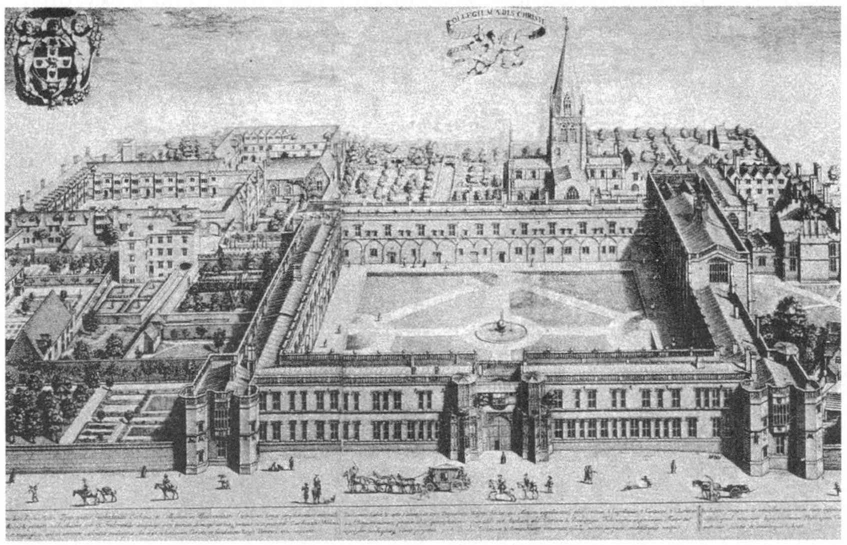

Fig. 3.7. Christ Church, Oxford, in 1673, with Tom Quad completed.

Diatribudae duae Medico-philosophicae, and in 1664 his monumental *Cerebri Anatome* – to which Lower, Hooke, Locke and Wren had contributed – embodying researches on the structure of the brain. More publications flowed from Willis's pen in these productive years. In December 1659, Boyle completed his book *New Experiments Physico-Mathematicall, Touching the Spring of Air and its Effects* (published in 1660), in which he described forty-three detailed experiments on the construction of the air-pump and its applications, leading to Boyle's Law. In 1662 an enlarged second edition appeared with addenda dealing with the acrimonious controversy with Hobbes over-interpretations of experimental results.

Boyle's seminal work, *The Sceptical Chemist*, which first appeared in 1661, was to be the foundation stone of chemistry as a coherent science setting out the concept of elements and of compounds formed from them.

Hooke's *magnum opus* was his *Micrographia* (1665), which summarised some of his inventive work in Oxford and in the few years following. Wren is believed to have provided some of its superb illustrations. Hooke was now aged thirty and a cooperative investigator sharing with colleagues his abounding imagination and inventiveness which became apparent to all. His mind teemed with ideas such that he wanted to press on to the next before having fully completed the exploration of the previous. In this he was markedly different from Isaac Newton (1642–1727), who was essentially an individualist and a perfectionist who pursued ideas to the most refined outcome achievable. As Hooke embarked on his work with the Royal Society, Newton entered Trinity College, Cambridge, in 1661, as an undergraduate, and became a Fellow in 1667. The readers of his *Principia Mathematica* (1687) had the advantage of the background provided by the earlier concepts of the Oxford scientists.

Richard Cromwell did not have his father's gifts of resolve and iron will, and was not destined to last long as Lord Protector. In 1659 petitions were addressed to him, from both Cambridge and Oxford Universities, against the Durham College proposal, on the grounds *inter alia* that the institution would be too small to be effective. The scheme was thus allowed to lapse.

At Oxford, Dean Owen resigned in 1658 – his predecessor Edward Reynolds being reappointed at Christ Church for a few months – and John Wilkins finally left Wadham to be (briefly) Master of Trinity College, Cambridge, in 1659–60, while Thomas Willis remained in Oxford for a few more years and became Sadlerian Professor of Natural Philosophy, still with some of his most productive years ahead.

Near the end of Hooke's time in Oxford, William Penn matriculated at Christ Church (26 October 1660) and came into residence. He had

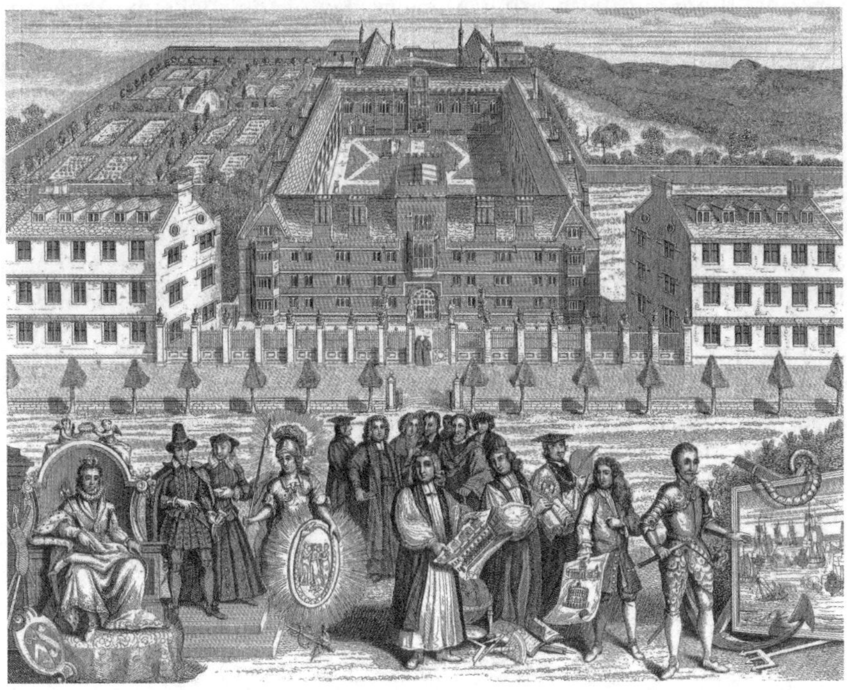

Fig. 3.8. Wadham College, Oxford, with the Warden, John Wilkins, and his 'Invisible College'. (*Left*) James I, Nicholas Wadham and his wife Dorothy; (*centre*) John Wilkins, Thomas Spratt (Bishop of Rochester), Seth Ward (Bishop of Salisbury), Sir Christopher Wren, and Admiral Blake; (*rear*) John Goodridge, Dr Bisse, Mr Godolphin, Dr Hody, and other principal benefactors. (G. Virtue, *Almanack*, 1738.)

been much influenced by Dean Owen and the Puritans such that at the Restoration he was sent down (1661) for nonconformity. Nevertheless, he was elected F.R.S. in 1681 when Hooke was an influential figure in the Society and after Penn's founding work in Pennsylvania had begun.

After 1659, most of the scientists in the Wilkins group began to drift towards London, holding their meetings in Gresham College. In March, Boyle took the air pump there to demonstrate its capabilities, and at a meeting on 28 November 1660 there was a proposal to found a Society for the advancement of scientific learning, which received an approving response from Charles II now restored.[45] Hooke seems to have been present at the meetings in 1661 and May 1662. In November 1662 he was appointed Curator of Experiments to the new Society, but initially with no salary: 'Mr Hooke should come and sit amongst them and both bring in every day of their meeting three or four experiments of his own and take care of such as should be mentioned to him by the Society.' The Society was incorporated by Royal Charter in 1662.

Hooke moved to London to live in Gresham College, the headquarters of the Royal Society, and in 1665 was appointed its Professor of Geometry.[46] He continued to be right-hand-man to Robert Boyle (a key figure in the Royal Society), who lived mainly in Oxford until 1668, after which he went to live permanently in London at his sister Lady Ranelagh's house. Willis, too, finally went to reside in the capital, where he ran a successful medical practice and published extensively on his clinical experiences.

Many of the senior members of the Oxford group of scientists associated with Wilkins, now returned to the Anglican fold, became bishops: Wilkins to Chester, Seth Ward to Exeter then Salisbury, and Spratt (Figure 3.8) to Rochester. Elevation did not diminish their scientific interests, and they continued actively in the affairs and discussions of the Royal Society of which they were Fellows, and to which they had contributed in its foundation.

For Hooke and his contemporaries, a new chapter had opened.[47, 48]

Notes and references

1 S. Inwood, *The Man Who Knew Too Much* (Macmillan, 2002).

2 S. R. Gardiner, *Constitutional Documents of the Puritan Revolution, 1628–1660* (London, 1889), p. 270.

3 H. Bettenson, *Documents of the Christian Church* (Oxford University Press, 1967), pp. 286–91.

4 A. L. Rowse, *Oxford in the History of the Nation* (Weidenfeld and Nicolson, 1975).

5 A. Clark (ed.), *The Life and Times of Anthony Wood, 1632–1695* (Clarendon Press, 1891).

6 H. L. Thompson, *Christ Church* (Robinson and Co., London, 1900), p. 73.

7 C. E. Whiting, *The University of Durham, 1832–1932* (Sheldon Press, 1932), pp. 17–29.

8 A. Hassall, *Christ Church, Oxford* (Hodder and Stoughton, 1911).

9 Mrs Fell, a lady of robust character, refused to leave the Deanery and had to be forcibly removed by being carried out on a chair (or some say, in a wheelbarrow) while her children were removed on boards.

10 P. Toon, *God's Statesman* (Paternoster Press, 1971); also *Correspondence of John Owen (1616–1683)* (Clarke and Co., Cambridge, 1970).

11 Library and Archives of Christ Church, Oxford, xii, 6, 86, ff. 72–4.

12 The Chapter Act Books at Christ Church survive only in a very incomplete state, and many of the Disbursement Books are missing for these years.

13 J. Skelton, *Oxonia Antiqua Restaurata* (second edition, J. B. Nichols, 1834), plate 103.

14 Vestiges of the earthworks are still to be seen in Mansfield Road and in the gardens behind the houses on the west side of St Giles.

15 Clark, *Anthony Wood* (ref. 5).

16 A Scottish soldier 'marvayled how the schollers could goe to their bukes for those painted idolatrous windows'.

17 'John Evelyn', *Dictionary of Scientific Biography*, **3** (Scribner, New York, 1981), pp. 494–97.

18 Alfred E. Jones, *Catalogue of the Plate of Christ Church Oxford* (Oxford University Press, 1939), pp. 1–3, plate 2.

19 Thompson, *Christ Church* (ref. 6), p. 76.

20 Anthony Wood, quoted in Thompson, *Christ Church* (ref. 6), p. 76.

21 J. Field, *The King's Nurseries: The Story of Westminster School* (James and James, 1989).

22 It was common practice for school masters to take pupils into their houses as paying lodgers, presumably to augment their meagre salaries.

23 J. Welch, *History of Scholars of St Peter's College, Westminster* (London, 1788).

24 Scholars elected to Christ Church from Westminster in 1653 were William White, Arthur Bret, John Salway and Richard Lucie.

25 The identity of Mr Goodman is uncertain. It is possible that he may have been a relative of the Revd Cardell Goodman, Rector of All Saints, Freshwater (Hooke's home parish) from 1644 until he was ejected from the benefice by order of Cromwell's Council of State in 1653. By coincidence, Samuel Fell (later Dean) had been Rector of Freshwater from 1615 until 1621, when he became Lady Margaret Professor of Divinity at Oxford.

26 Servitors existed as a category of the Colleges' community for a large part of Oxford's history, enabling boys from relatively poor homes to take degrees (E. G. W. Bill, *Education at Christ Church, Oxford, 1660–1800* (Clarendon Press, 1988), pp. 189–94) and survived into the nineteenth century (L. S. Sutherland, *The Last of the Servitors*, Christ Church Annual Report, 1975, pp. 35–9).

27 Richard Waller (ed.), *The Posthumous Works of Robert Hooke, M.D., F.R.S.* (London, 1705).

28 John Locke, born 29 August 1632, was elected having petitioned Dean Owen in elegant Latin prose and finishing with verse.

29 L. Jardine, *On a Grander Scale: the Outstanding Career of Sir Christopher Wren* (Harper Collins, 2002).

30 J. Hughes, *Thomas Willis: His Life and Works, 1621–1675* (Royal Society of Medicine, 1991).

31 R. W. Church, *Bacon* (Macmillan, 1888).

32 *Dictionary of Scientific Biography*, **13** (Scribner, New York, 1981), pp. 404–9.

33 P. Romanell, *John Locke and Medicine* (Prometheus Books, Buffalo, New York, 1989).

34 *Dictionary of Scientific Biography*, **13** (Scribner, New York, 1981), pp. 361–81.

35 Harvey retired from public life and became associated with George Bathurst at Trinity College, Oxford, where he carried out pioneering

investigation of the embryological development of fertilised hens' eggs. The results were published in 1651 under the title *De Generatione*. Harvey's inclinations were Aristotlean rather than Baconian, nevertheless.

36 John Wilkins, *Mathematicall Magick, or, The Wonders that may be Performed by Mechanicall Geometry* (London, 1648).

37 J. Fairvell, R. Flood and R. Wilson, *Oxford Figures* (Oxford University Press, 2000).

38 Robert Boyle, fourteenth offspring of the Earl of Cork, was born at Lismore, Ireland, on 25 January 1625. He was educated at Eton and then travelled extensively in Europe, following which he lived a studious life mostly in Dorset and Ireland before moving to Oxford in 1654.

39 R. E. W. Maddison, *The Life of the Honourable Robert Boyle, F.R.S.* (Taylor and Francis, 1969).

40 S. Shapen and S. Schaffer, *Leviathan and the Aër Pump* (Princeton University Press, 1985).

41 J. T. Fowler, *Durham University* (F. E. Robinson, 1904), pp. 15–21.

42 Bill, *Education at Christ Church* (ref. 26), pp. 17–36.

43 Thompson, *Christ Church* (ref. 6), p. 84.

44 W. G. Hiscock, *A Christ Church Miscellany* (Oxford University Press, 1946), pp. 215–6.

45 Thomas Spratt, *History of the Royal Society* (London, 1667; reprinted, Washington University Press, 1958).

46 R. Nichols, *The Diaries of Robert Hooke, the Leonardo of London (1635–1703)*, (Book Guild, Lewes, 1994).

47 J. A. Bennett, M. A. R. Cooper, M. Hunter and L. Jardine, *London's Leonardo: The Life and Work of Robert Hooke* (Oxford University Press, 2003).

48 P. W. Kent, *Some Scientists in the Life of Christ Church, Oxford* (Oxford University Press, 2001).

Chapter 4

Hooke and the Royal Society

Sir John Enderby F.R.S.

The preceding chapters set out the chronology, early life and some aspects of the personality of Robert Hooke. Born at Freshwater in 1635, Hooke was educated at Westminster School, then at Christ Church,[1] where he was awarded the degree of M.A. in 1663. It was during his time at Oxford that he became involved with 'new science' through his contacts with outstanding and able contemporaries and with the group around John Wilkins and Robert Boyle at Wadham College, and it was with Boyle that he came to London on the founding of the Royal Society.

The origins of the Royal Society can be traced back to 1645, when a group of scholars began regular meetings to discuss the New (experimental) Philosophy. For a time these meetings were held in Oxford, and Hooke certainly knew of their existence. After the Restoration they were moved back to London, and after the meeting held on 28 November 1660, those present withdrew to Lawrence Rooke's apartments and agreed to set up a College for 'the Promoting of Physico-Mathematicall, Experimental Learning'. Those present, as recorded in the journal book, were:

Viscount Brouncker	Jonathan Goddard
Robert Boyle	William Petty
David Bruce	Peter Ball
Sir Robert Moray	Lawrence Rooke
Sir Paul Neile	Christopher Wren
John Wilkins	Abraham Hill

These twelve men were the original founding Fellows, although they drew up a list of some forty other men who might be invited. It is not known whether Hooke was in the list. The first Royal Charter was granted in 1662, and the second, in 1663, made a grant of arms with the motto *Nullius In Verba*, and defined its name as 'The Royal Society of London for Improving Natural Knowledge'.

It is interesting to compare the basic statistics of the Society in the mid-seventeenth century with those of today, noting that the growth in membership and staff numbers has not been reflected in the number of Officers. The Officers listed in the Charters are the President, the two Secretaries and the Treasurer. It was not until 1723 that the position of Foreign Secretary was created (and to which Philip Zollman was elected), thus increasing the number of Officers to five.

	1677	2003
Fellows	327	~1,200
Officers	4	5
Premises	Gresham College	6–9 Carlton House Terrace
Staff	~4	~150
Publications	Transactions	Proc(A+B) and Trans(A+B)

One feature of today's Society not present in 1662 – and, indeed, one which would not have been understood by the Fellows of the day – is the A/B 'divide'. The provisions in the first and second Charters for two Secretaries make no specific reference to their areas of expertise. However, in the Council Minutes of 3 February 1887 it is recorded that 'The *Philosophical Transactions* be published in two independent series: one (A) containing those papers which are of a mathematical or physical character, the other (B) those of a biological nature'. No explicit reference to the titles of the Secretaries being altered officially can be traced, but it can be assumed that this is the point at which they became known respectively as 'Sec A' and 'Sec B'.

The new science

Before examining the role of Robert Hooke in the Royal Society, we must first consider the early Renaissance period and appreciate the political, social and intellectual turmoil which reached a peak in Stuart times. After 1492 the assaults on an all-encompassing explanation of the 'laws of nature' began to increase on many fronts: the discovery of America, discrediting ancient geography; the astronomical observations of Tycho Brahe, Galileo and others; Harvey's (1628) ideas about blood circulation rather than regarding the heart as a furnace; Earth-bound observations which characterise motions in the heavens.

Giordano Bruno (1548–1602) was born in Nola, Italy, studied in Paris and from there came to England to popularise the 'new' astronomy. Although he had an audience with Queen Elizabeth, she failed to be impressed, and on his return to Continental Europe he was burnt at the stake as a heretic.

A key English figure in the fundamental development of the new science and of the concept of an 'invisible college' of scholars was Francis Bacon (1561–1626), the son of Sir Nicholas Bacon, Keeper of the Seal of Queen Elizabeth. The career of Francis Bacon blossomed when James I succeeded Elizabeth, and until his arrest for bribery in 1621 he was an active exponent of the new science. Even though he was found guilty, he managed to keep his scientific interest active, though he was neither an inventor nor an experimentalist. It is said that the chill he caught while collecting snow to freeze chickens led to his death in 1626. He did not live to see the creation of the Royal Society, of which he would have undoubtedly approved.

But it was not just science that was in a state of turmoil. James I (James VI of Scotland, 1566–1625), who succeeded Elizabeth in 1603, was dubbed 'the wisest fool in Christendom'; and the political upheaval exemplified by the gunpowder plot and the continuing difficult relationship with Parliament was not diminished when in 1625 James was succeeded by his son Charles I (1600–1649). The background of challenge to authority (perhaps even relating back to the Reformation and the rejection of Rome by Henry VIII) carried with it its own momentum, so that the claim of Divine Right by James and Charles was no longer sustainable. The Civil War, the execution of Charles I, and the Protectorate of Cromwell, did not seem to inhibit those scholars of the day who attacked the Aristotlean world-view and wanted it replaced by a science based on experimental reason. Indeed, it has been argued that the political unrest actually stimulated those who wished to think (to use a modern expression) 'outside the box'.

In 1660 Charles II was restored to the throne, and soon became associated with the Royal Society. Having seen the fate of his father and being told about the unpopularity of his grandfather, he perhaps decided that the best course was to encourage the scientific endeavour of the day and so keep in touch with the times!

Finally, the coffee houses, which grew in numbers during the lifetime of Hooke, demand special mention. The first of them opened in London in 1652 and was known as Pasqua Rosee's Head. Coffee came to Oxford in 1654, to be sold at The Angel in High Street, close to Robert Boyle's house in which Hooke lodged. By 1663 there were eighty-two coffee houses in London, and at the time of Hooke's death there were probably at least five hundred. They were places where all manner of discussion could be held, and Hooke was a frequent visitor to one in particular: Garraways. Here he talked science, learned new intelligence from foreign parts, negotiated with builders and tradesmen, and even performed or practised experiments in preparation for his duties as Curator of the Royal Society – England's first salaried scientific research appointment.

It is of interest to trace the way in which Hooke interpreted his duties, and the currents and counter-currents that characterised his relationship with the Royal Society and its Principals between 1663 (the date of his election as a Fellow) and his death in 1703.

Hooke as Curator

Both the first and second Charters provided for the appointment of two or more Curators of Experiments, and towards the end of 1662 the Council of the Royal Society decided to fill one of the posts with a full-time professional scientist. The obvious person to take the position was Robert Hooke – all the more so because of his continuing links with Boyle and Wilkins. On 12 November 1662, Council accepted Sir Robert Moray's proposal that Hooke be appointed Curator with a notional salary of £30 per annum. He was elected a Fellow on 20 May 1663, and on 11 January 1665 was appointed Curator for life. His salary of £80 seems to have been paid jointly by the Royal Society (£30) and the wealthy financier Sir John Cutler F.R.S. (£50) – an unhappy arrangement which in 1683 led to legal action by Hooke to recover monies owing to him.

The Royal Society was not a rich organisation, and it was important to attract, as members, well-heeled financiers, landowners, merchants and the aristocracy. Hooke's job specification required him to 'furnish every day [the Society] met with three or more considerable experiments'. The object, of course, was to entertain the wealthy dignitaries and so extract from them sufficient cash to keep the Society afloat and meet the various expenses incurred by Hooke and others.

An important figure providing an insight into the early days of the Society was Samuel Pepys (1633–1703) – a Cambridge graduate with an abiding interest in the new science. After graduation (1654) Pepys was appointed as Clerk to the Exchequer in the last days of the Commonwealth, and at the Restoration became Clerk of the Acts to the Navy Board. This gave him access to, and influence with, the King and his circle. Pepys' Diary, written between 1660 and 1669, discloses forthright accounts of his life and feelings, as well as of his day-to-day activities, including his admission as a Fellow of the Royal Society. On 15 February 1665, he wrote:

> With Creed to Gresham College, where I had been by Mr Povy at the last week proposed to be a member; and was this day admitted, by signing a book and being taken by the hand by the Praesident, my Lord Brunkard, and some words of admittance said to me. But it is the most acceptable thing to me to hear their discourses and to see their experiments; which was this day on the nature of fire, and how it goes out in a place where the ayre is not free, and sooner out where the ayre is exhausted; which they showed by an engine on purpose ... Above all, Mr Boyle today was at the meeting, and above him Mr Hooke, who is the most, and promises the least, of any man in the world that I ever saw.[2]

Hooke's later role as Secretary was not without its difficulties, but his astonishing range of the experiments and demonstrations continue to amaze, even today. Pepys again describes his being fascinated by a meeting on 21 February 1666 (despite the plague being still rife in London):

> Thence with my Lord Brunker to Gresham College, the first time after the sickness [plague] that I was there, and the second time any met. And hear a good lecture of Mr Hooke's about the trade of Felt making, very pretty.[3]

Some months later, on 8 August 1666, Pepys

> Discoursed with Mr Hooke a little ... about the nature of musicall sounds made by strings, mightly prettily, and told me that having come to a certain Number of Vibracions proper to make any tone, he is able to tell how many strokes a fly makes with her wings (those flies that hum in their flying) by the note that it answers to in Musique during their flying. That, I suppose, is a little too much raffined; but his discourse in general of sound was mighty fine.[4]

Weighing machines, falling bodies, fossils, pressure cooking, blood transfusions, respiration ... all were grist to Hooke's mill. At another meeting on 2 April 1668, Pepys

> Went thence with Lord Brounker to the Royal Society, where they were just done; but there I was forced to subscribe to the building of a College, and did give 40l ... I did desire of Mr Hooke and my Lord an account of the reason of Concords and Discords in music – which they said is from the aequality of the vibrations.[5]

Imagine having to produce, week in and week out, three or four new experiments and to then describe and discuss them in front of learned and possibly not-so-learned gentlemen!

Hooke as Secretary

The successive dates of election of the two Secretaries allowed by the Charters is shown below, by which it can be seen that Hooke's immediate predecessor was Henry Oldenburg.

22 April 1663	John Wilkins	Henry Oldenburg
30 November 1668	Thomas Henshaw	Henry Oldenburg
30 November 1672	John Evelyn	Henry Oldenburg
30 November 1673	Abraham Hill	Henry Oldenburg
30 November 1675	Thomas Henshaw	Henry Oldenburg
30 November 1677	Nehemiah Grew	Robert Hooke
30 November 1679	Thomas Gale	Robert Hooke
30 November 1681	Francis Aston	Robert Hooke

Although the Council spelt out, in some detail, the duties of the two Secretaries, their approach reflected their individual personalities. From all accounts the first pair – John Wilkins and Henry Oldenburg – were very different. Wilkins, a charismatic man, was certainly in at the beginning of the new science, having prospered under the Commonwealth, no doubt helped by his marriage to Cromwell's sister, Robina. His brief appointment as Master of Trinity, Cambridge, came to a sudden end at the Restoration, but he survived, and ended his career as Bishop of Chester. As a man of the cloth, he was keen to show the consistency of the new science with religious belief, and found justification for his approach in the Book of Daniel 12.4: 'Many shall run to and fro and Knowledge shall be increased'.

Oldenburg, the son of Professor Heinrich Oldenburg of the Royal University of Dorpat, was born and educated in Bremen, Germany. At age twenty-three he came to England for four years, and travelled extensively. On his return to Bremen he was asked to negotiate with Cromwell (1653), and after a spell at Oxford became tutor to various sons of the aristocracy, including Richard Jones, the son of Robert Boyle's sister, Lady Ranelagh. His election to the Fellowship in 1663 was followed immediately by election to the Council and appointment as Secretary.

Oldenburg was an immensely successful Secretary, having helped to create, in 1665, the *Philosophical Transactions*, and managed, not without a little difficulty, to cool down disputes among the Fellowship, often centred on Hooke himself. His cosmopolitan background allowed him to liaise with scientists in the wider world on natural philosophy.

In short, Oldenburg's sudden death in September 1677 was a most serious blow to the Society. He appears to have contracted malaria on his estate, which, being located between Woolwich and Greenwich, was in the marshlands of the Thames estuary. However, the death of Oldenburg allowed Hooke to lobby for the vacant position, and he soon enlisted the help of the Society's heavyweights, Robert Boyle, Abraham Hill and John Hoskins. In previous years he had tried to secure a place on the Council, but his lack of success partly reflected the mutual distrust that existed between him and the President, Viscount Brouncker, who, as the first President, had already served for fifteen years. It was time for a shake-up among the Officers, and after much jockeying for position the following elections were agreed at the Council of 30 November 1677:

President	Sir Joseph Williamson
Vice President	Sir Christopher Wren
Treasurer	Abraham Hill
Secretaries	Robert Hooke and Nehemiah Grew

A potential source of difficulty (as will be seen) was that Hooke retained his position as Curator of Experiments.

Pepys maintained an active role in the Society, first serving on its Council and then as President 1684–86. Amongst his friends were included John Wallis, John Evelyn, Isaac Newton and Christopher Wren. It was Pepys' name, however, which appeared on the title-page of Newton's great work *Principia Mathematica* (1687) – the work which changed intellectual endeavour and gave exact sciences their foundation – 'Imprimater S. Pepys, Reg.Soc. Praeses. Julii 1686.'

It might be amusing to compare the brief *curriculum vitae* of the present Secretary with that of Hooke. The only two aspects I can find in common are first that we had both been in the Fellowship for exactly fourteen years before our election to the office of Secretary, and secondly, the five-year term of office.

	Robert Hooke	John Enderby
Place of birth	Isle of Wight	Lincolnshire
Father's occupation	Clergyman	Farmer/seed merchant
Education	Westminster/Oxford	Chester/London
Civil status	Bachelor	Married
Residence	London	Bristol
Scientific mentors	Boyle and Willis	Bernal and Cusack

Age at election to the Society	Twenty-eight	Fifty-four
Age at election as Secretary	Forty-two	Sixty-eight
Term of office	Five years	Five years
Reason for termination	Vote by Council	Statute 25
Paid by the Society	Yes	No
Other employment	Gresham College City of London	University of Bristol Various
Secretarial Duties	Organising demonstrations; maintaining records of experiments, discussions and Council's deliberations; (fund-raising through entertaining wealthy patrons with scientific novelties); advice to the City of London; and so on	Supervising 'A' side elections; medals and awards; Lead Officer for publications, archives, library and education; science advice
Time spent on Society affairs	Three(?) days per week	~Three days per week

It is interesting to consider how much time Hooke actually spent on Secretarial duties. He had extensive outside interests, which sometimes overlapped with his duties, but often did not. Beginning in 1666, following the Fire of London and his appointment as a City Surveyor, he had to balance his role as Curator with his heavy commitments to the grandees of London. From time to time Council grumbled that Hooke was not giving sufficient time to his demonstrations, and often, when he failed to deliver, Oldenburg stood in by reading letters from his foreign correspondents. In fact, Council lost patience with Hooke, and in November 1670 decided to censure him at their next meeting. However, it was perhaps realised that in spite of his weaknesses, Hooke's overall qualities were unique, and the proposed censure motion was quietly dropped. During his time as Curator Hooke became somewhat disillusioned with the Society, and tried, possibly in a half-hearted way, to set up a rival group with membership restricted to the more scientifically active Fellows.

His appointment as Secretary led to even more complications, for he retained his position as Curator. Thus, on the one hand, as a paid employee he was responsible to the Council, but as Secretary he was a member of the Council. Early on, an argument arose as to who should keep the minutes of the meetings. Some on Council thought that

Hooke's onerous duties as Curator would leave him little time to maintain proper records, and that the responsibility should be given to Grew. This greatly upset Hooke, who thought he had spotted a conspiracy; but eventually a compromise was reached whereby both Secretaries should make notes of the meetings, though the write-up would be Hooke's responsibility.

We thus have a picture of a complex and suspicious man, with a huge range of scientific and commercial interests, being asked to be a second Oldenburg by keeping records, maintaining foreign correspondence and ensuring the regular production of the *Philosophical Transactions*. As it happened, Grew was of little help and retired after two years, to be replaced by Thomas Gale, High Master of St Paul's.

In December 1679, Council instructed the Secretaries to bring order to the Society by focusing on one issue at each meeting and then preparing 'a distinct account and narrative'. A persistent complaint against Hooke was that his record-keeping was poor and that he failed to ensure that the *Philosphical Transactions* appeared on a regular basis. Matters came to a head in 1682 when it was clear that of the many and varied tasks required of Hooke, including looking at new premises for the Society, together with his outside interests, were really too much for a man of indifferent health. The detailed business of record-keeping was not of the highest priority so far as he was concerned. So, in November 1682 his time as Council member and Secretary came to an end, and he returned to his original position as in 1662, as Curator of Experiments.

In his recent account of Hooke's life (*The Man Who Knew Too Much*[6]), Stephen Inwood's metaphor that 'Hooke was a player, not a referee' is particularly apt. All in all, the consensus view is that in spite of his energy and his enormous grasp of science in all its manifestations, Hooke's period as Secretary was not a great success.

Postscript

Hooke's removal from the Council was by no means the end of his association with the Society. He retained his position as Curator, albeit with varying terms and conditions. until the post effectively disappeared in 1688. Nevertheless, he continued to play an important part in the affairs of the Society – not least in renting his rooms for meetings (for which he received a fee). He also, much to his pleasure as vindication of his struggles, received back-pay from Sir John Cutler, after a ruling by the Court of Chancery. His health continued to deteriorate in his last years, but he maintained his commitment to the Society and was frequently called on to solve practical problems that had defeated the other staff. In spite of his apparent poverty, Hooke actually died a wealthy man: Inwood estimated his estate to be worth £1 million in today's money.

Aspects of Hooke's scientific legacy are explored in this volume and elsewhere.[7, 8] His service to the Royal Society was, in spite of all the difficulties, enormous, and his brilliant demonstrations and inventions ensured that the Society was highly regarded as a new source of knowledge. Hooke, more than any of his contemporaries, showed how science was of direct concern to government, commerce, defence and civic policy, and not merely a branch of the entertainment industry. The fact that the Society today is seen as a source of independent advice and comment on issues ranging from GM foods to aspects of intellectual property can be traced back, in large part, to the energy, insight and ability of one of its early Secretaries: Mr Robert Hooke.

Acknowledgements

The author thanks the staff of the Royal Society library, and particularly Joanna Corden, for all their help in preparing this chapter.

Notes and references

1 P. W. Kent, *Some Scientists in the Life of Christ Church, Oxford* (Oxford University Press, 2001).

2 R. Latham and W. Matthews, *The Diary of Samuel Pepys*, **6** (Bell and Son, London, 1972), pp. 36–7.

3 Ref. 2, **7**, p. 57.

4 Ref. 2, **7**, p. 239.

5 Ref. 2, **9**, p. 147.

6 S. Inwood, *The Man Who Knew Too Much* (Macmillan, 2002).

7 J. A. Bennett, M. A. R. Cooper, M. Hunter and L. Jardine, *London's Leonardo: The Life and Work of Robert Hooke* (Oxford University Press, 2003).

8 L. Jardine, *The Curious Life of Robert Hooke: The Man Who Measured London* (Harper Collins, London, 2003).

Chapter 5

Hooke's concepts of the Earth in space

Ellen Tan Drake

Robert Hooke's accomplishments in his long career represent a synthesis of different scientific cultures, and even a summary of his scientific and technological contributions would require the space of a large volume. Aside from his prolific and fruitful ideas in physics, chemistry, biology, geology, astronomy, meteorology and architecture, he was a great inventor. He invented, or improved upon (to name but a few) the microscope, the spring-controlled balance wheel for watches, the universal joint found today in every vehicle and many instruments, the clock-driven telescope, the telescopic sight, the bubble level, the sextant, the air pump, the iris diaphragm, many meteorological instruments such as the thermometer, the wheel barometer, the wind gauge, and other instruments and devices. His focus on precision instrumentation, measurements, and the results of his experimentation, gave support to the original and creative ideas that sprang from his brilliant mind.

Many of Hooke's ideas contributed to the work and fame of others. His perceptive contributions in the Earth sciences have been shown to extend farther. and are more philosophically profound. than those of the much admired seventeenth-century Danish cleric/scientist Nicolaus Stenonis, known as Steno.[1] In geology, therefore, Hooke had no equal in the seventeenth century; nor, indeed, for many subsequent decades. More importantly, James Hutton (1726–1797) – recognised widely by geologists as the 'father' of modern geology – was influenced by Hooke's 'Discourses of Earthquakes', published posthumously in 1705.[2] That Hutton had read Hooke's ideas on geology is shown by the extent to which other eighteenth-century intelligentsia cited and adopted them; and although Hutton never mentioned Hooke by name, his texts in both his *Abstract* (1785) and his *Theory of the Earth* (1788) are reiterations of Hooke's ideas on the 'terraqueous globe'. The telling proof that Hutton was thoroughly familiar with Hooke's writings is that on those points where Hutton disagreed with Hooke, his style became polemic as he argued against them. Hooke's idea of 'axial displacement' – as polar wander was known at that time – was particularly disturbing to Hutton, even though in Hutton's century the concept of polar wander had not been supported by anyone since Hooke announced it, and had been all but forgotten. Hutton took it up, however, in order to debate it, as if with Hooke himself, in an attempt to bring about its final demise.[3]

This chapter relates some of Hooke's extraordinary and significant ideas about the Earth, specifically: (1) his 'perfect Theory of Heavens', first announced in 1666 and later shared with Newton in correspondence in 1679, providing the latter with the correct way to approach the gravitation problem; and (2) his highly original explanation of polar wander – a terrestrial surface phenomenon that is very important in modern geology. Newton went on to achieve international acclaim for his *Principia Mathematica*, considered a great revolutionary milestone in humanity's understanding of the Universe. On the other hand, Hooke's clearly expressed fundamental concepts about the Earth in space, generously shared with others, and especially with Newton, earned him only an obscure reputation today. At the same time, despite the rejection of the concept of polar wander by Hooke's contemporaries and by later writers such as Hutton, the idea proved significant in the development of modern geology. In the twentieth century, Alfred Wegener found polar wander to be essential to his hypothesis of continental drift in explaining the biogeography of geological periods and the distribution of climatic belts.

Hooke's ideas of the Earth in space

As early as 23 May 1666, Hooke read a paper to the Royal Society on 'The Inflexion of a direct Motion into a Curve by a Supervening Attractive Principle,' in which he said:

> I have often wondered why the Planets should move about the Sun according to Copernicus his Supposition, being not included in any solid orbs (which the Antients possibly for this reason might embrace) nor tyed to it, as their Centre, by any visible strings; and neither depart from it above such a degree, nor yet move in a streight line, as all bodies, that

have but one single impulse ought to doe: But all the Celestiall bodies, being regular solid bodies, and moved in a fluid, and yet moved in Circular or Elliptical Lines, and not streight, must have some other cause, besides the first imprest Impulse, that must bend their motion into that Curve.[4]

Note that implicit in the above quote is 'Newton's' First Law. Moreover, Hooke continued, the cause of deflecting the motion of a body into a curve is

An attractive property of the body placed in the centre; whereby it continually endeavours to attract or draw it to itself ... [and] ... all the phenomena of the planets seem possible to be explained by the common principle of mechanic motions, and ... we may be able to calculate them to the greatest exactness and certainty, that can be desired.'

He concluded that not only can the motions of the planets and satellites be solved, but also those of comets.

Then, in 1670 Hooke presented another lecture – published in 1674 as one of his Cutlerian Lectures – in which he expressed the clear statement regarding his principle of universal gravitation as follows:

That all Coelestial Bodies whatsoever, have an attraction or gravitating power towards their own Centres, whereby they attract not only their own parts, and keep them from flying from them, as we may observe the Earth to do, but that they do also attract all the other Coelestial Bodies that are within the sphere of their activity; and consequently that not only the Sun and Moon have an influence upon the body and motion of the Earth, and the Earth upon them, but that ☿ ♀ ♂ ♃ and ♄ [Mercury, Venus, Mars, Jupiter and Saturn] by their attractive powers, have a considerable influence upon its motion as in the same manner the corresponding attractive power of the Earth hath a considerable influence upon every one of their motions also.[5]

By contrast, Newton's writings on the subject were for some years vague and ill-defined, and his ideas, as revealed in his writing, were steeped in mystical terms and were what might be called 'fuzzy' – in line with his lifelong interest in the medieval practice of alchemy. He thought that the planets and the Sun were kept apart by 'some secret principle of unsociableness in the ethers of their vortices', and that gravity was due to a circulating ether that had to be replenished in the centre of the Earth by a process like 'fermentation or coagulation.' In a letter to Henry Oldenburg, dated 7 December 1675, more than five years after Hooke's lucid explanation of the problem as quoted above, Newton wrote :

So may the gravitating attraction of the Earth be caused by the continuall condensation of some other such like aethereall Spirit, not of the maine body of flegmatic aether, but of something very thinly and subtily diffused through it, perhaps of an unctuous or Gummy, tenacious & Springy nature, and bearing much the same relation to aether, wc the vitall aereall Spirit requisite for the conservation of flame & vitall motions (I mean not ye imaginary volatile saltpeter), does to Air. For if such an aethereall Spirit may be condensed in fermenting or burning bodies, or otherwise inspissated in ye pores of ye earth to a tender matter wch may be as it were ye succus nutritious of ye earth or primary substance out of wch things generable grow (or otherwise coagulated, in the pores of the earth and water, into some kind of humid active matter for the continuall uses of nature, adhereing to the sides of those pores after the manner that vapours condense on the sides of a Vessell subtily set); the vast body of the Earth, wch may be every where to the very centre in perpetuall working, may continually condense so much of this Spirit as to cause it from above to descend with great celerity for a supply.[6]

Further in the letter, Newton explains how the planets and the Sun are kept apart:

So some fluids (as Oyle and water) though their pores are in freedome enough to mix with one another. Yet by some secret principle of unsociablenes they keep asunder, & some that are Sociable may become unsociable by adding a third thing to one of them, as water to Spirit of Wine by dissolving Salt of Tartar in it. The like unsociablenes may be in aethereall Natures, as perhaps between the aethers in the vortices of the Sun and Planets.[7]

Newton thus applied his 'secret principle of unsociablenes' to the aethers and Cartesian vortices of the Solar System to explain how the Sun and the planets are kept 'asunder.' He thought that circular orbital motion is in a state of equilibrium between two equal and opposite forces, the *vis centrifuga* tending to fly out and the other to pull in. Hooke, on the other hand, correctly assumed that circular motion is the result of a disequilibrium of forces that causes the deflection of a body from its tangential straight path into a curve by a force (the Sun) at the centre; in other words, centripetal force. Newton therefore visualised the problem from within the rotating frame of reference of the Earth, while Hooke made a leap of imagination that propelled him outside of the Solar System to look inward. The distinguished biographer of Newton, the late Richard Westfall wrote: 'Without the concept of centripetal force, the theory of universal gravitation was inconceivable and Hooke's contribution to gravitation was not then insignificant.'[8] In the course of the correspondence between Newton and Hooke in 1679–80, Hooke presented Newton with a complete statement of these and other ideas on the gravitational problem.[9]

When comparing these Newtonian passages of 1675 with those of Hooke's (1666 and 1670) earlier and clear expressions of gravitational attraction, it is impossible to escape the conclusion that Hooke indeed understood the gravitation theory before the concept occurred to Newton. The date of Newton's *annus mirabilis* – 1665 or 1666 (it is not clear which plague year), claimed by Newton and his supporters and later writers for the date when he developed the Universal Law – is, therefore, suspect. There is apparently no independent corroboration of this claim.

Hooke's concept of polar wander

In a lecture presented early in 1687, Hooke summarised a number of facts concerning the Earth – facts generally known by the Fellows of the Royal Society – which he had discussed earlier, in 1684. First, that the Earth revolves around the Sun in the plane of the ecliptic, once in twelve months; second, that it rotates on its own axis $364\frac{1}{4}$ times during the year and that the Earth's axis is inclined to the plane of the ecliptic at $23\frac{1}{2}°$; third, that this axis is parallel to itself, or nearly so, in its journey around the Sun and at present points to a position in the heavens not far from 'the last Star of the Tail of the little Bear' – Polaris; and fourth, it proceeds by degrees nearer towards it, 'not directly, but in a Circle parallel to the Ecliptick, or whose Centre is the Pole of the Ecliptick' – the precession of the equinoxes. Hooke says at this point: 'Thus far I take the same with the Hypothesis of Copernicus and his Followers.'[10]

As a fifth point in his summary of what was known about the Solar System in his day, Hooke added an idea of his own:

> Fifthly, I suppose yet further, that the axis of the Diurnal Rotation of the Earth hath also had a progressive motion, and hath, in process of time, been chang'd in position within the Body of the Earth, and consequently that the Poler points upon the Surface of the Earth, have alter'd their Situation; so that the present Polar Points have formerly been distant from those Poles that were then; and consequently that these former Polar Points are now remov'd to a certain distance from the present, and move in Circles about the present.[11]

This is Hooke's statement of the concept of polar wander. Note that he refers to the 'polar points' upon the surface of the Earth – the geographic poles. The point that has confused people since the utterance of this idea is: how can the pole positions change with respect to the surface of the Earth without changing the orientation of the Earth's axis with respect to the plane of the orbital plane, the ecliptic? The answer, as Hooke conceived it, can only be that the surface of the Earth has shifted with respect to those pole positions. It is in this sense that Hooke asked his audience to consider:

> Whether it may not have been possible, that this very Land of England and Portland, did, at a certain time for some Ages past, lie within the Torrid Zone; and whilst it there resided, or during its Journying or Passage through it, whether it might not be covered with the Sea to a certain height above the tops of the highest Mountains.[12]

Hooke believed that sediments deposited on the floor of the ocean can be raised by degrees by 'earthquakes' to form mountains.[13] He came to this idea – of England having been, at some time in the past, in the torrid zone – from his knowledge of the large fossil ammonites found on the Isle of Wight (his birthplace) and on the Dorset coast at, for instance, Portland. Hooke reasoning that the huge fossil ammonites must have been produced in hot climates was based on his observation that tropical species are generally larger in size:

> All those extraordinary great Species are the productions of the Torrid Zone, or the hotter Climates, and not of the colder, and such as lie so far remov'd towards the Poles as Portland or England do, about which there are now no living Fishes, to be found that any wise come near to that Magnitude, but are of much smaller size and of different shapes.[14]

Hooke's idea of polar wander became known as his theory of 'axial displacement.' This term, however, is unfortunate, and could be misleading, as it implies a displacement of the axis of rotation with respect to the orbital plane. As a result of his experiments in twirling molten glass around a pipe, when a bulge developed at the 'equator' of the glass, Hooke postulated that the Earth is an oblate spheroid. This concept was again claimed by Newton and his followers to be Newton's; but the idea was clearly Hooke's. As late as 1680, Bishop Burnet questioned Newton about the shape of the Earth. Newton replied, in a letter, that he believed the Earth to be spherical, like all the planets that could be seen with telescopes, on the basis that if they were 'oval,' then Jupiter would be more so:

> The *vis centrifuga* at his equator caused by his diurnal motion being 20 or 30 times greater then the *vis centrifuga* at our equator caused by the diurnal motion of our Earth, as may be collected from the largeness of

his body & swiftness of his revolutions. The sun also has a motion about
his axis & yet is round.[15]

The date of this letter – January 1681 – is clear, yet in the third edition
(1727) of the *Principia Mathematica* Newton claimed he knew the true
figure shortly after 1672, when Jean Richer, on a voyage to Cayenne,
found that his pendulum clock had to be shortened at the equator, as it
lost time when approaching that region. The cause of this phenomenon was not understood until Hooke explained the oblateness of the
Earth and thus the decrease of gravity at the equator. Without dimin-
ishing the mighty impact of Newton's *Principia Mathematica*, therefore,
it can be concluded that much of what has been attributed to Newton
was perhaps the work of Hooke.

Polar wander, however, was an idea that no-one liked, so it was not
necessary or desirable for anyone else to claim to be its originator.
Hooke's concept of polar wandering on an oblate spheroidal Earth was
postulated by him to explain interchanges of land and sea areas. He
believed that, depending upon the positions of those parts with respect
to the polar points, the changed centre of gravity would cause 'sliding,
subsiding, sinking and changing of the Internal Parts of the Earth, as
well as External, tho' the latter will be more powerful, as being more
affected by the Rotation.' Such change would also cause 'an alteration
in the Magnetical Power and Vertue of the Body of the Earth, especially of such Parts as are more loose and of a more fluid Nature.' The
same principle, he thought, would cause swelling of the sea near the
equator and sinking near the poles, so that 'many submarine Regions
must become dry Land, and many other Lands will be overflown by the
Sea.' Furthermore, the 'many places which by degrees are made
Submarine, will be cover'd with Various Coats or Layers of Earth'
because the land is continually washed down, and 'by Rivers carried
into the Sea, and there deposited in the Submarine Regions' into
'Layers or stratifications of divers kinds of Substances.'[16]

Such major changes in the environment would cause changes in the
flora and fauna, but 'preserving in the mean time the Characterisks
and Marks of the former Qualifications, when in another Condition.'
Hooke recognised, therefore, that the ammonites were fossils of extinct
species – an astute observation that led him to express some of his
creative and original ideas on evolution.[17]

Reception of the theory of axial displacement

Hooke's contemporaries did not fully understand the concept of polar wander. Hooke clearly stated:

> There may be in the Rotation of the Body of the Earth, a change of the Axis of that Rotation, by a certain slow Progressive Motion thereof, whereby the Poles of the said Motion appear to be in superficial parts of the Earth, which heretofore were at some distance from the then polar Points or Parts.[18]

He was referring to the relative positions of the poles with respect to the surface – 'superficial parts' – of the Earth, and was clearly not advocating a wholesale multi-dimensional shift of the rotational axis with respect to the ecliptic. Polar wandering – the displacement of the poles relative to the surface of the Earth – is a totally distinct idea from axial displacement with respect to the heavens such as the precession of the equinoxes and the later recognised motion of nutation. However, Hooke's contemporaries, as well as some later and present-day writers, have not understood this distinction.

Edmond Halley (1656–1742) – successor to John Wallis in the Chair of Geometry at Oxford, and subsequently Astronomer Royal – must have been quite taken by Hooke's ideas, as he later conceived of an Earth model involving terrestrial shells, each having its own poles, sliding with respect to one another, to explain the problem of the secular variation of magnetic declination. Halley communicated Hooke's ideas, in a letter dated 15 February of the same year (1687), to John Wallis in Oxford. Wallis (1616–1703), Savilian Professor of Geometry – with whom the young Hooke, when at Oxford, studied mathematics – was the pre-eminent English mathematician before the rise of Newton. Reputedly, he was considered to be quarrelsome with others in regard to priority on subjects ranging from solutions of mathematical puzzles to curing a deaf-mute child. Wallis read Halley's communication to the Oxford Philosophical Society on the subject of axial displacement and, after discussion among the members, decided that Hooke's axial displacement idea was wrong. In his replies to Halley on 4 March and 26 April 1687 he reported his own reaction as well as the consensus of the Oxford group, saying, 'sure we are, that there is no evidence in history that ye top of ye Alps was ever sea; Except in Noah's Floud'; and the notion of the Earth changing its axis 'seems too extravagant for us to admit.' To Wallis and his adherents, therefore, the Earth's surface had been the same since Noah's flood:

Sea where now is sea, and Land where now is Land: so that (unless it
were before ye Creation of Adam) we cannot find a time wherein the
Earth should be (so often) have been tossed & turned upside down, (for
ye Equator & Poles to change places) & the top of ye Alps become a sea
only to enable us to give an account of some Fish-shels found there.[19]

Wallis conceded that 'some little alteration may have been in the
Earth's axis from that different obliquity of it to the Plain of the
Ecliptick', but that 'so vast a change as is now suggested, could not
possibly have been' without some historical record of it. The connect-
ing of these two separate and distinct ideas in proximity to each other
suggests that Wallis and his company confused an astronomical axial
displacement with Hooke's pole-wander on the surface of the Earth. In
the first instance, in referring to the obliquity of the Earth's axis to the
plane of the ecliptic Wallis obviously meant the orientation of the
Earth's axis with respect to the Solar System. He seems not to have
realised that Hooke's polar wander concept did not imply that the axis
had undergone changes in its position with respect to the heavens
except that already noted by astronomers: precession.

Since the terrestrial effects of either of these actions – whether the
axis undergoes a multi-dimensional shift or the Earth's surface moves
with respect to the axis – would have been the same, it did not matter
how Wallis interpreted Hooke's idea. As far as Wallis was concerned,
Hooke's axial displacement was non-existent. If it did exist, he insisted,
it would have been recorded somewhere in the Bible or in some other
historical text. Wallis's complaints, however, were sufficiently disturbing to Hooke to prompt him into scrutinising the classics in a search for
historical evidence of polar wander. Wallis's allusion to Noah's Flood
and a biblical chronology as proof against an axial shift demonstrates
that Wallis and Hooke were debating past each other on different
planes. The age of the Earth was a subject of great interest to Hooke,
and his writings indicate that he thought much about the problem of
the limited time-span allowed by the biblical chronology for the age of
the Earth. He certainly, at least, was considering a different time-scale
from Wallis. While there is no evidence that Hooke conceived of the
billions of years we now know to be the age of the Earth, he made
many objections to the biblical chronology as providing insufficient
time for all that he had observed of terrestrial processes. His writings
show that he would have had no difficulty thinking in terms of many
millions of years to accommodate geological processes as well as polar
wandering and organic evolution.

Hooke often mollified his audience on the point of Earth's chronology – especially after 1689, during the reign of William and Mary,

when the general political and religious climate of England became more rigid in religious dogma. James II (Duke of York), who succeeded his brother Charles II in 1685, was a Catholic, and at first attempted to encourage the nation and Parliament to adopt toleration towards Catholicism; but he soon changed to a policy of making England Roman Catholic, in opposition to Parliament and most of the people. The resultant climate of growing tension and resentment led to the Glorious Revolution of 1688, at which point James was deposed and exiled. He was succeeded by his Protestant daughter Mary, who ruled jointly with her husband William of Orange, and the atmosphere in the country then became one of religious conformity.[20]

In his adresses to the Royal Society, Hooke felt it politic to add such phrases as 'if their chronology may be granted' in reference to the 'space of time' since the beginning allowed by other peoples of the world. He repeatedly told his audience that such people – he called them 'Heathens' – such as the Chaldeans, the Egyptians, and especially the Chinese, allowed a much greater 'space of time.' He particularly admired the Chinese for their history, their inventions and their language, and even attempted to learn Chinese; and, with obvious approval, said that the Chinese 'do make the World 88,640,000 years old.'[21]

Another point of difference between Wallis and Hooke was the adherence of the Oxford group to a spherical (or near-spherical) Earth; but as reported by Wallis they conceded that if it were a spheroid they would prefer a 'prolated' Earth (with a long axis from pole to pole) to an 'oblated' one. Apparently in an attempt to ridicule Hooke, Wallis then told Halley of a 'Dr. of Physick of good credit' who was present at the Oxford meeting and showed the group what seemed 'to all appearances' the shell of a fish taken by the good doctor from the kidney of a woman. It is more probable, Wallis commented rather sarcastically, that the fish-shell was formed in the woman's kidney 'than that this kidney had once been sea.'[22] It is almost possible to hear the derisive laughter in the halls of the Oxford Philosophical Society.

Considering the ridicule in which Wallis held Hooke's ideas, the latter's defence of his hypothesis seems rather mild and justified, although it has been characterised by his critics as extreme, vitriolic and unreasonable. Hooke defended his notion of a 'flatted ovall figure' for the Earth (an oblate spheroid), and had discussed extensively on the subject in 1675, attributing the cause of the equatorial bulge to the centrifugal effect. Further, he emphasised, 'The Alteration of the Axis of rotation doth not tumble or tosse or turne the earth upside down' as Wallis and his group claimed. With apparent wounded feelings due to Wallis's criticism and ridicule, Hooke took a parting shot: 'And since the Dr is willing to give as well as to take a Liberty of Censuring, I conceive that the Deriding of an hypothesis is neither a philosophicall nor Geometricall answering or disproving thereof nor soe praiseworthy a qualification in a professor of Both.'[23]

Probably because of the treatment that Hooke's hypothesis suffered at the hands of Wallis and his group, the idea was not prevalent in the ensuing centuries. The eighteenth century's colourful character Erich Rudolf Raspé reviewed (1763) and applauded much of Hooke's theories about Earth science, but made a point of singling out the axial displacement idea as not worthy and therefore to be ignored and discarded.[24] James Hutton made a point of attacking it, demonstrating that he must have read Hooke and probably also Raspé, whose writing he cited.[25] Hutton must have been considerably bothered by the concept, as it is, after all, not usually necessary to debate vehemently against an idea that had been rejected for almost a century.

The idea vindicated

While the mechanism of polar wandering was not, and is still not, clear, its effect is evident. Hooke cites as evidence the occurrence of tropical and subtropical flora and fauna in England. To him, it is evident that England must have been in a hot climatic zone some time in the past. And since climatic belts have a strong relationship to the positions of the poles, then the north pole must, in the past, have been at a different place relative to the surface of the Earth.

The concept of the north pole wandering over the globe is a highly imaginative one – an idea that was important for Alfred Wegener in explaining (1929) his hypothesis of continental drift. Wegener defined the phenomenon as follows:

> Since only the uppermost layer of the crust is accessible to geologists, and since the former site of the poles can only be estimated by means of fossil evidence as to climate, which originates on the surface of the Earth, we have to define polar migration as a surface phenomenon; that is, as a rotation of the system of parallels of latitude relative to the whole surface of the globe, or otherwise as a rotation of the whole surface relative to the system of parallels (which amounts to the same thing because all movements are relative).[26]

Continental drift and polar wander are two distinct and separate ideas, but this distinction has not been understood by some. A large shift in mass within the mantle due to convection could cause continental drift and a shift of the spin axis with respect to the surface of the Earth as a result of a change in its moment of inertia. Continental drift/sea-floor spreading/plate tectonics, however, involve horizontal motions of the terrestrial plates relative to each other, while polar wander is a shift of the whole surface of the Earth with respect to the positions of the poles. Being an astute experimenter and observer, Hooke must have noticed the effect of mass shifting in his experiments with twirling molten glass, and noted the shift in the equatorial bulge. While Hooke did not exclude any possible movement of the terrestrial crust, his tectonics was essentially vertical, and he cannot, therefore, be considered an early proponent of the hypothesis of continental drift. Polar wander, however, is a necessary component in drift hypothesis and in plate tectonics. It is evidenced by the observed patterns of paleoclimate and biogeography in the distribution of flora, fauna and sediment types. On the other hand, continental drift involving horizontal movements of continents, relative to each other, was found to be a complication in deciphering the distribution patterns at various geological periods during which the climatic belts changed with respect to the varying pole positions. While the two concepts – continental drift and polar wandering – are distinct from each other, the distribution patterns could not be interpreted coherently unless the continents were assembled more or less the way Wegener had proposed as the land mass of Pangæa in his drift theory. Figure 5.1 schematically illustrates the interconnection of polar wandering, biogeography and continental drift/sea-floor spreading/plate tectonics. It can be seen that in order to reconstruct the arrangement of continents and climatic belts of the past, both continental drift and polar wander need to be taken into consideration. Note also that such reconstruction does not involve any change in the position of the axis of rotation with respect to the orbital plane, the understanding of which has escaped many. Wegener's writing clearly shows his frustration at the general lack of comprehension of these ideas during his lifetime, and he bemoaned: 'Some opponents still rejected this view … with a severity which is hard to understand.' He pointed out that 'if one starts out from the standpoint of drift theory, and if one maps the fossil evidence for climates on a chart developed for the relevant period by means of the theory, these contradictions completely vanish, and all the climatic evidence arranges itself to form the pattern of climatic zones which is familiar to us today.'[27] Wegener's reputation has now been restored to its place of prominence in the history of geology for his highly imaginative idea of continental drift – the embryonic idea for today's geological paradigm of plate tectonics.

At the risk of being labeled 'anachronistic,' it should be pointed out that today Hooke's polar wander concept is still useful and fruitful in

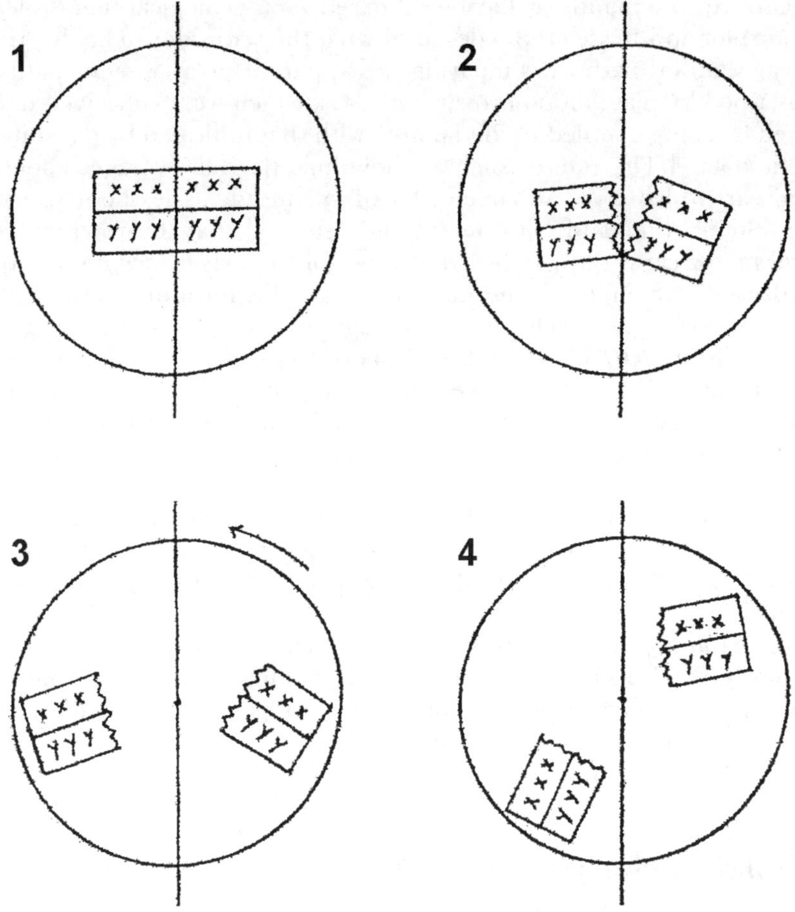

Fig. 5.1. The relationships among continental drift, polar wandering and biogeography: 1, the position of the original continent with its assemblage of flora and fauna (xs and ys); 2, the beginning of continental drift/seafloor spreading; 3, continued drifting, and simultaneously, polar wandering (direction shown by arrow); 4, the continent and the biogeography (geographical distribution of the biota) as it appears today. In order to reconstruct the original scene, both drift and polar wandering must be taken into consideration.

the plate tectonics paradigm. Paleomagnetic data, like the paleoclimatic zones, can only be explained by displaced poles in the past. Goldreich and Toomre (1969) lent mathematical support to the concept of large angular displacements of the Earth's rotational axis relative to the mantle as having occurred on a geological time-scale.[28] Courtillot and Besse (1987) deduced what they consider to be the 'true polar wander' path by comparing the apparent polar wander path as described by plate motions over hot-spots, which were conceived to be fixed by being coupled to the mantle, with that indicated by paleomagnetic data.[29] The rate of such a whole 'mantle roll' averages about 5 cm/year, which is of the same order of magnitude as sea-floor spreading. Steinberger and O'Connell (1997) showed that the rotation axis 'will follow closely any imposed changes of the axis of maximum non-hydrostatic moment of inertia,' and that 'the resulting path of the rotation axis agrees well with paleomagnetic results.'[30] On a voyage of the drillship *JOIDES Resolution*, Robert Duncan and his co-workers (1991), using their data on the Réunion hot-spot in the Indian Ocean, measured the amount of true polar wander or a whole Earth shift of 8–12°, during the last 66 million years, around a pole on the equator at 60° E.[31]

Scientists on a recent leg of the Ocean Drilling Program (ODP), Leg no. 197, investigating the Hawaiian–Emperor chain of islands, have shown that while hot-spots do not appear to be fixed as had been thought, their data suggest a combination of motions including polar wander, although so far there are insufficient data to determine the extent of each factor involved.[32] The fact remains, however, that the concept of polar wander, though still widely misunderstood, has proved to be an important and necessary component of the plate tectonics paradigm.

Hooke's undeserved obscurity

It seems that today most people have never heard of Hooke; and even among scientists, few are aware of his many significant achievements beyond his eponymous Law. Hooke was highly respected in his day, but was plagued by extraordinarily bad luck – not least of which was that he was a contemporary of Newton. His obscurity today is surely due partly to this bad luck, but it is also due to a consistently 'bad press' over the last 300 years. Newton has always been pictured as a god-like heroic figure, especially in children's books, bolstered by such powerful tales as the legend of the apple. Hooke has usually been represented by later writers with all his warts and human foibles, and is rarely mentioned in children's books. Yet of all the great luminaries of the seventeenth century, Hooke was the least hampered by superstition, mysticism or traditional authorities, and probably contributed the most to science and technology.

Hooke's bad luck is evidenced by numerous examples,[33] and the following are but a few examples in his professional life. (1) He was the first to prove the Power and Towneley hypothesis by experimentation; but it is now known as Boyle's Law. (2) He was the first to invent a pocket-watch using a spring-balance wheel; but Christiaan Huygens is generally credited with the invention, and the date-inscribed pocket-watch which Hooke presented to Charles II in 1675, to prove his priority, is now lost. (3) In 1664–65 he was the first to track a comet. He proposed that it was the same comet that appeared in 1618, and predicted that it would return after another interim of the same duration; but the discovery of the periodicity of some comets is attributed to Edmond Halley, who was nine years old at that time. (4) He was the first to express, clearly and concisely, a theory of combustion based on experimentation; but John Mayow has been assigned the credit. (5) He anticipated Newton in some of the fundamental ideas underlying the Universal Law of Gravitation – notably, the concept of centripetal force as an opposite and equal force to the familiar centrifugal effect – and communicated his ideas to Newton; but he never received credit. (6) He was the first to describe the iridescent interference colours seen when light falls on a layer of air between two thin glass plates; but, ironically, these are known as 'Newton's rings'. (7) He designed the great dome of St Paul's Cathedral and the Monument to the Fire of London of 1666; but both are attributed to Sir Christopher Wren. (8) He was the true founder of the science of geology; but Steno is generally praised for this role. And further, he profoundly influenced James Hutton's writings; while the latter is revered as the 'father' of modern geology.

Hooke was also unlucky in other, more personal, ways. (1) He had poor health throughout his life, suffering from headaches, indigestion, colds, dizziness, and insomnia, and how he could have accomplished as much as he did while suffering such a constant array of debilitating symptoms (not helped by self-medication) is remarkable indeed. (2) His position as the Royal Society's Curator of Experiments supposedly earned him a salary of £80 per annum, but he hardly ever received it, especially in the early years. (3) When the miserly 'philanthropist' John Cutler offered him £50 per annum to present a series of lectures, the Royal Society promptly reduced his ephemeral £80 to £30 per annum. Hooke gave his lectures, but Cutler never paid up during his lifetime, and Hooke had to sue Cutler's estate, although by the time he won he was an old man and did not need the money. (4) When Hooke died he was buried with due respect at St Helen's, Bishopsgate, but his grave was dug up and removed in the nineteenth century, and its location was lost. (5) A commemorative stained glass window at St Helen's, funded by a German firm, featured Hooke as one of the church's Worthies; but it was destroyed during the Irish Republican Army's bombing of London's financial district in April 1992. So far neither the church nor any other group is sufficiently interested to contribute to its replacement, so (at the moment) the window is simply plain glass. (6) None of the thousands of instruments and models that Hooke constructed, nor the fossil specimens he collected, survived Newton's presidency of the Royal Society and the move from Gresham College. (7) So, too, is missing the portrait of Hooke which certainly existed at one time, and which should have been in the possession of the Royal Society to be displayed along with other prominent members and Officers of the Society. It is as if Fate, in collaboration with his detractors in the literature, also wished to erase his memory.

Conclusion

Historians place scientists of the past in their own chronological, intellectual and social milieu. Someone with an influential idea during his time but which was later proved to lead nowhere, was simply wrong, or was positively detrimental to the progress of a science, is rightly considered an important person worthy of study in the history of science. Human beings, after all, can learn from their mistakes as well as their successes. It is interesting to study how scientists can be misled, as well as succeed, as a result of interrelationships among a closely-knit community and hierarchy of scientists. The characterisation of a person of the past as 'genius' by a later writer because his ideas proved to be right and fruitful, however, is considered judging with 'modern' standards and therefore 'anachronistic' and to be avoided. For this reason it is best if a writer does not admire his subject too much. Yet, at very rare times in the past there have been extraordinary individuals of science who were so remarkable, on target, and fruitful in the intellectual development of our own age, that these people should be remembered, honoured, and admired. These were the great scientists of all times. On occasion, historians might allow the words 'ahead of his time' in relation to the development of an idea or an invention, as if such foresight is almost fortuitous – the result of serendipity. Hooke was sometimes wrong, of course, but almost always for the right reasons. He was guided by the data from his experiments, conducted with instrumentation of the greatest precision for his age and designed by himself, and he was not influenced by superstitious or religious prejudices. Hooke can be labeled as 'on target' for a huge array of human intellectual accomplishments – too large, in my opinion, to be considered serendipitous. Newton has been almost deified because his *Principia Mathematica* provided a dramatic turning point in our thinking that culminated in our present state of knowledge. Hooke, in contrast, has an undeservedly obscure reputation today, in spite of the brilliant and fundamental contributions he made to Newton's achievements as well as in many other areas of human endeavour. While Newton's failures or character defects are either overlooked or positively swept aside, writers have had a field day with Hooke, often judging on the basis of his telegraphic notes to himself in the privacy of his Diary. He has been ridiculed and branded with all sorts of negative labels that resulted in detracting from, and minimising the significance of, his achievements in so many fields.

Hooke's ideas on the Earth in space laid the foundation for the mechanical age and the conviction that everything around us is knowable. In geology, his single concept of polar wander represents a synthesis of different scientific cultures – climatology, biogeography and drifting continents – and it must be recognised as a necessary and important component of the geologists' modern paradigm: plate tectonics. Without this concept we cannot make sense of the biogeographic distributions in our world or reconstruct coherent climatic belts for ancient land masses. If for nothing else, this single contribution of Robert Hooke should ensure him a place of honour in our history. But we know he contributed far, far more.

Acknowledgments

It is with pleasure that I participate in this commemoration of Robert Hooke. The distinguished engineer, the late Edmund C. Hambly, called Hooke 'London's Leonardo'; Dr Allan Chapman named him 'England's Leonardo'; and Christ Church is rightly proud of its remarkable alumnus. Indeed, like Leonardo, Hooke was a scientist of all times. I thank Dr Paul W. Kent for his fine organisation of the commemmorative meeting, and Dr Allan Chapman for his kind advice on manuscript style. I am hopeful that the event in Oxford in October 2003, together with the Gresham College conference that took place at the Royal Society in July 2003, will do much to restore Hooke's reputation and prestige in the annals of science and history.

Notes and references

1 Steno is much admired by geologists as the 'founder' of their science, even though he published only a short pamphlet on the subject, *De Solido intra Solidum Naturaliter contento Dissertationis Prodromus* (known simply as *Prodromus*), (Florence, 1669), 76 pp. A discussion by Drake and Komar, however, shows a much more profound understanding of the subject by Hooke than by Steno. See Ellen Tan Drake and Paul D. Komar, 'A Comparison of the Geological Contributions of Nicolaus Steno and Robert Hooke,' *Journal of Geological Education*, **29** (1981), 127–34.

2 Robert Hooke, 'Lectures and Discourses of Earthquakes, and Subterraneous Eruptions, Explicating the Causes of the Rugged and Uneven Face of the Earth; and What Reasons May be Given for the Frequent Finding of Shells and Other Sea and Land Petrified Substances, Scattered Over the Whole Terrestrial Superfices', in Richard Waller (ed.), *The Posthumous Works of Robert Hooke, M.D., F.R.S.* (London, 1705), pp. 279–450.

3 James Hutton, 'Abstract of a Dissertation', reproduced in facsimile in George W. White (ed.), *Contributions to the History of Geology*, **5** (Hafner, Darien, Connecticut, 1970), 30 pp; James Hutton, 'Theory of the Earth,' *Transactions of the Royal Society of Edinburgh*, **1**, part II (1788), 209–304. For a discussion of Hutton's debate with Hooke's ideas of axial displacement, see Ellen Tan Drake, 'The Hooke Imprint on the Huttonian Theory', *American Journal of Science*, **281** (1981), 963–73.

4 Royal Society (London) MS No. RBO.RBC.2.242.

5 For Hooke's published Cutlerian Lectures, see Robert T. Gunther, *Early Science in Oxford*, **8** (Oxford, 1931).

6 Letter from Newton to Henry Oldenburg, Secretary of the Royal Society, 7 December 1675, in H. W. Turnbull (ed.), *The Correspondence of Isaac Newton*, **1** (Cambridge, 1959), pp. 365–6.

7 Turnbull, *Correspondence* (ref. 6), p. 368.

8 Richard Westfall, 'Hooke and the Law of Universal Gravitation: a Reappraisal of the Reappraisal,' *British Journal for the History of Science*, **3** (1967), 245–61.

9 H. W. Turnbull (ed.), *The Correspondence of Isaac Newton*, **2** (Cambridge, 1960), pp. 297–313; see also Louise D. Patterson, 'Hooke's Gravitation Theory and Its Influence on Newton, I: Hooke's Gravitation Theory,' *Isis*, **40** (1949), 327–41, and 'Hooke's Gravitation Theory and Its Influence on Newton, II: The Insufficiency of the Traditional Estimate,' *Isis*, **41** (1950), 304–5. Patterson persuasively argues that Newton's debt to Hooke was no small matter.

10 *Posthumous Works* (ref. 2), p. 346, Hooke's proposition (supposition) No. 4.

11 *Posthumous Works* (ref. 2), p. 346, Hooke's proposition (supposition) No. 5.

12 *Posthumous Works* (ref. 2), p. 343.

13 For a complete discussion of Hooke's contributions to geology, see Ellen Tan Drake, *Restless Genius. Robert Hooke and his Earthly Thoughts* (Oxford University Press, 1996). Hooke believed that sediments deposited on the

floor of the ocean can be raised to form mountains by 'earthquakes' – a word used by Hooke to denote a variety of processes, and not limited to catastrophic seismic events. By 'earthquakes' he meant every manner of Earth movement, whether by violent 'slipping, sliding, or subsiding' (faulting) or by volcanic eruptions, or slowly and imperceptibly 'by degrees,' such as those erosional or depositional changes effected by the forces of wind, water or ice.

14 *Posthumous Works* (ref. 2), p. 343.

15 Letter from Newton to Bishop Burnett, January 1680/81, in Turnbull, *Correspondence* (ref. 6) **2**, 329. It should be noted that at the time, the term 'oblate' did not exist – but Hooke's meaning is clear in his statement that the form of the Earth is 'somewhat flatter towards the Poles than towards the Equinoctial', *Posthumous Works* (ref. 2), p. 343.

16 *Posthumous Works* (ref. 2), p. 347–8.

17 The Royal Society, in association with Gresham College, held a Hooke tercentenary conference on 6–10 July 2003. A paper on Hooke's theory of evolution was presented by Ellen Tan Drake, and is scheduled to be published under the aegis of that conference.

18 *Posthumous Works* (ref. 2), p. 357.

19 A. J. Turner, 'Hooke's Theory of the Earth's Axial Displacement: Some Contemporary Opinions,' *British Journal for the History of Science*, **7** (1974), 166–70.

20 For a more detailed discussion of the history of this period in England, see Roger Lockyer, *Tudor and Stuart Britain, 1471–1714* (St Martin's Press, 1964), pp. 355–63.

21 For a discussion of Hooke's concept of time, see Drake, *Restless Genius* (ref. 13), pp. 100–3.

22 David Oldroyd has quoted at length the acrimonious letters on both sides, and discussed the Wallis–Hooke debate in 'Geological Controversy in the Seventeenth Century: 'Hooke vs. Wallis' and its aftermath', in Michael Hunter and Simon Schaffer (eds.), *Robert Hooke: New Studies* (Boydell Press, Woodbridge, 1989), pp. 207–33. The 'Dr. of Physick' quote appears on p. 212.

23 Oldroyd (ref. 22), p. 224.

24 Rudolf Erich Raspé, *Specimen Historiae Naturalis Globi Terraquei, Praecipue de Novis e Maris Natis Insulis, et ex his Exactius Descriptis et Observatis, Ulterius Confirmanda, Hookiana Telluris Hypothesi, de Origine Montium et Corporum Petrefactorum* (Amsterdam and Leipzig, 1763), translated and edited by A. N. Iversen and A. V. Carozzi (New York, 1970).

25 Drake, 'The Hooke Imprint . . .' (ref. 3).

26 Alfred Wegener, *Die Entstehung der Kontinente und Ozeane* (New York, 1929), p. 148.

27 Wegener, *Die Entstehung* (ref. 26), pp. 129–30.

28 Peter Goldreich and Alan Toomre, 'Some Remarks on Polar Wandering', *Journal of Geophysical Research*, **74** (1969), 2555–67.

29 Vincent Courtillot and Jean Besse, 'Magnetic Field Reversals, Polar Wander, and Core–Mantle Coupling', *Science*, **237** (1987), 1140–7.

30 Bernard Steinberger and Richard J. O'Connell, 'Changes of the Earth's Rotation Axis owing to Advection of Mantle Density Heterogeneities', *Nature*, **387** (1997), 169–73.
31 Robert Duncan and M. A. Richards, 'Hotspots, Mantle Plumes, Flood Basalts, and True Polar Wander,' *Review of Geophysics*, **29** (1991), 31–50.
32 Robert Duncan, personal communication (2002).
33 An updated biography of Hooke is included in Drake, *Restless Genius* (ref. 13), pp. 9–59; for a more detailed discussion of examples of Hooke's bad luck, see specific subject entries in that work. See also Margaret Espinasse, *Robert Hooke: New Studies* (London, 1956) – an excellent overview of Hooke's life, his personality, and his time.

Chapter 6

Hooke's telescopic observations of Solar System bodies

Allan Chapman

Robert Hooke's fame as an observer of the natural world is primarily associated with his microscopical researches, although at the same time as he was assembling that corpus of discoveries that would immortalise him in *Micrographia*, he was also making a series of cutting-edge astronomical observations. While Hooke never produced a single volume of structured researches into astronomy as he did for the microscopical realm, nonetheless most of his 'Lectiones Cutlerianae', published between 1674 and 1679, dealt with astronomical physics, while about half of his contributions to *Philosophical Transactions* were concerned with celestial phenomena in one way or another.

Robert Hooke belonged to the 'next generation' of telescopic astronomical discoverers after Galileo, who, after 1610, applied new evidence acquired by the telescope to advance a radically different understanding of the nature of the Universe from that which had been inherited from classical antiquity.

This classical Universe, which had been given its definitive formulation by Claudius Ptolemy around A.D. 150, envisaged the Earth as a motionless sphere set at the centre of a series of concentric spheres that carried the Sun, Moon, planets and stars around us. In 1543, however, the Polish cathedral dignitary Nicholas Copernicus, in an attempt to account for some of the persistent anomalies of the Ptolemaic geocentric system, proposed a geometrical model for the Solar System in which the Sun was placed at the centre, while the Earth and planets rotated around it. Copernicus's heliocentric cosmology possessed a definite advantage when it came to explaining the observed motions of the planets and incorporating them into a coherent geometrical model, though as the Earth did not seem to be spinning through space on a common-sense level, Copernicanism appeared to fly in the face of everyday experience. In consequence, European astronomers became very much aware of the need to demonstrate conclusively the physical truth or falsehood of the heliocentric system. They recognised, moreover, that this could only be done after amassing new observational data on the motions of the stars and planets that were vastly more accurate than any that had been collected so far.[1]

By 1600, Tycho Brahe of Denmark, who was one of the last great naked-eye observers, had built up a body of observational data about the motions of the planets that was ten times more accurate than that which had been available when he established his great observatory, Uraniborg, in 1576.[2] Yet even these observations, accurate to a single arcminute, were insufficiently precise to convince the meticulous Tycho that a six-monthly displacement of star positions, such as was predicated by the Copernican theory, really existed. While Tycho remained loyal to his own modified version of the geocentric cosmology, his assistant Johannes Kepler became a convinced Copernican. Not only that, but Kepler's analysis of the Tychonic observations of Mars convinced him, between 1608 and 1619, that the Red Planet rotated around the Sun not in a circular orbit but in an elliptical one. What is more, the observed acceleration and deceleration of Mars as it moved around the Sun enabled Kepler to formulate his three Laws of Planetary Motion which would come to transform the subsequent history of astronomy and lay the foundation for Hooke's and Newton's gravitational researches.[3]

Galileo's telescopic discoveries widened the Copernican debate by setting forth new observational evidence which, even if it could not supply clear proof for the heliocentric theory, was fundamentally at odds with Ptolemy's geocentricism, and effectively provided pro-Copernican ammunition by analogy. The spherical, world-like appearances of the planets, the rugged topography of the Moon, Saturn's *ansae* ('handles', or peculiar projections, later discovered to be rings), Venus's phases, the spots and axial rotation of the Sun, the dense star-fields of the Milky Way, and the seeming infinity of the stellar Universe when viewed through telescopes of increasing power – all could be used to support the Copernican case simply because they were at odds with Ptolemy.[4] And Galileo, who became what might be called an 'evangelical' convert to Copernicanism, used these new telescopic evidences to and beyond the point of reasonable scientific argument in his zeal to trounce the conservative astronomers of the great Italian Renaissance universities, and in doing so provoked a famous backlash when the Church warned him that he could not teach as fact that which he could not actually prove.

The astronomical revolution of the sixteenth and seventeenth centuries, indeed, was no less a part of that broad movement which we call the Renaissance than were the works of Michelangelo, the plays of Shakespeare, or the theology of Luther, for like the age's great works of art, literature, and theology, astronomy lay at the heart of mankind's attempt to understand its place with relation to antiquity, to the natural world, and to God. By the time that Hooke was beginning to make serious contributions to science in the late 1650s, rapid improvements in telescope technology were adding enormous new evidence in favour of the Copernican theory. The telescopic Universe seemed to go on for ever and ever; educated opinion was coming to accept the idea that the stars were indeed remote incandescent bodies that resembled our Sun; while if the planets were worlds, then was there not a possibility that they could be inhabited? The Revd Dr John Wilkins, Warden of Wadham College, Oxford, and one of the great formative influences on the young Robert Hooke, was the first great populariser of Galileo's ideas in the English language, and Wilkins' books are replete with discussions about telescopic discoveries, Copernican cosmology, possibly inhabited worlds, and even space travel.[5]

Moreover, all of these astronomical discoveries – together with equally intellectually powerful discoveries in scientific subjects as diverse as geography, geomagnetism, physics and physiology – were made with newly developed scientific instruments. These instruments – which included the microscope, air pump, barometer, pendulum clock and magnetic compass, as well as the telescope – were all significant because, as Hooke said, they made the human senses more acute, enabling us to inquire deeper into the inner structures of nature. Indeed, they were what Hooke was to call 'artificial organs', in so far as they strengthened our natural organs of sense.[6] As far as astronomy was concerned, the key innovation after 1650 was the development of telescopes with long-focus object-glasses, through which very high-magnification observations of planetary bodies could be made.

Telescopic instrumentation

The long refracting telescopes which came into being by the mid-1650s, moreover, provided the first significantly improved 'artificial organs' of astronomical perception since those available to Galileo and his contemporaries around 1610. The improvements in glass-making and grinding that had taken place primarily in Holland and Italy at the hands of Christiaan Huygens, Giuseppe Campani, Eustachio Divini and others suddenly made it possible, by the mid-seventeenth century, to break through the earlier optical 'ceiling' under which Galileo and his contemporaries had laboured, and in whose time telescope-making had been technologically dominated by the craft of the spectacle maker. The bigger optical apertures and longer focal lengths that came into being after 1655, however, gave the telescope a new lease of life which for the first time permitted the examination of Solar-System bodies under relatively high magnifications. While most of these post-Galilean telescopic researches were conducted in continental Europe by the Huygens brothers, G. D. Cassini and Johannes Hevelius, the foremost English researcher of the period was undoubtedly Robert Hooke.[7]

It is probable (though no firm confirmatory evidence survives) that Hooke's first telescopic observations of Solar-System bodies were made at Oxford during the late 1650s. In Oxford, around 1656 so he later told Richard Waller (his obituarist) – he was encouraged by Seth Ward, Savilian Professor of Astronomy, and by John Wilkins, while it was also in Oxford that he formed his lifelong friendship with Sir Christopher Wren, whose pre-architectural fame derived from his astronomical and related physical researches.[8] Shortly after Hooke's establishment at the Royal Society in the early 1660s, he had access to at least five long refracting telescopes possessing focal lengths of 6, 12, 15, 36 and 60 sixty feet respectively, though it is not known who owned them. It is also clear that by May 1664 he had thoroughly mastered the art of making sustained and detailed observations with these extremely unwieldy instruments, one of which (probably the 60–footer) he later sketched as it stood erected in the quadrangle of Gresham College, complete with all of its pulleys and adjusting tackle (Figure 6.1).[9] Hooke had learned to track a planet in right ascension and declination with a 60–foot wooden tube hanging from a vertical pole, to move his eye around within the cone of light exiting the eyepiece so as to maximise image clarity upon his retina, and to estimate the comparatively apparent angular diameters of the planetary and cometary bodies thus observed. (I have tried to replicate some of these types of observations, using single-element lenses of considerably shorter focal length than those described by Hooke, and can vouch from personal experience for the enormous amount of manipulative dexterity and sheer patience that must have been required to observe the planets with long telescopes.)

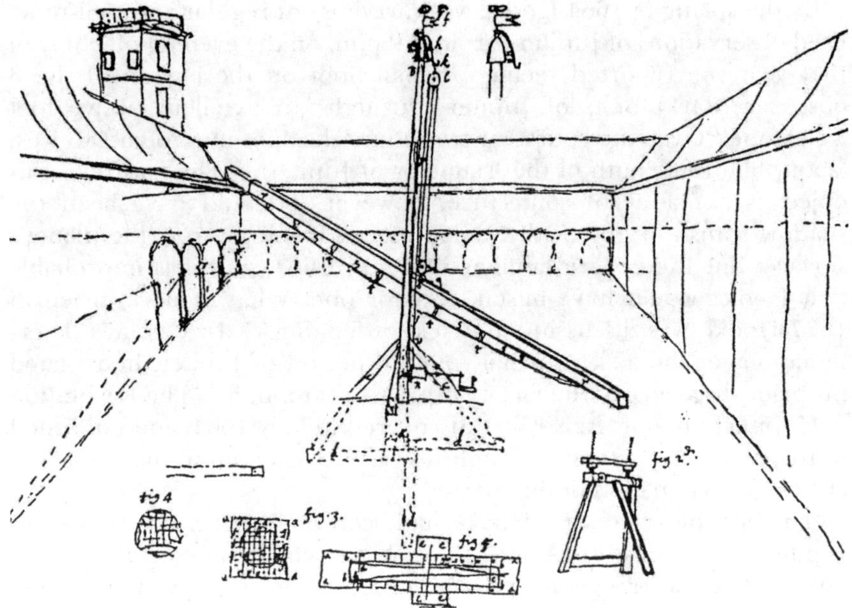

Fig. 6.1. Hooke's drawing of his 60-foot telescope erected in the quadrangle of Gresham College. (Courtesy Royal Society.)

Jupiter

In the early 1660s, European scientists saw planetary surface astronomy as possessing a pivotal significance in the cosmological debate of the period; for if planets such as Mars, Jupiter and Saturn were found to be rotating upon their polar axes, these rotations would, said Hooke, *à propos* of Giuseppe Campani's prior remark, 'serve much to confirm the opinion of Copernicus'.[10]

While Galileo's 1610 observations of the moons of Jupiter, and Christiaan Huygens' discovery of Saturn's satellite Titan in 1655, had clearly demonstrated that the Earth was not the only centre of rotation in the Universe, no-one before the late 1650s had possessed telescopes of sufficient optical quality to reveal clear topographical features on the actual surfaces of the planets and thereby demonstrate that the planets possess diurnal rotations in their own right. While such observations provided no definitive proof that the Earth actually moves around the Sun, when they were added to Galileo's 1611 discovery of the solar rotation, as well as a developing knowledge of the jovian and saturnian satellite systems, these observations fundamentally challenged the concept of terrestrial primacy which lay at the heart of the geocentric Universe.

By the spring of 1664 Hooke was carrying out regular and well-practised observations of Jupiter. Around 9 p.m. on the evening of 9 May of that year, he reported seeing 'a small Spot on the biggest of the 3 obscurer [dark] Belts of Jupiter' through 'an excellent twelve foot Telescope'. Over the course of two hours the spot moved east to west 'about half the length of the Diameter of Jupiter'.[11] The nature of this object is a matter of conjecture, however. It could have been the shadow transit of one of the jovian moons passing across the planet's surface; but these were familiar sights by 1664, and it is improbable that Hooke would have mistaken it for one. What is more, when in 1677 Hooke was discussing and acknowledging G. D. Cassini's determinations of the exact diurnal rotation period of Jupiter, he restated his prior discovery of the fact of Jupiter's rotation, for 'The Revolution of [Jupiter] upon its Axis I first discovered in May 1664, and published in the first Transactions', though he was not claiming to have made a critical determination of that period.[12]

It is possible that what Hooke had seen moving across the face of Jupiter on 9 May 1664 was that object which nineteenth-century astronomers, working with greatly superior telescopes, would call the 'Great Red Spot', which is located 22° south of the jovian equator, on the edge of the southern equatorial belt. This spot is the most conspicuous and long-lasting discrete object on the jovian surface, though it is impossible to be certain that this is what Hooke (and soon after, Cassini) actually saw. For one thing, Hooke assigns no colour or size to the spot he observed in 1664, while even more tantalisingly, he does not even specify the hemisphere in which it was located. Modern astronomers know that Jupiter's system of belts, and the spots which develop within them, are the products of the planet's violent and anticyclonic meteorology. The two great equatorial belts, which stand one above and one below Jupiter's equator, can, indeed, vary in size and darkness, thereby making it impossible to know which was the most conspicuous or dark in May 1664. Furthermore, Jupiter's anticyclonic belts are now known to generate large conspicuous cloud structures that can last for weeks or more before breaking up, but which are not permanent features.

It is clear, however, that Hooke saw a relatively permanent object on the jovian surface, and that it moved almost a quarter way around the planet in two hours. This would indeed be a reasonable observation and an approximate rotation period for a planet which Cassini, by the beginning of 1666, had determined possessed an axial rotation period of 9 hours 55 minutes 56 seconds.[13] Indeed, quite contrary to the popular assumption that Hooke resented other scientists who developed what he perceived to be his own initial discoveries, he warmly applauded Cassini's exact timings, for 'we are obliged to him for the perfecting the Theory [of Jupiter's rotation] as we are also for many other rare Discoveries and excellent improvements in Astronomy'. Hooke expresses this praise, moreover, in an appendix to his own published Cutlerian Lecture, *Cometa*, in 1678.[14]

Some of Hooke's best observations of Jupiter, however, were made on the night of 26 June 1666, with a 60-foot-focus refracting telescope. Hooke tells us that through this instrument, Jupiter appeared four times larger than does the Moon to the naked eye, subtending an apparent 2° of arc. This would suggest that Hooke was working at a magnification of around 173, though as the 41.48-arcsecond naked-eye diameter of Jupiter would have produced a prime-focus image of around 3.67 mm, a very powerful eyepiece would have been required to obtain a high magnification.[15] During this observation – which seemed to extend throughout most of the short midsummer night – Hooke recorded the position of four belt systems around Jupiter, and drew attention to the differences in luminosity of the brighter zones between the darker belts. He also observed the shadow transit of what was probably Jupiter's innermost satellite, which in the space of ten minutes passed across about one-sixth of the body of the planet, while the brilliant satellite itself slowly moved towards the eastern limb of Jupiter.[16]

Hooke was always cognisant of the difference between spots that were the products of satellite shadow transits, and those which were clearly objects on the surface of the planet and had no correlation with satellite positions. On the night of 26 June 1666, at about 1.30 a.m., he recorded the presence of what he believed to be a permanent spot on the larger equatorial belt of Jupiter, which moved westwards and disappeared around the limb. However, 'about a week before' (around 18 June) he also recorded that he saw two spots in both the northern and southern equatorial belts simultaneously, which seemed to keep pace with each other prior to their disappearance around the western limb.[17]

From our modern perspective, Hooke is often infuriatingly imprecise about the exact locations and physical descriptions of the 'permanent spots' which he recorded on Jupiter's surface. This did not in any way derive from a wish to confuse his readers, however, but from the simple fact that the astronomers of the 1660s knew nothing about Jupiter's complex meteorology, and were primarily concerned with finding enduring spots – anywhere on the planet's surface – which could be used to demonstrate the existence of an axial rotation and thereby add weight to the Copernican theory. Very soon after these initial observations, moreover, astronomers came to realise that, for

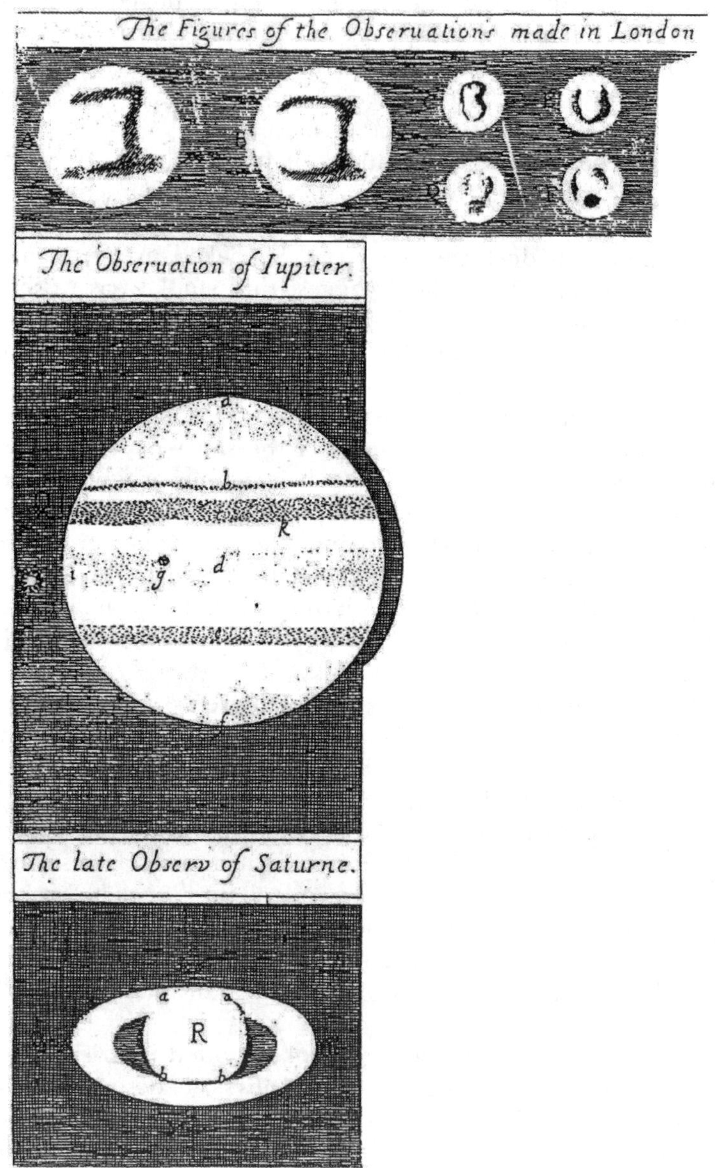

Fig. 6.2. Observations by Hooke. (*Top*) Mars, 3 March 1666. (*Middle*) Jupiter, 26 June 1666. The letter 'k' denotes the position where he reported seeing a large spot which in two hours moved off the planet's limb. (*Bottom*) Saturn, 29 June 1666. (*Philosophical Transactions of the Royal Society*, no. 14, 2 July 1666.)

whatever reason, well-marked spots sometimes vanished from the jovian surface. Indeed, Cassini recorded that the conspicuous spot which he, and no doubt Hooke, had been observing for eight months or so, suddenly disappeared in the early months of 1666, and did not reappear until 1672.[18]

Fortunately, however, Hooke supplied a drawing to accompany his observation of 26 June 1666, even though the coordinates are not without ambiguity (Figure 6.2). In this drawing – which clearly delineates the position of six polar and longitudinal dark zones – Hooke indicates with a letter 'k' a position on the edge of the supposed northern hemisphere belt where he had seen 'a large darker spot' two hours prior to the time of the drawing, but which, in the meantime, had rotated westwards and around the jovian limb. Hooke seemed to time this drawing at between 3.15 a.m. and 3.25 a.m., 26 June, from the rapidly moving shadow transit of a jovian moon passing across Jupiter's surface (the moon itself, which he also included in the drawing, standing a few arcseconds eastward of the planet's limb). But was this 'k' spot the same spot that he first observed in May 1664,[19] the same spot as that which Cassini was observing, or the same as that subsequently called the Great Red Spot? Hooke's drawing is further tantalising, among other things, because he tells us nothing about the optical characteristics of the eyepiece he was using with his 60-foot-focus object-glass. If it were a convex positive Keplerian eyepiece, or one of the two-lens Huygenian eyepieces with which he elsewhere spoke of 'charging' his large-aperture telescopes in his dispute with Auzout in 1665,[20] he would have obtained an inverted image of Jupiter, in which the 'k' position would have been on the southern equatorial belt, rather than the supposed northern as depicted.[21] As the position of 'k' is about 22° south of the planet's equator, Hooke could well have seen Jupiter's Great Red Spot on the night of 26 June 1666, if not in May 1664. Hooke's observations of Jupiter remind us that what might especially interest a modern person when analysing a 340–year-old scientific observation is not necessarily the same as that which interested the original observer.

Saturn

The planet Saturn was also an object of intense curiosity to seventeenth-century astronomers, this bafflement being compounded by the planet's extreme distance (was twice as far away from the Sun as Jupiter) and consequently smaller telescopic image size, and by the peculiar behaviour or its *ansae* ('handles'). These saturnian *ansae* had baffled Galileo back in November 1610, though in 1659 Christiaan Huygens, after using a long-focus refracting telescope, announced that they consisted of 'a ring, thin, plane, nowhere attached, and inclined to the Ecliptic'.[22] Then, between 11 o'clock and midnight on 29 June 1666, and probably maximising the same run of good observing weather which had allowed him to make such excellent observations of Jupiter, Hooke recorded his own observations of Saturn made with his 60–foot telescope (Figure 6.2). He confirmed that a clear, thin detached ring was visible, as previously reported by Huygens, but then proceeded to point out the presence of a series of black lines which were clearly visible between the body of Saturn and the ring. These black lines would have been produced in the front of the visible image by the shadow of the ring falling on the body of Saturn, and behind the planet by the shadow of Saturn falling on the ring. 'Whether Shadows or not, I dispute not', concluded Hooke![23] It is also clear from this observation that Hooke possessed acute colour and light-intensity vision, for he noted that the ring appeared slightly lighter in colour than did the body of the planet. While later astronomers were to discover that Saturn also has a complex system of longitudinal belts like those of Jupiter, these less pronounced saturnian structures were not observed by Hooke or his contemporaries.[24]

Mars

Although it is possible that Christiaan Huygens was the first to observe a permanent surface feature on Mars – the subsequently named Syrtis Major – Robert Hooke was quick to insert a 'stop press' communication 'since the Printing of the former sheets' in the April 1666 number of *Philosophical Transactions*, reporting his sighting of *maculae* (spots) on the martian surface. He had seen them in late February and March 1666, and wanted to alert the astronomical community 'before Mars gets out of sight' and lost its conspicuousness in the spring sky.[25] As in the case of Jupiter, the supposed newly discovered martian spots could be used to help substantiate the Copernican theory, 'whence it may be collected, that Mars (as well as Jupiter, and the Earth, &c.) does move about his own Axis.' Hooke promised a fuller communication of his martian researches, 'God permitting', which he supplied to the Royal Society in July 1666.[26]

Hooke made his principal martian observations with his refracting telescope of 36 feet focal length. This seems, indeed, to have been one of Hooke's favourite object-glasses, for he used it in various research configurations, including his study of the Pleiades cluster, in his discovery of five distinct stars (the Trapezium) in the Sword of Orion (wherein Huygens only found three stars), and, in 1669, as a vertical zenith sector in his attempt to measure the parallax of the star γ Draconis. This 36-foot-focus lens – which was probably the work of Hooke's favourite London optician, Richard Reeves – was a 'good one' in spite of the thickest part of its curvature not being in the geometrical centre of the glass, and could give good images at an aperture of 3½ English inches.[27]

By early March 1666, Mars was approaching opposition, and was relatively close to the Earth. Believing that he could now improve upon some previous observations of Mars made with his 12-foot telescope, Hooke directed his 36-foot instrument at the planet. But as with his observations of Jupiter and Saturn, Hooke is tantalisingly vague as to the exact optical magnifications with which he 'charged' his telescope (speaking only of 'shallow', 'deep', and 'greater charge' glasses), though when the larger instrument was fully 'charged', the martian disk 'appear'd very near as big as that of the Moon to the naked eye'.[28] Observing conditions were not good, however, but on 3 March he believed that he saw a clear set of martian surface features, of which he made two drawings, ten minutes apart. Then, over the remainder of March he made about eighteen or twenty further observations. These varied in quality, depending on the state of the air and the magnification that the martian image would bear. The two consecutive drawings which he made on 3 March both show a curious dark feature which has a resemblance to the three sides of a square in the full-Moon-sized image produced by his telescope (Figure 6.2). It is possible that this really could have been a continental structure on the martian surface, part of which belonged to that feature which nineteenth-century martian cartographers, working with greatly superior telescopes, would name the Syrtis Major (which was also observed by Huygens). The dark Syrtis Major, Sinus Sabaeus and Acidalis Planitia can form a shape resembling the three sides of a square when seen against the lighter-coloured terrain; but it is difficult to judge whether this is what Hooke actually saw, in whole or in part, and how much he might have been misled by aberrated images.

The features on the martian drawings which Hooke made later in March 1666, for which seeing conditions obliged him to use lower magnifications, look suspiciously like central-field circular aberrations, though Hooke believed them to be real martian features such as those which Francisco Fontana thought he had seen on Venus and Mars in the 1630s and 1640s.[29] It should never be forgotten, however, that Hooke was a cautious and critical observer who invariably noted the steadiness, transparency and humidity of the air and the rate of star 'twinckling' at the time of an observation. He also recognised the need to check the telescope's image for optical aberrations by placing his eye at different spots within the cone of light exiting the eyepiece, 'changing my eye into various positions, so that there might be no kind of Fallacy in it'.[30] While we now know that features on Jupiter can change as a result of that planet's anticyclonic upper atmosphere, so we also know that Mars, with its thin atmosphere, is often disturbed by planet-encircling dust storms whipped up from its arid surface. Modern observers know that the martian surface can become seemingly blank when dust storms obscure the now familiar features; and how can we know what disturbances were raging in the Red Planet's atmosphere in March 1666?

It is quite clear, however, that Hooke believed that he had found topographical features on the surface of Mars, although some of them – such as those seen on 28 March – were 'not reconcilable to the Appearances, unless we allow a Turbinated motion of Mars upon its Center'. Did Mars have, instead of a simple axial rotation, 'some kind of Librating motion'[31] which made it difficult to be certain when the same features could be seen from exactly the same position?

Hooke never attempted to determine Mars' diurnal rotation from observations of his supposed spots, though during the same opposition, in February and March 1666, Cassini, in Bologna, was successfully doing so. In addition to working with lenses by two of Europe's leading astronomical opticians, Eustachio Divini and Giuseppe Campani, Cassini had the advantage of a much more favourable observing station. Not only was the air on the outskirts of Bologna steadier and more transparent than that of central London, but because Bologna is some 7° closer to the Earth's equator than is London, Mars would have been correspondingly higher in the sky (about fourteen full-Moon diameters higher), and would therefore be seen through less atmosphere.

In this world of rapidly advancing scientific discovery, the fruits of Cassini's martian studies reached the Royal Society – via the good graces of the Venetian Ambassador in Paris – on 3 June 1666. Cassini could see distinct marks on the martian surface, as could Campani, over February and March 1666, from which the conclusion was drawn 'that the Period of this Conversion [rotation] is made in the said space of 24 h. 40 m.; and not oftener than one within that time'.[32]

The Moon

As early as October 1664, Hooke had been drawing the lunar surface using 'a thirty foot Glass' (probably his well-documented 36-foot), and when he gained access to the above-mentioned 60-foot instrument he produced even better. Hooke's lunar drawings are important for a variety of reasons. Perhaps most obvious is that his drawing of the region around the lunar crater Hipparchus shows what a superlative astronomical draughtsman he really was. It is not always easy to evaluate his skill as a telescopic astronomer from his tangled reports of jovian or martian spots, but lunar craters do not change, and to assess the scientific quality of his drawing it is only necessary to compare it to a modern photograph of Hipparchus lit at the same angle, on a Moon about 8 days old (Figure 6.3). It is true that we may not compare the Hipparchian terrain to the 'short Sheep pasture which covers the Hills of Salisbury Plains',[33] but as his correspondence with Auzout made clear, Hooke was not averse to the idea of an inhabited Moon.

Another aspect emphasised by Hooke's lunar drawings is the remarkable quality of definition which these unwieldy telescopes really could produce, if skilfully and patiently handled. The complex of craters around Hipparchus subtends an angle (to a terrestrial observer) of about 1.5 arcminutes – slightly less than twice the apparent mean angular diameter of Jupiter. Yet within this region, Hooke was clearly seeing and drawing details which were in themselves no more than a few arcseconds across; details, morever, that cannot be attributed to telescopic aberration or observer's imagination, for they can still be distinguished through modern telescopes or seen on lunar

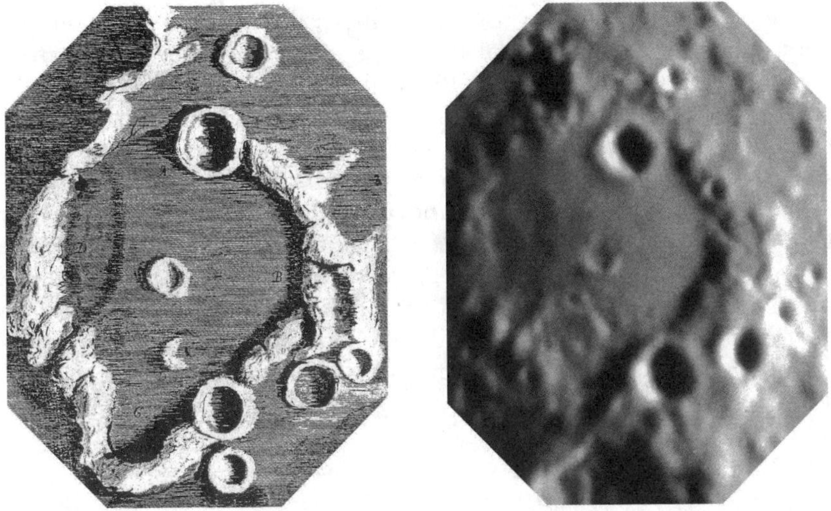

Fig. 6.3. (*Left*) Hooke's drawing of the lunar crater Hipparchus; (*right*) a photograph of the same crater, taken by Kenneth Kennedy in 2004. (Hooke's drawing courtesy Royal Society.)

photographs. It is true that the stark, hard monochromatic features of the lunar terrain form a less rigorous test of telescopic resolving power than do features on the surfaces of the atmospherically turbulent outer planets, yet nonetheless they provide us with an objective yardstick with which to assess Hooke's skill as a telescopic astronomer, and also reveal much about the quality of the object-glasses which he used.

The third and perhaps most radical consequence of Hooke's lunar studies was his concept of modelling the lunar surface in the laboratory. In his lunar crater studies published at the end of *Micrographia* he describes two sets of such experiments. Firstly, he dropped bullets (musket balls) into tubs of viscous pipe-clay and found that the resulting impact structures resembled the 'pits' of the lunar landscape. However, as asteroids and space debris were not known in 1665 he abandoned the impact model of lunar crater formation simply because he had no knowledge of any eligible projectiles which could produce them. Secondly, he noticed that the air bubbles bursting on the top of a pot of boiling alabaster (gypsum) also looked like lunar craters, which led him to consider that the Moon had once been a volcanically active body.

I am not aware of any scientist before Hooke who attempted to model planetary surface phenomena by means of dynamic laboratory experiments, although he must have been familiar with Christopher Wren's previous attempts to make sense of the *ansae* of Saturn by means of illuminated spheres and cardboard projections. Nor am I aware of anyone else who used the spherical shape of the Moon and telescopically visible spherical planets to draw evidence for the presence of a 'gravitating force' in the Universe. As early as 1664 Hooke had argued that the Moon must indeed possess a power of gravity in so far as all the matter of which the Moon was formed is tightly and symmetrically packed around a central point of attraction.[34] This was a remarkably astute observation, and it might be conjectured whether Hooke's awareness of such a force and its manifestation was due to the ideas of his own Oxford mentor, Dr John Wilkins – who had discussed this gravitating power in the 1640s – and in those flying experiments performed in the gardens of Wadham College in which Hooke subsequently recorded his collaboration.[35]

Comets

Hooke's telescopic researches were nowhere more ingeniously allied to laboratory researches than in his study of comets. The bright comet of 1664 had seized the attention of Europe's astronomers, as Hevelius,

Huygens, Cassini and others debated the nature of its glowing and apparently fiery substance and the possible shape of its orbit. Had the comet been shot out of the Sun? Was it produced from planetary effluvia? And was its orbit a straight line, or did it correspond to an open conic section such as an hyperbola or a parabola?[36]

Surprisingly, Hooke published nothing on the comet at the time (though he presented his findings to the Royal Society), but in 1677, when another brilliant comet swept through the skies of the northern hemisphere, he responded to Royal Society solicitations by publishing his treatise *Cometa*, which dealt in particular with his studies of the comet of 1664. Later, in 1705, Richard Waller published some of Hooke's manuscript lectures and other documents on comets.[37] What is especially relevant in the present context, however, is not Hooke's ideas on the orbits of comets so much as on their actual substance, source of illumination, and relation to space physics. It was from his observations of cometary nuclei and tails that Hooke was to proceed not only to laboratory experiments, but also to a series of ingenious physical analogies that encompassed geology, vulcanism, combustion chemistry and optics.

Central to Hooke's ideas on comets was the nature of the nucleus and its relationship with the coma (head) and tail. Though he does not tell us the specifications of the telescopes with which he observed the comet of 1664, he tells us that he used 6-foot and 15–foot telescopes to observe the comet of April and May 1677 (Figure 6.4). Through his telescopes, the nucleus of the 1677 comet looked 'like the shining of a star through thin cloud'. The brilliant, starry nucleus then projected a long thin medulla, or stem, which arose out of it in a direction away from the Sun, to form the second-brightest region of the comet. And then there was the coma, which burgeoned out into a long and relatively compact tail – a tail, moreover, which was so impressive that 'people commonly ghessed [was] about two yards long'.[38]

As this long thin comet approached the horizon, Hooke noticed that he could position his 6-foot telescope to align the comet behind a distant weather vane. By this means he was able to establish the physical proportions of the comet, either by measuring the diameter of the iron vane and its heavier vertical timber support (and triangulating the angles which they subtended from his place of observation), to use them as simple but effective measuring bars, or by accurately timing the comet as it passed behind the two verticals and reappeared. The coma was found to be 4 arcminutes 10 arcseconds across, whereas the starry nucleus within it was only 25 arcseconds.[39]

These 1677 observations prompted him to return to his studies of 1664, to ask such questions as: what are comets made of, what is the

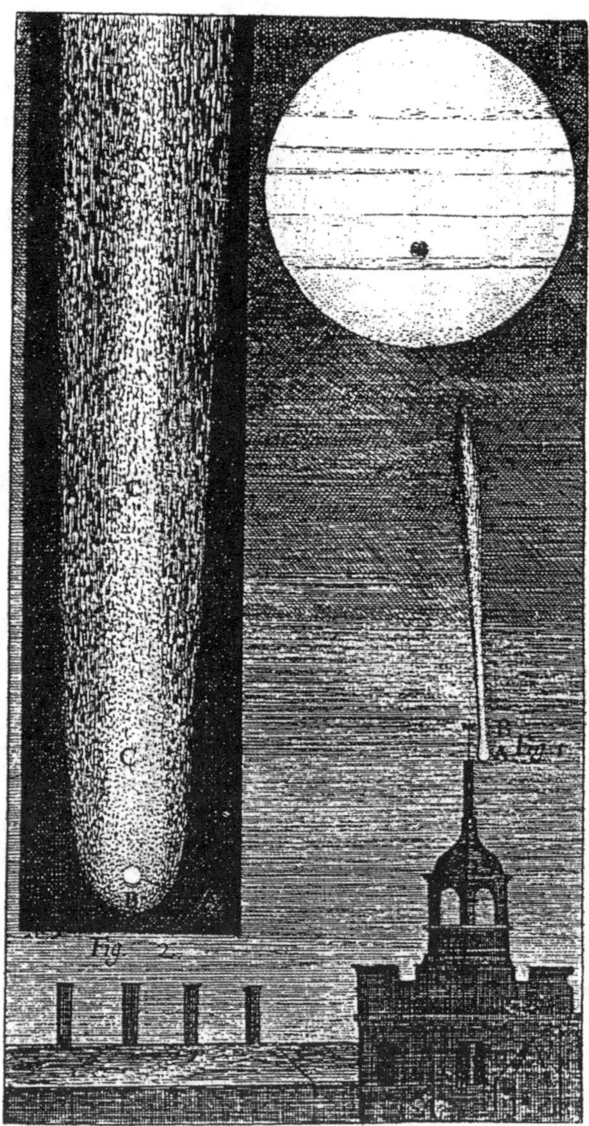

Fig. 6.4. Observations by Hooke. (*Left*) The comet of
April 1677. (*Right*) The horizon view drawing illustrates the way in which Hooke used a distant weather
vane and post to measure the diameter of the comet's
coma aond nucleus. (*Top*) It is not clear whether the
drawing of Jupiter, showing a conspicuous spot in the
southern (?) belt, was Hooke's or Cassini's.
(Hooke, *Cometa*, London, 1678).

source and nature of their light, and do they possess gravity like the planets? These questions took Hooke beyond the usual mathematical descriptions of astronomical phenomena, and opened up a range of possibilities about the nature of celestial matter, along with considering forms of what nineteenth-century physicists would come to call energy exchange. Comets, indeed, provided a powerful stimulus to Hooke's prodigious scientific imagination and his capacity for lateral thinking.

Hooke concluded from his careful telescopic studies that cometary nuclei consist of solid matter. However, terrestrial volcanic activity suggested that the Earth had a soft interior beneath its hard surface. Could a comet's nucleus, therefore, consist of similarly soft subterranean material of 'a loose and spongy nature'? If this were so, it could explain how a comet generates its light, for as Hooke's telescopic observations had made abundantly clear, a comet's nucleus is light-generating in its own right, as it is equally bright on its sunward and contra-sunward sides.[40]

Hooke very significantly realised that the light of a comet is fundamentally different from that of a flame. As he reminds us in *Lampas*[41] (1677), the middle of a candle flame is darker than the surrounding glowing envelope. Indeed, common combustive flames usually had, at their centres, hot yet dark sooty regions rather than brilliant light regions.

Hooke explained comets by invoking one of his favourite physical scenarios: his fascination with menstruums (solvents), whereby a corrosive agent mechanically abraded or shook up a hard substance placed within it and thereby created motion, light, and even heat. This idea is first encountered in his experiments on nitrous airs and combustion, expounded in *Micrographia* (Observation XVI), by which, so Hooke argued, the agitated or corrosive parts of the air tear apart the sulphurous or inflammable bodies placed within it. And was not the aether which suffused space such a menstruum? Was not even the Earth's own atmosphere the result of this aether gradually wearing the rocks away as we are spun through space, thereby producing an effluvium?[42] Also, was not this aether dissolving comets and making their nuclei erode away to produce a light-suffused and agitated tail? Hooke even suggested that if the material of cometary nuclei was spongy and permeable, then it would be easier for the aether to enter into them.

Indeed, Hooke was fascinated by these aetherial menstruums (a word derived from a medieval dog-Latin alchemical term). He saw them as being intimately bound up with his perceived vital forces of the Cosmos – light, magnetism, gravity and such – and acting in a vibrative or wave pattern; and it was not for nothing that he considered light itself as engendered when a wave force moves through the aether, thereby inflecting the sensations of redness and blueness from opposite ends of its sinusoidal vibration within the beholder's eye.[43] While this motion was most obvious in the dissolving menstruums of flames, even the apparently static phosphorescence produced by rotting fish, decaying wood, and phosphorus itself, belied the presence of microscopically small light-generating motions, so argued Hooke; and the same dissolving motion which caused a rotten fish to glow in the dark[44] also probably produced the glow of cometary nuclei and tails. Hooke even suggested a musical analogy. In the same way as a unison string on a viol will produce a sympathetic 'tremulation' in other strings when it is struck, could not the vibrative nature of the aether be imagined as such a universal unison note to which comets and other glowing bodies respond, vibrate, and emit light?[45]

In addition to analogies drawn from experiments on flames (described in *Lampas*) and observations of glowing substances, Hooke also devised an ingenious laboratory experiment to simulate cometary dissolution. First he took a wax ball and encrusted it with iron filings, after which the ball was suspended in a weak solution of sulphuric acid, inside a long glass cylindrical vessel. Hooke noted that as the acid attacked the iron filings, bubbles began to ascend from the ball to the top of the glass. As the bubbles ascended they began to spread out in the weak acid solution, producing a flow pattern from the ball which looked like a comet's tail. Ignorant as he was of the existence of hydrogen and the way that its bubbles always rise up through water, one cannot help but marvel at Hooke's ingenuity in devising an experiment which so clearly produced many of the basic structural components of a comet – albeit for the wrong reasons.

He also suggested that in spite of its dissolution and conversion into light, there must still remain some part of a cometary nucleus which was not destroyed by the menstruum. This, indeed, must be the part which possessed that 'gravitating principle'[46] which made it susceptible to being attracted towards the Sun, pulled it out of its original straight line of motion, and 'incurvated' it somewhat into a concave orbit about the Sun, 'though it were not wholly stayed and circumflected into a Circle'.[47] While a brilliant comet might be substantially dissolved away as it nears the Sun, it was clear that for over a month after the comet of 1664 had lost its tail and ceased to be a naked eye object that it could still be observed through the telescope, though appearing as no more than a dim star shining through a tiny patch of haze. Hooke traced this comet well into February 1665, and could have done so for longer, so he claimed, had he not lost it in the glare when the Moon moved into the field. He then suggested that the earlier brilliant comet of 1618 – which had blazed across the skies of northern Europe seventeen years before he was born, and which had been the most memorable relatively recent comet – could no doubt have also been traced (had anyone thought of following it) with telescopes as it flew off tailless into space.[48]

Hooke was probably the first astronomer to track a comet from its naked-eye blaze into distant fuzziness, though it was not clear to him why, if the aether were uniformly distributed throughout space, a comet only produced a great tail when it was near the Sun. He was, however, the first to admit that much more needed to be learned before we could even begin to really understand the nature of comets; and like the great experimentalist that he was, he admitted the need for 'a much greater stock of observations to build upon'[49] before firm conclusions could be drawn.

The Sun

As a telescopic observer of the Solar System, Hooke is surprisingly silent about the Sun. He was, of course, fully aware of the Copernican implications of Galileo's sunspot discoveries of fifty years earlier, and would have been familiar with the detailed solar researches of Christoph Scheiner which were published in 1626.[50] Yet surprisingly, Hooke never seems to have studied the solar surface, although in his lecture *A Description of Helioscopes, And some Other Instruments*, presented to the Royal Society in 1676, he dealt at length with the possible construction of a 'folded' refracting telescope, the darkened internal mirrors of which would remove the blinding glare of the Sun.

In these experiments in folded telescope designs, Hooke used his familiar 60-foot focus object-glass, which he attempted to reduce to the more manageable dimensions of a flat 12-foot box by a series of internal mirrors inside the optical train, as he claimed to have originally demonstrated to the Royal Society in 1668.[51] While he had used various bright speculum alloys and even mercury-backed glass mirrors when using this instrument on planetary bodies, he fitted it with mirrors of black glass, black marble, and 'Glass of Antimony' for viewing the Sun.[52]

Although this 'Helioscope' was not a success because of the difficulty in making optically flat mirrors at that time, it is surprising that Hooke never seems to have studied the Sun by the more conventional technique of telescopic projection onto a white screen, such as had been used by Galileo and his contemporaries, and which was also used by Flamsteed at Greenwich after 1676. It is possible, however, that the reason for Hooke's lack of attention was that during the 1660s and 1670s the Sun was one of the least interesting bodies in the Solar

System. This extended period of extremely low sunspot activity during the middle and late seventeenth century was later discovered and researched by the English solar physicist E. Walter Maunder (1851–1928), and was subsequently named the 'Maunder Minimum'.[53] It would, however, be interesting to know what conclusions about the Sun Hooke would have drawn had he lived during a period of greater solar activity, as he would probably have devoted more time to its study.

Miscellaneous astronomical observations

In addition to the above telescopic studies of the planets, all of which were directly connected with Hooke's favourite scientific agenda – Copernicanism, vulcanism, and the chemistry and physics of light and gravity – he also left a variety of references to astronomical observations in his Diary and elsewhere.

On 1 January 1675, for example, he was at Sir Jonas Moore's house, in the Tower of London, with Viscount Brouncker and other Royal Society luminaries, to observe an eclipse of the Moon with an 8-foot telescope. It seems, however, that in reporting this observation Hooke was also keen to emphasise his claimed priority as a horological inventor, for the eclipse was timed with 'my pocket-Watch, whose ballance is regulated with springs'.[54] Eclipses were, however, important events in the seventeenth century, as their exact timing provided key physical checks on the still-developing theory of Copernican and Keplerian elliptical orbits, and astronomers were always keen to compare predictions for the various phases of an eclipse with what actually took place.

Mercury

Considering the importance of eclipses and similar phenomena, it is all the more unfortunate that Hooke was unable to observe the transit of Mercury across the disk of the Sun that took place on 7 November 1677. The preceding transits of Mercury, in 1631, 1651 and 1661, had been carefully observed and measured by astronomers because of the ideal opportunity which the transits provided to accurately establish the nodal point of Mercury's orbit with reference to the centre of the Sun and the Earth. Establishing the exact elements of a planet's orbit was always a problem in the seventeenth century, though as the Sun's position was known better than that of any other Solar-System body it could be used as a comparative benchmark whereby the Sun's position could be used to fix a planet's position with relation to an exact place against the starry sphere.

Hooke was certainly very interested in the transit, and in *Cometa* he reported the successful observations of Johannes Carolus Gallet in Avignon and Edmond Halley in Saint Helena.[55] On 7 November 1677 (or 28 October 1677, in the Old Style calendar then in use in England) it was cloudy, and Hooke recorded that 'The eclipse of ☉ [Sun] by ☿ [Mercury] appeared not.' Down the river at Greenwich, John Flamsteed fared a little better, though the first part of the transit was clouded out for him as well.[56]

Stellar observations

While this chapter is primarily concerned with Robert Hooke's observations of Solar System bodies, it should not be forgotten that his interest in telescopic astronomy also extended to stellar and nebulous objects. In *Micrographia* (Observation LIX) he described the Pleiades Cluster as seen through his 12-foot telescope, and compared it to Galileo's observation and drawing of the same cluster as recounted in *Siderius Nuncius* (1610). Galileo, with his modest refractor of around 30 times magnification, could see thirty-six stars in the Pleiades, but Hooke, with his 12-foot instrument (though he does not specify the diameter of the object-glass), could see seventy-eight; and with his 36-foot telescope he was able to see a great many more faint stars in the Pleiades beyond those visible in the 12-foot instrument. Hooke also claimed that this same 36-foot telescope, when its object-glass was unstopped to its full $3\frac{1}{2}$-inch aperture, could detect five stars shining in the heart of the Nebula in Orion's Sword (the misty patch directly below Orion's Belt), whereas Christiaan Huygens had reported being able to see only three. These stellar researches, indeed, led Hooke into ground-breaking concepts regarding scientific instrumentation, when he began to ask whether our ability to detect extremely dim stars was not only a function of the focal length in feet and the magnification of telescopes, but also of the aperture of the telescope's object-glass. In this respect Hooke became one of the first astronomers (and perhaps the first) to approach an understanding of what the astronomers of later centuries would call the resolving power of a lens.

Hooke clearly enjoyed working with powerful telescopes to observe the heavens, and his earlier Diary entries in particular contain numerous brief reports of his doing so with apparently no explicit research motive in view. He was, for example, delighted by the sheer visual beauty of Venus and the crescent Moon on the night of 10 April 1673, while fifteen days later he 'viewed ♀ [Venus] and ♃ [Jupiter] with telescope with Harry [Hunt]', his young Gresham College assistant.[57] On 22 January 1673 he mentioned the 'New planet observed about ♄ Planet' – no doubt the saturnian satellite discovered by Cassini in 1672 and subsequently named Rhea, which Hooke was surely keen to see for himself. One of his most remarkable telescope activities, however, came at the end of one of those days of gruelling self-medication which Hooke sometimes inflicted upon himself, when on 19 August 1675 he 'Took Hewks vomit it made me incline to vomit after 1 hours taking. It made me strain after 2 houres but brought up nothing. With drinking broth and feather I vomited a little but my head and eyes much worse. Raised Telescope Pole to the Turret. Was well refresht after vomit.' It would seem that after a day of heroic vomiting he repaired to his observing turret to look at the heavens!

Unlike Cassini and Huygens, Hooke did not devote great expanses of his working life to viewing astronomical bodies with the new long refracting telescopes, and this probably derived in part from the multitudinous responsibilities which the Royal Society, Gresham College and his City of London architectural commitments placed upon him, not to mention his own roving curiosity. His most serious and sustained telescopic observations of Solar-System bodies in fact seem to have been performed between early 1664 and 1667, and were briefly resumed during the time of the comet of 1677. While within that time Hooke made no great and singular telescopic discoveries, his jovian and martian observations nonetheless added new weight to the Copernican theory, his instrumental innovations were quite simply beyond the manufacturing capabilities of the age, and his work on lunar craters and gravity opened up all kinds of new avenues of investigation. But most of all, his observations of the bright comets of 1664 and 1677, and the brilliant and inspired experimental conclusions which he drew from them, simply confirm Robert Hooke as one of the most original physical scientists of the Scientific Revolution, and perhaps the first to think of astronomy as an experimental science.

Notes and references

1 Many historians of astronomy have dealt at length with the pivotal significance of Copernicus: see Thomas S. Kuhn, *The Copernican Revolution. Planetary Astronomy in the Development of Western Thought* (Harvard University Press, 1966); Michael Hoskin (ed.), *The Cambridge Illustrated History of Astronomy* (Cambridge University Press, 1997); and John D. North, *The Fontana History of Astronomy and Cosmology* (Fontana, London, 1994).

2 Tycho Brahe, *Astronomiae Instauratae Mechanica* (Wandesburgi, 1598), trans-

lated by H. Raeder and E. and B. Strömgren as *Tycho Brahe's Description of his Instruments and Scientific Work* (Copenhagen, 1946); J. L. E. Dreyer, *Tycho Brahe. A Picture of Scientific Life and Work in the Sixteenth Century* (1890; reprinted, Dover, New York, 1963); Victor E. Thoren, *The Lord of Uraniborg. A Biography of Tycho Brahe* (Cambridge University Press, 1990).

3 Hoskin, *Cambridge Illustrated History* (ref. 1), pp. 117–9; Max Caspar, *Kepler* (second English edition, Dover, New York, 1993).

4 Galileo Galilei, *The Starry Messenger* (1610); 'Letter on Sunspots', in *Discoveries and Opinions of Galileo*, translated and introduced by Stillman Drake (Doubleday, Anchor, New York, 1957).

5 John Wilkins, *A Discourse Concerning A New World & Another Planet* (London, 1640); Allan Chapman, "A World in the Moon': John Wilkins and his Lunar Voyage of 1640', *Quarterly Journal of the Royal Astronomical Society*, **32** (1991), 121–32.

6 Robert Hooke, *Micrographia, or Some Physiological Descriptions of Minute Bodies Made by Magnifying Glasses with Observations and Inquiries Thereupon* (London, 1665), 'Preface' (unpaginated), sig. a̲ a̲ r̲.

7 Much scholarly attention has been devoted to the early history of the telescope. See Albert Van Helden, 'The invention of the telescope', *Transactions of the American Philosophical Society*, **67**(4) (Philadelphia, 1977), 1–64, and Henry C. King, *The History of the Telescope* (London, 1955), pp. 50–9, for early work of Hevelius, Huygens and Cassini. Mary G. Winkler and Albert Van Helden, 'Johannes Hevelius and the visual language of astronomy', in J. V. Field and Frank A. J. L. James (eds.), *Renaissance and Revolution. Humanists, Scholars, Craftsmen, and Natural Philosophers in Early Modern Europe* (Cambridge University Press, 1993), pp. 97–116. Albert Van Helden, 'The telescope in the seventeenth century', *Isis*, **65**, 226 (1974) discusses the optical quality of several surviving lenses (pp. 45–6) as well as the 'average' telescopic focal lengths from the 1640s to the 1670s (pp. 46–8).

8 It is difficult to overestimate the influence of the contemporary Sir Christopher Wren on the young Hooke, both of whom, as a young don and an undergraduate respectively, were part of John Wilkins' Wadham group at Oxford in the mid-1650s. In the 'Preface' to *Micrographia* (1665), unpaginated, 14r, he spells out his indebtedness to Wilkins and Wren, while their continuing lifelong friendship and collaboration is made clear in Henry W. Robinson and Walter Adams (eds.), *The Diary of Robert Hooke, M.A., M.D., F.R.S., 1672–80 (transcribed from the original ... in Guildhall Library)* (Taylor and Francis, London, 1935, reprinted 1968). Wren had been observing Saturn in particular since 1649, as he stated in his *De Corpore Saturni*: Albert Van Helden, 'Christopher Wren's De Corpore Saturni', *Notes and Records of the Royal Society*, **23** (1968), 221. Also J. A. Bennett, 'Christopher Wren: Astronomy, Architecture and the Mathematical Sciences', *Journal for the History of Astronomy*, **6** (1975), 154–60. According to Richard Waller, in *The Posthumous Works of Robert Hooke, M.D., F.R.S.* (London, 1705), Hooke 'began to shew himself to the World' in Oxford in 1655, p. iii, while he was encouraged to do pendulum researches by Seth Ward in 1656–57, pp. iv–v.

Hooke also spoke of telescopic observations in the 'Preface' to *Micrographia* (1665), unpaginated, sigs a̲ a̲ v̲, e̲-e̲ v.

9 In a subsequent attack on Cassini's claims, which Hooke may have written in the 1690s, Hooke asserted that Sir Paul Neile, Dr Jonathan Goddard and Sir Christopher Wren were improving and using telescopes in London before the same had happened in France (though in reality innovation was taking place in Holland, Italy, France and England more or less simultaneously during the 1650s): William Derham (ed.), *Philosophical Experiments and Observations of Dr Robert Hooke* (London, 1726), pp. 260, 390. Dr Jonathan Goddard and Sir Paul Neile were active in the development of English astronomical telescope-making from the mid-1650s. John Ward, *The Lives of the Professors of Gresham College* (London, 1740), in which Seth Ward spoke of Goddard's early telescopic work; and Colin A. Ronan and Sir Harold Hartley, 'Sir Paul Neile F.R.S. (1613–1686)', *Notes and Records of the Royal Society*, **15** (1960), 159–65. See W. S. C. Copeman, 'Dr Jonathan Goddard, F.R.S.', *Notes and Records of the Royal Society*, **15** (1960), 69–77. The young Hooke, of course, in Oxford and in London, would have known all these men. The particular telescopes used by Hooke were mentioned in his *Micrographia* (1665), *Cometa* (1678), *A Description of Helioscopes* (1676), *An Attempt to Prove the Motion of the Earth from Observations* (1674), and other sources. It is probable that the telescopes used by Hooke were owned by Wren, Boyle, Neile, Ward, Goddard, and other prominent and wealthy Fellows of the Royal Society, all of whom possessed substantial telescopes. See also Alan D. C. Simpson, 'Robert Hooke and practical optics: technical support at a scientific frontier', in Michael Hunter and Simon Schaffer (ed.), *Robert Hooke: New Studies* (Boydell Press, Woodbridge, 1989) pp. 33–61.

10 Robert Hooke (?), 'An Accompt of the Improvement of Optick Glasses', *Philosophical Transactions of the Royal Society*, **1**(1) (1665), 3. Quite a number of seventeenth-century object-glasses survive in British and European museum collections. The Royal Society owns several of them. One of the Royal Society's lenses has a clear diameter of about $8\frac{1}{2}$ inches and a focal length of 170 feet. The other is $9\frac{1}{2}$ inches in diameter and of 210 feet focus, and is signed and dated on the edge of the glass with a diamond, 'Constantine Huygens, 1686'. While both lenses have a distinct green tinge and quite a lot of striation and bubbles, the overall area of the glass possesses a remarkable transparency and evenness when small print is examined through it. See especially Allan A. Mills, 'Three lenses by Constantine Huygens in the Royal Society', *Annals of Science*, **46** (1989), 173–82.

11 Hooke, 'A Spot in one of the Belts of Jupiter', *Philosophical Transactions of the Royal Society*, **1**(1) (1665), 3.

12 Hooke, *Cometa, or Remarks about Comets* (London, 1678), p. 78.

13 Hooke, *Cometa* (ref. 12), pp. 78–9.

14 Hooke, *Cometa* (ref. 12), p. 78.

15 Hooke, 'Some Observations Lately made at London concerning the Planet Jupiter', *Philosophical Transactions of the Royal Society*, **1**(14) (2 July 1666),

245–6. I am indebted to Tony Morris of the Mexborough and Swinton Astronomical Society, Yorkshire, who is a skilled and experienced observational astronomer and practical optician, for calculating the above data for me. Mr Morris has calculated from a planetary orbital computer program that on 26 June 1666 Jupiter subtended an angle of 41.48 arcseconds. At a focal length of 60 feet it would have produced a prime-focus image of Jupiter 3.67 mm across, and with a 105.35–mm (4.15–inch) focal length eyepiece, would have produced a magnification of 173 times, resulting in an apparent image of Jupiter four times larger than the full Moon, or 2° of arc. Hooke's technique of comparing the apparent size of a planetary object as it appears through the telescope with the size of the Moon as seen with the naked eye is a quick and easy method of relating the proportionate sizes of planets. As seen from Earth, the Moon always subtends an angle of around 30 arcminutes ($^1/_2°$), so when Hooke said that Jupiter appeared in the telescope to be four times bigger than the Moon, he meant that its image seemed to subtend 2°. The technique is very easy to perform for anyone who is familiar with practical telescopic astronomy, provided that the Moon, at any phase, is visible in the sky. One simply looks at the telescopic image of Jupiter, or any other planet, until one's retina has recorded a clear impression of the planet's size. Then, by looking at the Moon, often by switching the eyes in an alternate planet–Moon sequence, one compares the planetary impression to the half-degree disk or crescent. I have used the technique many times. Following Robert Hooke's popularisation of the late William Gascoigne's eyepiece micrometer announced by Richard Townley, however, astronomers had a much more exact technique whereby they could measure the apparent angular diameters of planets, as seen through telescopes: R. Townley, 'A description of an instrument for dividing a foot into many thousand parts, and thereby measuring the diameter of the planets to a great exactness', *Philosophical Transactions of the Royal Society*, **2** (1667), 541–4.

16 Hooke, 'Some observations ... Jupiter' (ref. 15), 246.

17 Hooke, 'Some observations ... Jupiter' (ref. 15), 246. On this page Hooke records a variety of features on Jupiter's surface.

18 Hooke, *Cometa* (ref. 12), 79.

19 Hooke, 'Some observations ... Jupiter' (ref. 15), 246. For Hooke's drawing of Jupiter, see *Philosophical Transactions of the Royal Society*, **1**(14) (2 July 1666), frontispiece.

20 Hooke's references to his eyepieces are often vague or completely absent, as his attention clearly centred on the object-glass. In his response to Adrien Auzout (1665), however, he spoke of a 2–inch focal length double convex eyepiece with his 12–foot focus object-glass: 'Mr Hook's [*sic*] answer to Monsieur Auzout's Consideration ...', *Philosophical Transactions of the Royal Society*, **1**(1) (1665), 69. Such a lens would, of course, have produced an inverted image. Likewise, in his observations of Mars in 1666, he stipulated that the image 'was inverted by the Telescope, according to the appearances': Hooke, 'The Particulars Of those Observations of the Planet Mars intimated to have been made at London in the Months of February

and March A. 1665/66', *Philosophical Transactions of the Royal Society*, **1**(14) (2 July 1666), 241.

21 *Philosophical Transactions of the Royal Society*, **1**(14) (2 July 1666), frontispiece.

22 Huygens had realised the ring-like character of Saturn's *ansae* by early 1656, though the full discovery was not announced until three years later in his *Systema Saturni* (1659). See *Oeuvres Complètes de Christiaan Huygens*, **15** (Amsterdam, 1967), p. 299. Also Van Helden, 'Christopher Wren's De Corpore Saturni' (ref. 8) 217.

23 Hooke, 'A late Observation about Saturn made at the same' [time as his Jupiter observation, June 1666], *Philosophical Transactions of the Royal Society* **1**(14) (2 July 1666), 247. At the time of Hooke's observations on 29 June 1666, Saturn was almost 17° above the horizon – rather low in the sky, especially when viewed through the polluted air of central London – and would have subtended an angle of 18.35 arcseconds. Its rings would have been fully open, as Hooke described. Positional information computed by Morris (ref. 15).

24 In spite of the detailed attention which Sir Christopher Wren, William Ball, Huygens, Cassini, and others paid to Saturn, Hooke has left few records of his own observations of Saturn, apart from those of 1666. By 1675, however, telescopes had improved sufficiently to enable G. D. Cassini to observe, as Saturn emerged from the solar glare, the famous division in the ring system that bears his name. He communicated his results to the Royal Society some months later, in a letter to Henry Oldenburg, 26 August 1676: *Philosophical Transactions of the Royal Society*, **11**(128) (1676), 689–90. The brothers William and Dr Peter Ball (or Balle) F.R.S., of Mamhead, near Exeter, Devon, in October 1665, for instance, were reporting their observations made 'with a very good Telescope near 38 feet long, and a double Eye-glass': *Philosophical Transactions of the Royal Society*, **1**(9) (1666), 152–3. The Ball brothers were suggesting, on the strength of their observations (incorrectly, as we now know), that Saturn had a pair of asymmetric rings, both of which embraced the planet, but which extended into space away from the body of Saturn along a 180-degree line, and looked rather like the two *ansae* which Galileo and others had believed might be attached to Saturn. The 'double Eye glass' described by Ball was most probably an early Huygenian eyepiece, consisting of a pair of separated plano-convex lenses close to the observer's eye, and which reduced chromatic aberration. Huygens had devised this double eyepiece around 1660, and it soon came to be widely used amongst astronomers. William Ball had certainly been in the company of the visiting Huygens on 3 May 1661, as part of a meeting recorded in John Evelyn's Diary. The Ball brothers tried to persuade Hooke to visit them in Devon, to assist them with their telescopic observations, but he lacked the time.

25 Hooke, 'Some New observations about the Planet Mars, communicated since the Printing of the former sheets', *Philosophical Transactions of the Royal Society*, **1**(12) (2 April 1666), 198.

26 Hooke, 'Some New Observations …' (ref. 25). In March 1666, Mars was approaching a very favourable opposition, as its orbit brought it relatively

close to Earth. To a terrestrial observer, Mars would have subtended an apparent angular diameter of about 14.43 arcseconds; Morris's calculations (ref. 15).

27 Hooke specifies Richard Reeves as the optician who made the best lenses for Goddard, Neile and Wren in the 1650s: Derham, *Philosophical Experiments ... of Robert Hooke* (ref. 9), p. 390. Hooke, 'The Particulars of those Observations of the Planet Mars, formerly intimated to have been made at London in the Months of February and March A. 1665/66', *Philosophical Transactions of the Royal Society*, **1**(14) (2 July 1666), 239–42. For the optical and operational characteristics of the 36–foot glass, see 'Mr Hook's answer ...' (ref. 20), 69, and *Micrographia* (1665), p. 242, in which he mentions observing the Orion Nebula with this instrument at its full aperture of 3½ inches. This seems to have been one of several 36-foot lenses made by Reeves: Simpson, 'Robert Hooke and practical optics ...' (ref. 9), p. 38. By the 1670s, however, Christopher Cocks (or Coxe) had taken over the lead as pre-eminent optician.

28 Hooke, 'The Particulars ...' (ref. 27), 240. If Mars was exhibiting an angular diameter of 14.43 arcseconds, and appearing almost as large as the Moon appears to the naked eye, then it is probable that Hooke was working at a magnification of around 124; Morris (ref. 15), for calculation of martian diameter in early March 1666, and telescope magnification. About midnight on the night of 12 September 2003, when Mars was at one of its closest ever oppositions to the Earth, I compared its apparent image as seen through a good refracting telescope with that of the rising Moon, using the same technique described in ref. 15. On that night, Mars subtended an angular diameter of 24 arcseconds, but when I compared the martian image on my retina to that of the Moon (30 arcminutes) as seen in the sky, I estimated that the image of Mars seemed just over two-thirds the size of the Moon.

29 Hooke, 'The Particulars ...' (ref. 27), p. 241–2. Drawings of Mars in *Philosophical Transactions of the Royal Society*, **1**(14) (2 July 1666), frontispiece. Francesco Fontana, *New Discoveries made with his own Telescopes and Microscopes* (Naples, 1646), translated from the Latin by Sally Beaumont and Peter Fay (private publication by Beaumont and Fay, Levens, Cumbria and Sonning Common, Reading, 2001).

30 Hooke, 'The Particulars ...' (ref. 27), 240.

31 Hooke, 'The Particulars ...' (ref. 27), 241.

32 'Observations made in Italy, confirming the former, and withal fixing the Period of the Revolution of Mars', *Philosophical Transactions of the Royal Society*, **1**(14) (2 July 1666), 242–5. In spite of the *Philosophical Transactions* editor's wish to portray Cassini's observations as 'confirming' Hooke's, they were indeed much more decisive in the discoveries which they conveyed.

33 Hooke, *Micrographia* (ref. 8), 243.

34 Hooke, *Micrographia* (ref. 8), 246.

35 Hooke described 'my way of flying by vanes [wings] tryd at Wadham' twenty years earlier with Dr Wilkins: *Diary ... 1672–1680* (ref. 8), p. 146, 11

February 1675. Early flight experiments were always performed within the context of overcoming gravity: see Allan Chapman, '"A World in the Moon": John Wilkins and his Lunar Voyage of 1640', *Quarterly Journal of the Royal Astronomical Society*, **32** (1991), 121–32.

36 Donald W. Yeomans, *Comets: A Chronological History of Observation, Science, Myth, and Folklore* (John Wiley, New York, Chichester, 1991), pp. 78–94.

37 Hooke, *Posthumous Works* (ref. 8), pp. 150–90.

38 Hooke, *Cometa* (ref. 12), p. 1. Although Hooke was probably the first scientist to attempt to model the assumed chemistry and physics of planetary body surfaces, his initial inspiration for using models to solve planetary problems may have derived from the wax and cardboard models which Wren had devised in the late 1650s as a way of trying to make sense of Saturn's ring, as mentioned in Van Helden, 'Christopher Wren's De Corpore Saturni' (ref. 8).

39 Hooke, *Cometa* (ref. 12), pp. 4–5.

40 Hooke, *Cometa* (ref. 12), pp. 10–12, 47.

41 Hooke, *Lampas, or, Description of Some Mechanical Improvements of Lamps and Waterpoises. Together with some other Physical and Mechanical Discoveries* (London, 1677), p. 7. Hooke, *Cometa* (ref. 12), p. 47.

42 Hooke, *Cometa* (ref. 12), p. 51.

43 Hooke, *Micrographia* (ref. 8), p. 58, 225ff.

44 Hooke, *Micrographia* (ref. 8), p. 54. Hooke, *Posthumous Works* (ref. 8), p. 117.

45 Hooke, *Cometa* (ref. 12), p. 46.

46 Hooke, *Cometa* (ref. 12), p. 14.

47 Hooke, *Cometa* (ref. 12), p. 44. Hooke had argued from the motions of the comet of 1664 that the curve of the comet's orbit was the product of two gravitationally-related forces, as he informed the Royal Society on 23 May 1666. Hooke, *Posthumous Works* (ref. 8), p. xii.

48 Hooke, *Cometa* (ref. 12), p. 44.

49 Hooke, *Cometa* (ref. 12), p. 46.

50 Christoph Scheiner, *Rosa Ursina* (Bracciani, 1626–30).

51 Robert Hooke, *A Description of Helioscopes, And some Other Instruments* (London, 1676) pp. 4–5.

52 Hooke, *Helioscopes* (ref. 51), p. 6.

53 E. Walter Maunder, 'A Prolonged Sunspot Minimum', *Knowledge*, **17** (1 August 1894), 173–6; 'The Prolonged Sunspot Minimum, 1645–1715', *Journal of the British Astronomical Association*, **32**(4) (January 1922), 140–5.

54 Hooke, *Helioscopes* (ref. 51), p. 23; also *Diary ... 1672–1680* (ref. 8), 1 January 1674/75, p. 139.

55 Hooke, *Cometa* (ref. 12), p. 65–77. It must never be forgotten, however, that because of the very pluralistic character of Hooke's scientific career, spanning simultaneously half a dozen sciences, as well as a lucrative architectural practice, his astronomical observations were performed spasmodically, and were usually stimulated by the occurrence of an interesting astronomical event such as the close opposition of Mars in 1666, the fully open rings of Saturn, also in 1666, and the brilliant comets of 1664 and 1677. Men such as Huygens, Cassini and Hevelius, however, devoted the

greater part of their professional lives to telescopic astronomy, thereby accumulating a night-by-night knowledge of astronomical bodies over a period of forty years or more.

56 Hooke, *Diary ... 1672–80* (ref. 8), 28 October 1677. Also John Flamsteed to Sir Jonas Moore, 6 November 1677, in *The Correspondence of Sir John Flamsteed, the First Astronomer Royal*, 1, 1666–1682, compiled and edited by Eric G. Forbes and (for Maria Forbes) by Lesley Murdin and Frances Willmoth (Institute of Physics, Bristol and Philadelphia, 1995), Letter 306, pp. 575–6.
57 All the above dated entries appear in *Diary ... 1672–80* (ref. 8).

Chapter 7

The impact of Hooke's *Micrographia* and its influence on microscopy

Gerard L'E. Turner

Robert Hooke won the title of the 'father of microscopy' by publishing, in 1665, the first book devoted to the instrument, which had been invented in the first decade of the seventeenth century. But he was not a serious microscopist in the sense that the Dutchman, Antoni van Leeuwenhoek, or the Italian, Marcello Malpighi, deserve the title. Hooke was a polymath – a true natural philosopher, attracted by the novelty and possibilities of an unfamiliar instrument, and ready to demonstrate and then to write about what it could achieve. His success was instant, and also far-reaching, for it established the popularity of the microscope with generations of observers, and this in turn supported the serious, scientific use of the instrument and ensured that it was manufactured in quantity and steadily improved in design.

The invention of the microscope closely followed that of the tele-scope, credited to spectacle-makers in Middelburg in the Netherlands around 1608. It is curious that three centuries elapsed between the first recorded use of spectacles, which make use of the magnifying effect of ground and polished glass, in about 1286, and the time of the late Renaissance, when the use of lenses for the investigation of the very distant and the very small was achieved. It is probable that chance led to the placing in line of two lenses – a positive for correcting long sight and a negative for correcting short sight – thus achieving the Dutch or Galilean form of telescope. Once the creation of lenses was stimulated by the success of the telescope, the idea arose of reducing the size of a lens to a diameter as small as 3 mm, with the resultant increase in magnification to a possible 100 times. To extend the eye's capacity to see small objects, either a single lens or a combination of two or three lenses may be used. Since the telescope was the forerunner of the microscope, the idea of using combinations of lenses to form a compound microscope might be expected to arise. Nevertheless, in the seventeenth century there were serious drawbacks to the use of the compound instrument; so serious, that better results could be achieved with the single lens of the simple microscope.

The ability of glass lenses to enhance sight is diminished by the properties of light itself, by the quality and type of glass used, and by the method of making lenses. A lens to some extent breaks up the light into its component colours, with the result that the image has coloured edges, causing the defect known as chromatic aberration. It was not until the 1750s that John Dollond in London devised a telescope lens that was achromatic. The much smaller achromatic lenses for the microscope were more difficult to make, and were not produced commercially until around 1810, the result of work by the Amsterdam optical instrument maker, Harmanus van Deijl (1738–1809). Another defect – spherical aberration – produces a slight blurring of the image, resulting from the spherical curvature of the lens. This defect was corrected by the scientific design of optical systems in the 1830s.

Glass for optical purposes should have no colour, and should be of completely uniform composition throughout. It is difficult to avoid contamination, as some metallic compounds, in quite small quantities, will colour the glass. Optical glass of high quality needs a furnace much hotter than that required to make window or bottle glass, but such furnaces were not available until the early nineteenth century, and techniques had also to be evolved to ensure thorough mixing. The simple, single-lens microscope was, during the early period of the instrument's development, less affected by all these problems than was the compound microscope. Chromatic aberration was minimised because with a single lens a virtual image is seen by the eye, and the different colours are superimposed. Spherical aberration can also be rendered less significant in the simple microscope by reducing the aperture while using an intense light source. Finally, finding suitable pieces of glass for the tiny lenses, only 2 or 3 mm in diameter, of a simple microscope was less of a problem than creating the large compound instrument lenses. For these reasons, the resolving power achievable by the simple over the compound microscope in Hooke's time was something in the order of five to one. Despite this superiority of performance, the difficulty of using the single lens microscope was such that the future lay with the compound instrument.

Hooke was aware of the difference in performance between the two types of microscope. His own was a large compound microscope, of the type illustrated in the frontispiece of *Micrographia* (Figure 7.1). The

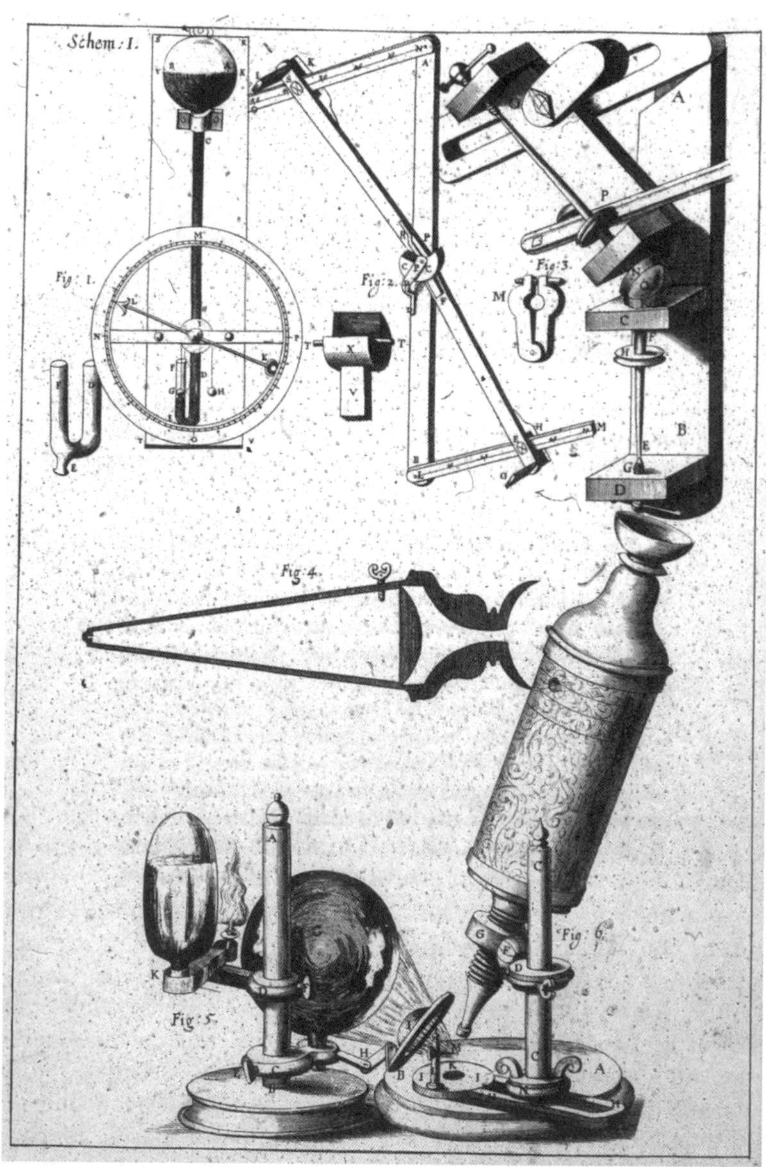

Fig. 7.1. Robert Hooke's microscope with illumination globe. The barometer and horizontal tube are irrelevant. (*Micrographia*, 1665.)

simple, single-lens microscope was the only type employed by Van Leeuwenhoek, who began his long series of letters to the Royal Society in 1673. In a lecture in 1679, Hooke commented:

> I have found the use of them [simple microscopes] offensive to my eye, and to have much strained and weakened the sight, which was the reason why I omitted to make use of them though in truth they do make the object more clear and distinct, and magnify as much as the double Microscope; nay, to those whose eyes can well endure it, it is possible with a single [simple] Microscope to make discoveries much better than with a double one, because the colours which do much disturb the vision in double Microscopes is clearly avoided and prevented in the single.

Hooke's comment that he suffered eye strain from using a single microscope sounds like an excuse, as to use it effectively would have taken much time and effort, both of which were in short supply for the busy Curator of Experiments to the Royal Society. Whatever the reason, he chose to use the large, side-pillar compound instrument (illustrated in *Micrographia*) equipped with an oil lamp and a condensing lens – a commercial product which at the time could be bought from the London optician, Richard Reeves, in Longacre. Hooke worked on improvements to the instrument, and designed his own compound microscope that was made by Christopher Cock and eventually bought from Cock by the Royal Society.

In effect, two microscopical traditions developed. The compound microscope, close relative of the telescope, came into its own for observing solid objects by reflected light at relatively low magnifications. All of Hooke's observations described in *Micrographia* were made by light reflected from the object. The simple microscope, focusing close to the object, was best suited for looking at transparent specimens with transmitted light. Its use required a high level of skill and concentration in the observer that was repaid by the ability to make significant scientific observations. It was the compound microscope, however, that was generally used throughout the eighteenth century for education and recreation.

The side-pillar design of the compound microscope persisted – no doubt because of the popularity of *Micrographia* – and from 1690 to 1710 the leading London optical instrument makers, John Yarwell and John Marshall, continued to make them to the Hooke pattern (Figure 7.2). They also engaged in an advertising war, claiming much for the quality of their lenses and for the capacity of their microscopes to show the circulation of the blood in the capillaries of a fish's tail. In the 1620s, William Harvey (1578–1657) had discovered the circulation of the blood by direct observation, and in 1660 the discovery was

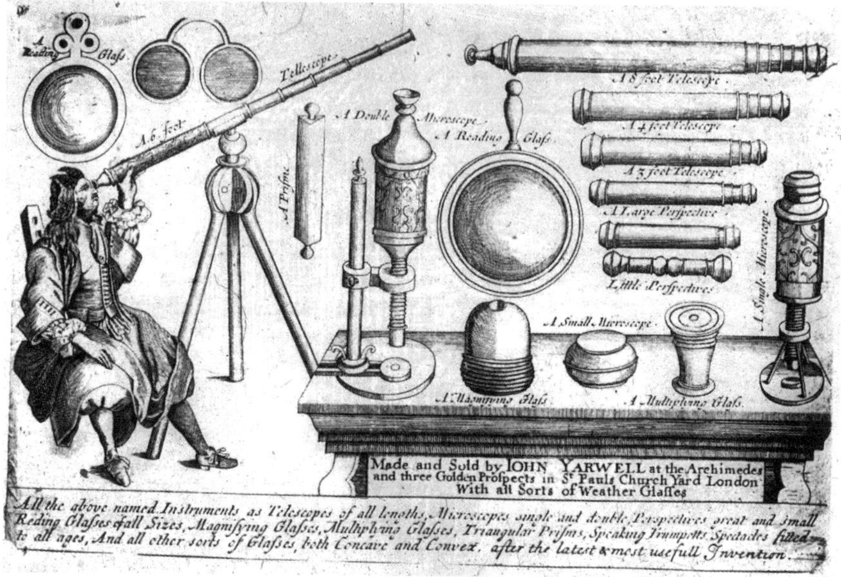

Fig. 7.2. The trade card of the optician John Yarwell (c.1648–1712), printed in 1683. There is no consistent scale to the objects. The microscope on the left of the table is based on Hooke's type. (Robert S. Whipple, 'John Yarwell, or the Story of a Trade Card', in *Annals of Science*, **7** (1951), 62–9, pl. viii.)

confirmed by Marcello Malpighi with the aid of a microscope. Malpighi's early and fundamental work was to study the structure of the lung, and to discover the connections between the arteries and the veins. His main treatise on the blood, *De Polypo Cordis*, appeared in 1666. At much the same time, Antoni van Leeuwenhoek, working in Delft in The Netherlands, was using the small, simple microscopes which he made himself to observe his 'little animals', including bacteria, protozoa and rotifers, the subjects of his letters to the Royal Society in London. He was also, inevitably, interested in the study of the blood, and in the 1670s he devised an aquatic microscope – which he called an 'aalkijker', or eel-viewer – to make it easier to observe the circulation of the blood *in vivo*. This was the background to the optical instrument makers' rivalry. Marshall scored a significant victory when his microscope and the possibility of viewing the circulation of the blood with it were described and illustrated in the first English technical encyclopaedia: John Harris's *Lexicon Technicum*, published in London in 1704. This established the compound microscope as one of the foremost instruments for experimental philosophy.

However, the compound microscope as used in the early eighteenth century was unnecessarily large, following the pattern set by Hooke, and it had a wide field lens, three inches in diameter, which spoilt the image by imparting too much colour. It was designed for viewing solid objects, and when, for example, the tail of a fish was to be viewed, Marshall was obliged to make drastic modifications. The barrel had to be turned off axis, and the box foot of the instrument had to be weighted with lead to counterbalance the body (Figure 7.3). The instrument had to be placed at the edge of a table, so that a candle could be placed at a lower level to enable light to pass through a lens to the fish tail. It was only in the 1720s that a sub-stage mirror – the obvious solution for viewing transparent objects – was provided. The 'double reflecting microscope', as the instrument came to be called, was provided with the sub-stage mirror and a bull's-eye lens, so that it was equally effective for transparent and solid objects, and this model was in use throughout the century for experimental philosophy. The simple microscope developed into the so-called 'screw-barrel' instrument, devised by the Dutchman, Nicolaas Hartsoeker, and introduced into England by James Wilson in 1702. The name derives from the wide thread used to focus the specimen, and it, too, was featured in *Lexicon Technicum*. This design had high-powered lenses and could be used for serious observations, while a low-powered version of the simple instrument was popular for examining plants and pond life.

It is not surprising that Hooke interested himself in optical instruments, for these represented the new technologies of his age; the telescope and microscope made accessible new worlds to be explored – irresistible attractions to a natural philosopher. The devising of special skills and procedures in the use of the instruments appealed to a man essentially practical, and *Micrographia* was the final outcome of a lengthy process of experiment and demonstration. The group of natural philosophers loosely based around Wadham College, Oxford, in the 1650s included Christopher Wren, who engaged in detailed microscopic work as well as observations with the telescope in the Wadham observatory. Wren later demonstrated to Charles II his drawings of microscopic observations, and was asked to make a book of them, although he declined the task. Hooke joined the Oxford group as assistant to the Hon. Robert Boyle (1627–1691), and was soon also involved in optical research. In 1661 Wren asked Hooke to take over the task of completing and preparing for publication his (Wren's) 'micrographic observations'. In March 1663 the Council of the Royal Society formally requested Hooke, as its Curator of Experiments, to 'prosecute his microscopical observations', and in the following year Hooke presented about forty observations – more than one a week. He was therefore ready to fulfil the Council's next requirement: to print his microscopical discourses. The involvement of the Royal Society in

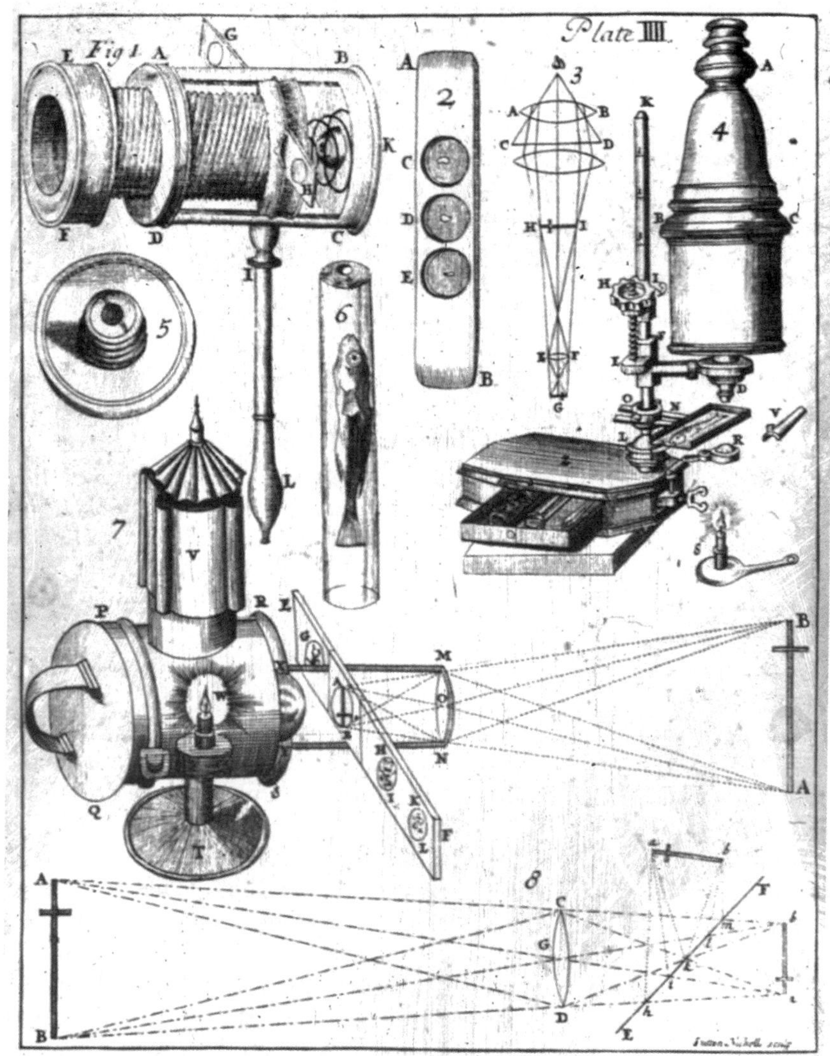

Fig. 7.3. The syllabus (1714) devised by William Whiston (1667{5?}–1752) for a course of lectures on experimental philosophy included this plate in the section on 'Opticks', showing (*top right*) a Marshall microscope and (*top left*) a Wilson screwbarrel. This student 'hand-out' occurs in several places over several years. (William Whiston, *A Course of Mechanical, Optical, Hydrostatical, and Pneumatical Experiments to be performed by Francis Hawksbee; and the Explanatory Lectures read by William Whiston, M.A.* (London, 1714) ... (bound with) *The Figures and Descriptions of the principal Instruments used in this Course of Experiments.*)

the publication of *Micrographia* was total, and extended to prolonged and careful editing before it appeared. The Society was also careful not to allow itself to be held responsible for the theories and hypotheses presented by Hooke in his text, which were to be presented 'not as certainties, but as conjectures'. Despite this institutional caution, Hooke's volume satisfied, to a remarkable degree, the aims of the Royal Society. The book showed the Society as being closely involved in practical inquiry using new technology, while the publication of this research provided excellent publicity.

Dedicated to Charles II, approved by the Royal Society, and a best-seller from its first appearance in January 1665, what qualities ensured the lasting appeal of *Micrographia*? Its first charm is its variety, and the almost haphazard selection of the objects studied. There are sixty Observations accompanied by thirty-eight plates ('schema'), the best known subjects being the insects, of which twenty are described, ranging from the famous flea and louse to flies, gnats, moths, ants and silverfish (Figures 7.4, 7.5 and 7.6). There are some related creatures, the teeth of a snail, the scales of a sole and other fish, and, by special request of Fellows of the Royal Society, 'the little fishes swimming in vinegar' – nematodes, which were objects of fascination to natural philosophers.

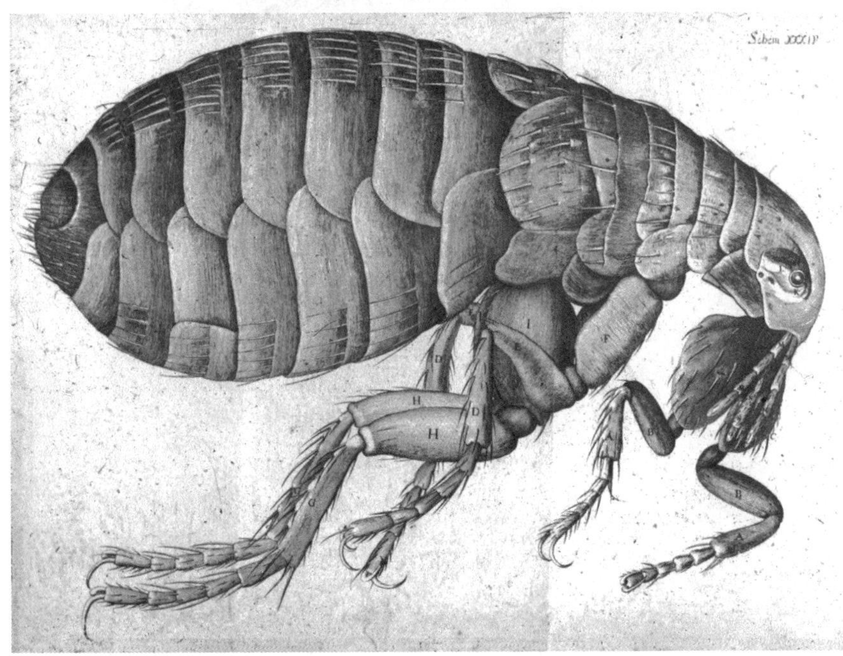

Fig. 7.4. Robert Hooke, *Micrographia* (1665), schem. XXXIV, 'Of a Flea'.

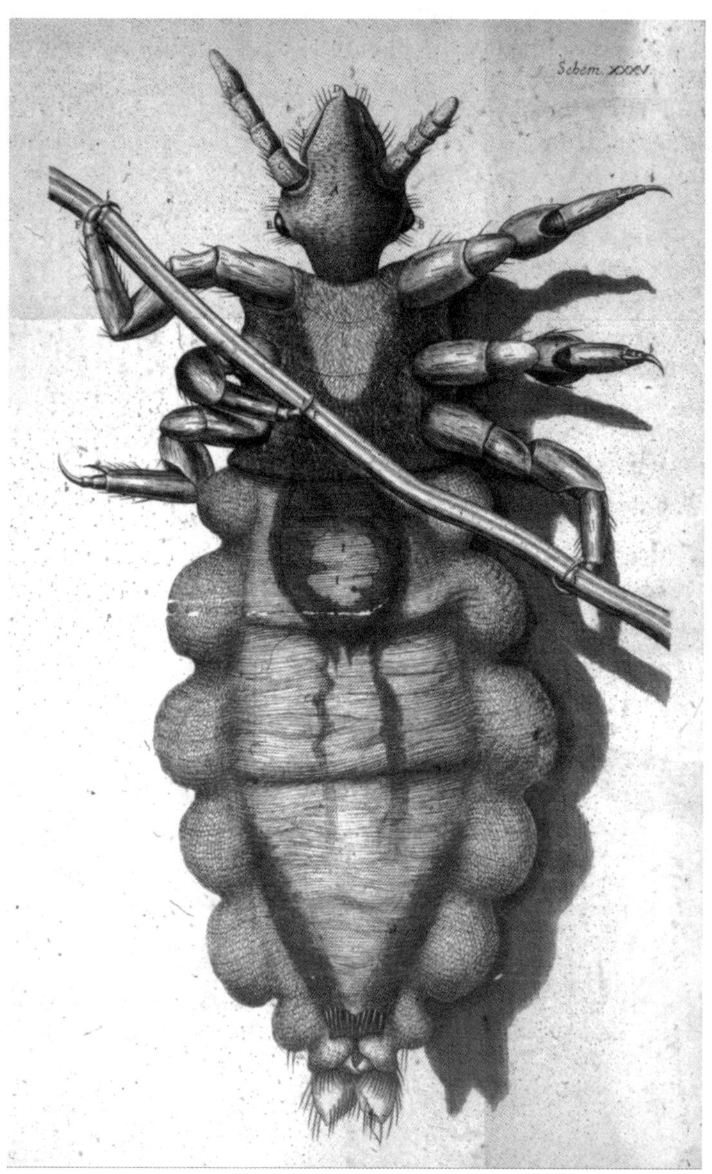

Fig. 7.5. Robert Hooke, *Micrographia* (1665), schem. XXXV, 'Of a Louse'.

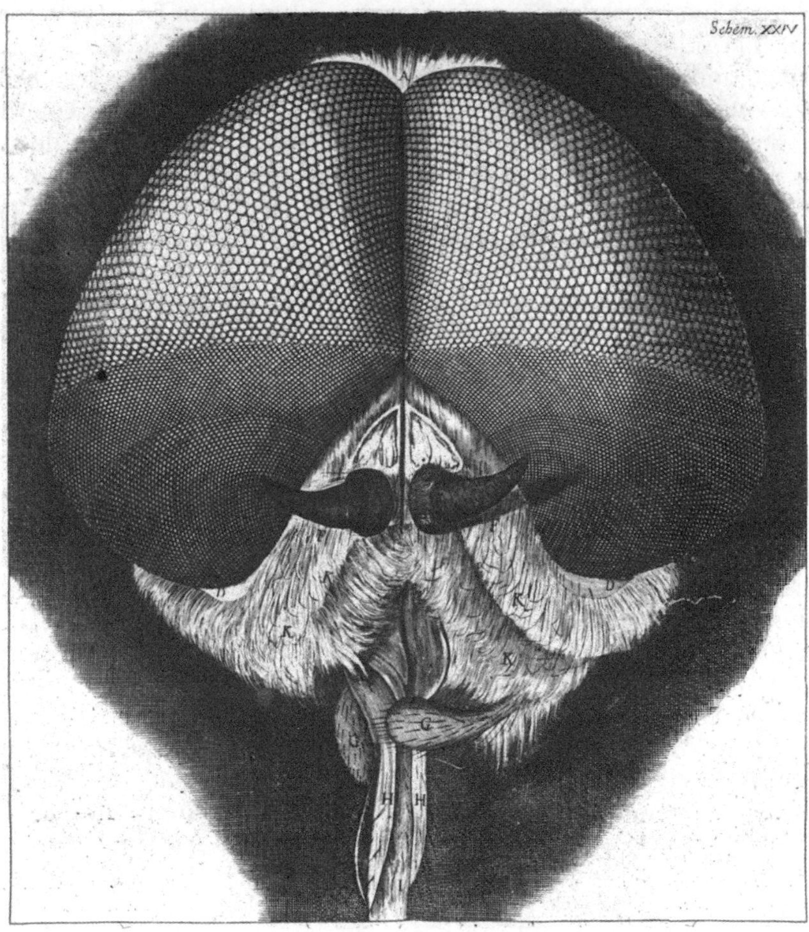

Fig. 7.6. Robert Hooke, *Micrographia* (1665), schem. XXIV, 'Of the Eyes and Head of a Drone-Fly'.

Also of great interest were plants, including flower seeds, moss, mould, and particularly the structure of wood and cork, accounting for fifteen Observations. Yet it is interesting that these two categories of object occur in the latter half of the book. The first fifteen objects are chosen apparently at random, as if Hooke looked around a room and picked up everyday objects that were to hand. Observation I is the point of a needle, followed by the edge of a razor (Figure 7.7) and examples of different types of cloth. Glass objects are examined, as are snow flakes and human urine. Hooke abandons the microscope completely for the last three Observations, which deal with refraction and other experiments on the nature of light, the fixed stars, and the Moon – the latter two involving the use of the telescope. This serves to emphasise the difference in approach of the experimental philosopher from that of the microscopical scientist. Hooke was not pursuing a clear line of study, but using the new technology simply to produce marvellous things to observe in the whole of Creation. It is this sense of the marvellous that is another aspect of the book's appeal: it conveys enthusiasm even to the modern reader, who may find its dense and wordy style rather difficult.

Hooke's 'Preface' to *Micrographia* is strictly Baconian. The Lord Chancellor, Francis Bacon (1561–1626), contributed so much to the development of scientific method that he may be said to be the herald of modern experimental science. In his great work *Novum Organum* (1620) he wrote: 'Neither the naked hand, nor the understanding left to itself, can do much; the work is accomplished by instruments and helps; of which the need is not less for the understanding than for the hand.' The Royal Society, with its motto *Nullius in Verba*, was the embodiment of Baconian thought. Hooke, in the same vein, contrasts the achievements of experimental philosophy, which traces 'the footsteps of Nature' with 'the philosophy of discourse and reason', which, he says, 'chiefly aims at the subtilty of its Deductions and Conclusions, without much regard to the first groundwork, which ought to be well laid on the Sense and Memory.' He sums up: 'The truth is, the Science of Nature has been already too long made only a work of the Brain and the Fancy: It is now high time that it should return to the plainness and soundness of Observations on material and obvious things.' This principle, he points out, has been greatly advanced by the invention of optical glasses: 'By the means of Telescopes, there is nothing so far distant but may be represented to our view; and by the help of Microscopes, there is nothing so small, as to escape our inquiry; hence there is a new visible World discovered to the understanding.' Just how amazing and exciting this was to the first users of optical instruments is difficult for us to appreciate today, but *Micrographia* gives us at least some concept of this experience.

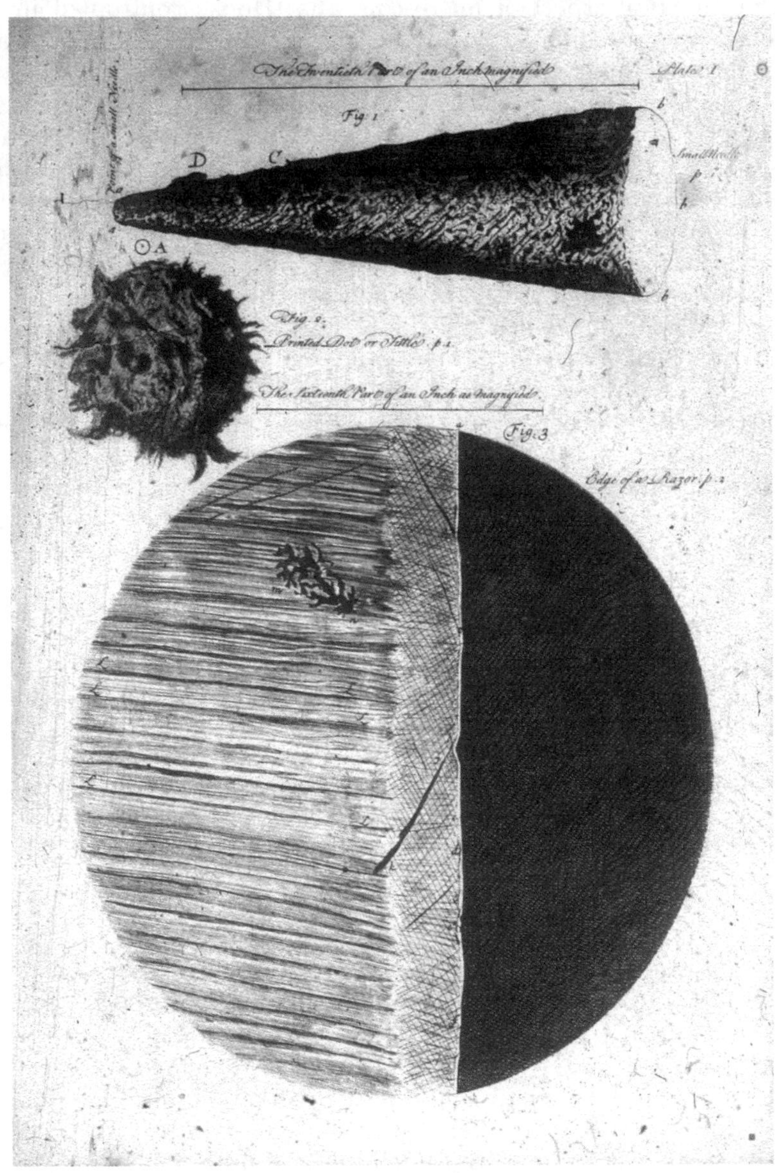

Fig. 7.7. This plate represents Hooke's schem. II, and is taken from
Henry Baker's *Micrographia Restaurata* (1745), where each object is
named adjacent to it. The engraving of the objects is identical to
Hooke's *Micrographia* (1665). 'Of the Point of a sharp small Needle';
'Printed Dot or Tittle' (full stop); 'Edge of a Razor'.

One practical aspect of microscopy that Hooke confronted in his 'Preface' was the difficulty of conveying to another person an image seen through the microscope. Microscopists found verbal descriptions inadequate in communicating to others what was observed, and so some form of illustration had to be attempted. Before the invention of photography, only two possibilities existed. One was for the microscopist to look down his instrument, and then turn away to draw what he remembered having seen. The other method was to place a drawing pad alongside the stage of the microscope, and to view the image with one eye and the pad with the other, so effecting a conjunction of images (a technique which was still being taught in the mid-twentieth century). Hooke describes the second method in *Micrographia*. He made his own drawings meticulously, and passed them to an engraver. Leewenhoek, however, was unskilled at drawing, and had to employ a draughtsman to illustrate his letters to the Royal Society.

Hooke pointed out some of the difficulties that he faced in discovering the true appearance of what he observed and in then producing a representation of it:

> Of these kind of Objects there is much more difficulty to discover the true shape, then of those visible to the naked eye, the same Object seeming quite differing, in one position to the Light, from what it really is, and may be discovered in another. And therefore I never began to make any draught before by many examinations in several lights, and in several positions to those lights, I had discover'd the true form. For it is exceeding difficult in some Objects, to distinguish between a prominency and a depression, between a shadow and a black stain, or a reflection and a whiteness in the colour. Besides, the transparency of most Objects renders them much more difficult then if they were opacous.

All early microscopists recognised the vital importance of recording and illustrating what was observed. The success achieved by *Micrographia* would have been impossible without the superb engravings that turned familiar insects into marvellous creatures and a mouldy surface into a flower garden. It was the choice of everyday specimens, and the engravings of them, that ensured the book's immortality. Eighty years after the publication of *Micrographia* , thirty-three of its plates were reprinted in a work called *Micrographia Restaurata*, the text of which was the work of Henry Baker, though he did not put his name to it. Baker was a typical eighteenth-century polymath, who made his living as a successful teacher of the deaf, and also participated to the full in the literary and scientific life of London. The continuing popularity of the microscope made it an obvious choice for Baker's attention, and he made a typically successful contribution to its development. In 1742 he published *The Microscope Made Easy* – the ideal layman's book, describing the best instrument to choose, and what results can be obtained. In dealing with which specimens to choose, Baker drew heavily on the work of his predecessors, notably Hooke. The purpose of microscopic study, as described by Baker and by Hooke, was to marvel at the wonders of God's Creation, and not to pursue any systematic study. Baker, however, carried out some serious observations of crystal growth – for which he was a elected a Fellow of the Royal Society in 1741 – and also designed an improved compound microscope made entirely from brass and therefore much more stable than the wood and pasteboard models that preceded it.

Baker's first book was most successful, running through four editions, and being translated into both Dutch and French. It is interesting to note his reason for involving himself, three years later, with the republication of the surviving plates from *Micrographia*, in the form that was chosen. Editions of the original were scarce and therefore expensive, and a cheap, briefly annotated reprint of the plates alone would be welcome. He also considered that Hooke's text was verbose, and that some of the opinions and hypotheses were out of date. If he felt superior to Hooke, his own pre-eminence as the author of a bestseller on the microscope was quickly challenged when the successful instrument maker George Adams published his *Micrographia Illustrata* in January 1746. Baker was furious, and attempted to have Adams' book suppressed as plagiarism. It is true that Adams definitely had engravings from both Hooke and Baker redrawn (Figures 7.8, 7.9 and 7.10), and that some of his commentary is similar to Baker's; but neither book contained original research, and both continued to sell extremely well, showing just how large a popular market existed in the mid-eighteenth century.

In 1753 Baker published his last book, *Employment for the Microscope*, which dealt with choosing and preparing specimens. But then Adams had the last word, for George Adams' son (also George) published, in 1787, his *Essays on the Microscope*, which included descriptions of 379 animalcula. Here again, the majority of the plates derive from Hooke, via Baker, and this became the standard work on the microscope into the nineteenth century. Nor was Hooke's influence confined to England. Baker's and Adams' books were translated on the Continent, and there were local authors too. A notable German example was Martin Ledermüller, who in 1763 published, in Nuremberg, *Mikroskopische Gemüths- und Augen- Ergötzung*, with engravings clearly modelled on, and even copied from, Hooke's illustrations (Figure 7.11). Into the nineteenth century, Hooke's plates continued to be used (Figure 7.12). Rees's *Cyclopaedia* – published in parts between 1802 and 1820 – names Adams

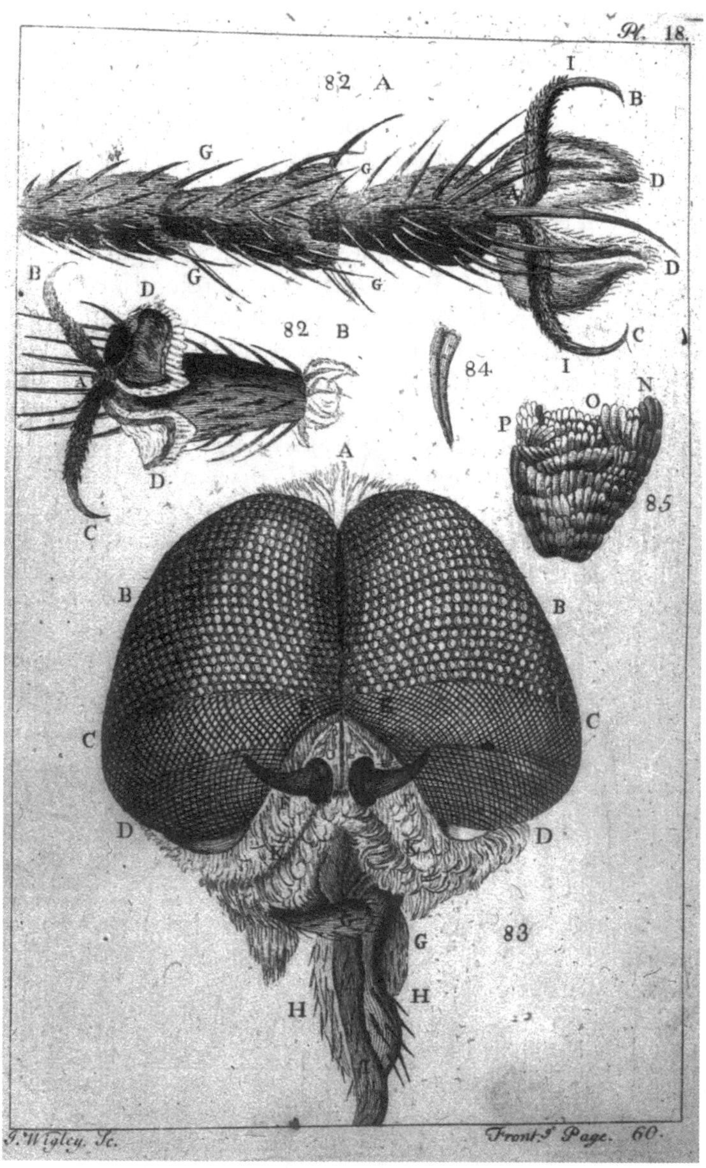

Fig. 7.8. George Adams, *Micrographia Illustrata* (1746), pl. 18, foot and head of a fly engraved on copper exactly as seen in Hooke's *Micrographia* (1665), and so reversed when printed.

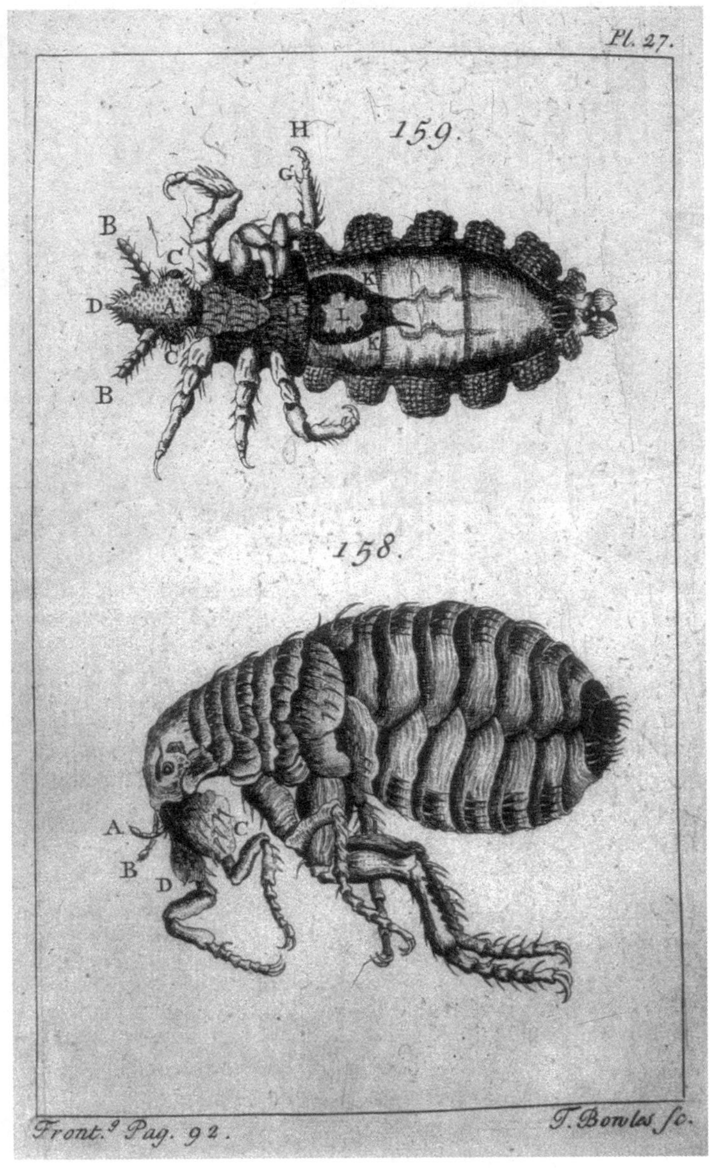

Fig. 7.9. George Adams, *Micrographia Illustrata* (1746), pl. 27, louse and flea copied from Hooke's *Micrographia* (1665), printed in reverse.

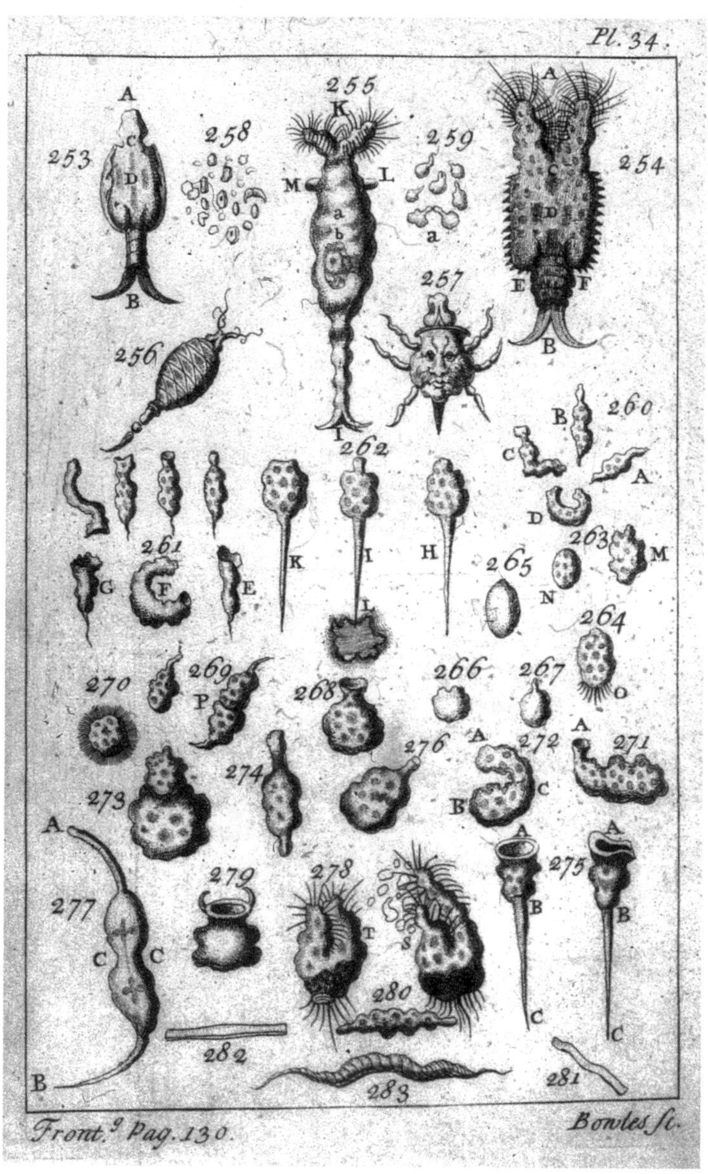

Fig. 7.10. George Adams, *Micrographia Illustrata* (1746), pl. 34, infusoria copied from Joblot's *Descriptions* (1718). Note the mask like a human face, derived from Joblot.

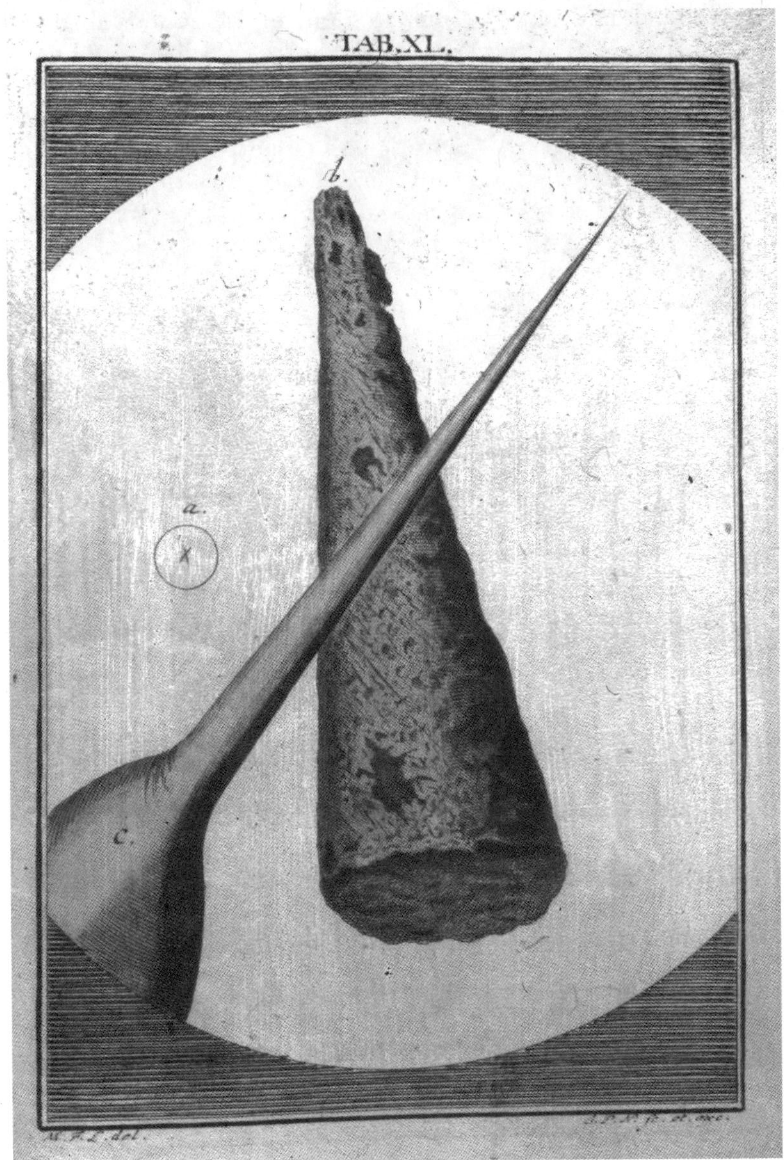

Fig. 7.11. Martin Ledermüller, *Mikroskopische Gemüths- und Augen-Ergötzung* (1763), Tab. XL, sting of a bee and point of a needle, copied from *Micrographia*.

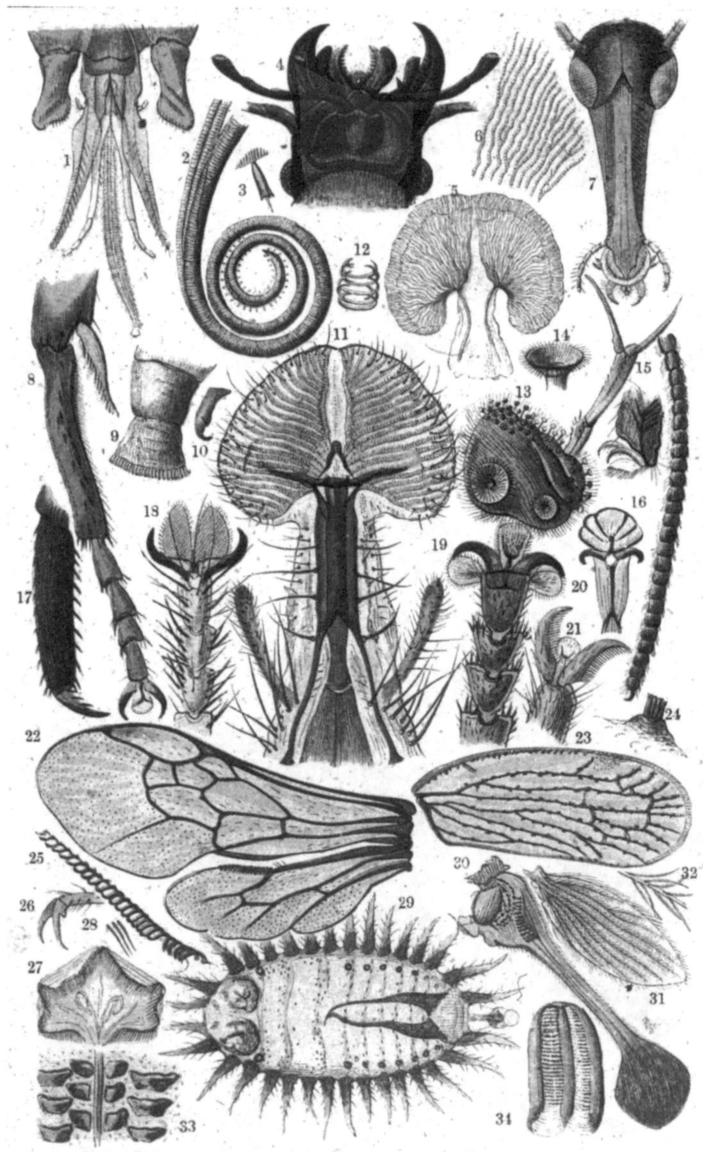

Fig. 7.12. J. G. Wood, *Common Objects of the Microscope*, pl. vii. From the first edition in 1861 until 1949, the same plates persisted.

and Baker as sources; and The Juvenile and School Library, of 157 Bond
Street, London, copied Hooke's plates in its anonymous *The Wonders of
the Microscope*, which first appeared in 1811.

Early in the nineteenth century came two developments that revolu-
tionised both the microscope itself and the interpretation of
observations made with it. Between 1830 and 1860, the microscope
became almost as good a scientific instrument as was possible, thanks to
the design of optical systems of J. J. Lister (1786–1869). In 1839, the
first permanent photomicrograph was successfully made by Fox
Talbot; and the following year, 1840, Alfred Donné, a French doctor of
medicine, showed to the French Academy the first daguerreotype
photomicrograph (Figure 7.13). Even so, the processes required much
light and long exposures, and suitable emulsions only became available
during the 1850s, allowing the earliest photomicrographs to be
published in a scientific journal, *Transactions of the Microscopical Society
of London*, in 1853. The first book with genuine photographs of microscopical images was published by William Olley in 1861, under the title
The Wonders of the Microscope Photographically Revealed. This still
contained the flea, the louse, and other old friends, but change was
under way. With photographic recording, the reproduction of the old
images became a thing of the past.

Robert Hooke was not a microscopist, even in the sense of his own
time. If he can be categorised at all, he was a physicist, but to use such a
description is anachronistic. He was a man of his time: clever, practical,
ambitious, endlessly curious, and endlessly ingenious. He took up the

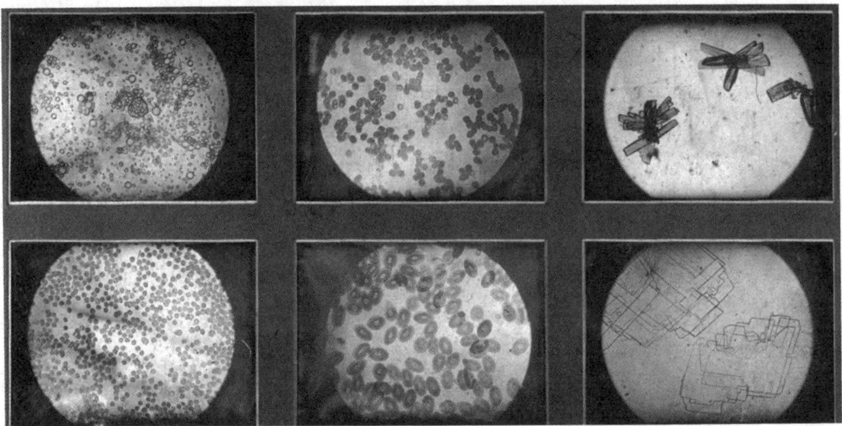

Fig. 7.13. In February 1840 A. Donné demonstrated to the French Academy
the first daguerrotype photomicrograph, and in 1844 six daguerreotype plates
were made by J. B. L. Foucault. This set was presented by A. Nachet to the
Royal Microscopical Society in 1905. The subjects are 'Blood, Milk, Corpuscle,
Crystals, etc.'

microscope as a subject of experimental philosophy, the popular appeal of which, to Fellows of the Royal Society and to the public at large, he fully recognised. Being meticulous, he ensured that his drawings and the engraver's finished work were of the highest standard. There do not exist better or more telling copper-plate engravings of microscopical subjects. Indeed, the great debt owed to the *Micrographia* is by virtue of its illustrations, which set a model for the eighteenth century. They could not be improved upon, and they are still admired today.

Bibliography

Adams, George, *Micrographia Illustrata: or, the Knowledge of the Microscope Explained* (first edition, London, 1746; fourth edition, 1771).

Adams, George, Jnr, *Essays on the Microscope; containing a Practical Description of the most Improved Microscopes: a General History of Insects, their Transformations, peculiar Habits, and Oeconomy . . .* (London, 1787).

Baker, Henry, *The Microscope Made Easy; or, I. The Nature, Uses, and Magnifying Powers of the best Kinds of Microscopes Described, Calculated, and Explained: For the Instruction of such, particularly, as desire to search into the Wonders of the Minute Creation, tho' they are not acquainted with Optics . . . II. An Account of what surprising Discoveries have been already made by the Microscope . . .* (London, 1742).

[Baker, Henry], *Micrographia Restaurata; or, the Copper-Plates of Dr Hooke's Wonderful Discoveries by the Microscope, Reprinted and fully Explained; Whereby the most Valuable Particulars in that Celebrated Author's Micrographia Are brought together in a narrow Compass; and Intermixed, occasionally, with many Entertaining and Instructive Discourses and Observations in Natural History* (London, 1745).

Baker, Henry, *Employment for the Microscope: In two Parts. I. An Examination of Salts and Saline Substances . . . II. An Account of various Animalcules never before described . . .* (London, 1753).

Bryden, David J. and Simms, D. L., 'Spectacles Improved to Perfection and Approved of by the Royal Society', *Annals of Science*, **50** (1993), 1–32.

Delves, J. and Highley, S., 'On the application of Photography to the representation of Microscopic Objects', *Transactions of the Microscopical Society of London*, n.s. **1** (1853), 57, plate 7. The first print of a photomicrograph published in a journal.

Dobell, Clifford, 'Leeuwenhoek's draughtsmen', in *Antoni van Leeuwenhoek and his 'Little Animals'* (London, 1932; reprinted New York, 1960), pp. 342–5.

Donné, Alfred, *Cours de Microscopie* (Paris, 1844).

Engelsman, S. B. (ed.), *Antoni van Leeuwenhoek, 1632–1723; Tentoonstelling in het Museum Boerhaave van 26 november 1982 tot en met 1 mei 1983* (Leiden, 1982); English translation by Brian Bracegirdle (ed.), *Beads of Glass: Leeuwenhoek and the Early Microscope* (Leiden, 1983).

Fournier, Marian, *Early Microscopes: A Descriptive Catalogue* (Boerhaave

Museum, Leiden, 2003).

Harris, John, *Lexicon Technicum: or, An Universal English Dictionary of Arts and Sciences* (two volumes, London, 1704 and 1710).

Hooke, Robert, *Micrographia, or Some Physiological Descriptions of Minute Bodies Made by Magnifying Glasses with Observations and Inquiries Thereupon* (London, 1665).

Joblot, Louis, *Descriptions et Usages de Plusieurs Nouveaux Microscopes* ... (Paris, 1718).

Ledermüller, Martin, *Mikroskopische Gemüths- und Augen- Ergötzung* (Nuremberg, 1763).

Malpighi, Marcello, *De Polypo Cordis* (Bologna, 1666).

Martin, Benjamin, *A New and Compendious System of Optics. In three Parts, viz. Part I. Catoptrics ... Part II. Dioptrics ... III. A Practical Description of ... Optical Instruments and Machines* (London, 1740).

Olley, W. H., *The Wonders of the Microscope, Photographically Revealed* (London, 1861).

Power, Henry, *Experimental Philosophy in Three Books: containing New Experiments, Microscopial, Mercurial, Magnetical* ... (London, 1663).

Spitta, Edmund J., *Photo-micrography* (London, 1899).

Turner, Gerard L'E., 'Henry Baker, F.R.S.: Founder of the Bakerian Lecture', in *Notes and Records of the Royal Society*, **29** (1974), 53–79.

Turner, Gerard L'E., *Essays on the History of the Microscope* (Oxford, 1980).

Turner, Gerard L'E., *Collecting Microscopes* (London, 1981); also published in Dutch, German and Italian.

Turner, Gerard L'E., *The Great Age of the Microscope* (Bristol and New York, 1989).

Varley, Cornelius, *Treatise on Optical Drawing Instruments* (London, 1845).

Wood, J. G., *Common Objects of the Microscope* (first edition, London, 1861; second revised edition, 1899; third edition, revised and rewritten 1938, reprinted 1949).

Zuylen, J. van, 'The Microscopes of Antoni van Leeuwenhoek', in *Journal of Microscopy*, **121** (1980), 309–28. Technical data on the extant simple microscopes.

Chapter 8

Springs, and Hooke's mechanical genius

Allan A. Mills

Hooke's place in the late Renaissance fell at a time when experimentation was being actively pursued and when fundamental advances were being made in basic new theories. It was in such circumstances that he not only joined in developing some of the theories but, almost uniquely, in discovering a profusion of ways in which their outcome could be pragmatically applied. In terms of everyday life, this aspect of his activities was the useful work of a brilliant technologist.

Amongst Hooke's many discoveries his name is probably most widely associated with the concept and use of springs and with Hooke's Law. His early work at Oxford, and later work, not only dealt with the 'springiness of air' – findings which led to Boyle's Law – but also with examples of what appeared to be 'springiness' in liquids. One of his earliest discoveries was that of surface tension, which appeared to show the existence of an elastic 'skin' on the surface of liquids. In an open-ended glass tube dipped into water the water rose somewhat, showing a positive meniscus, whereas when dipped into mercury the liquid lowered and showed a negative meniscus.

His chief exploits with mechanical springs included the investigation of simple straight wires and helical and spiral springs, and a study of the underlying principles of elasticity. Centuries passed before non-linear springs of the constant-tension and constant-force types were developed.

Such were Hooke's crucial contributions in a field which would provide some of the most basic engineering components and relationships.

Ordinary springs

Hooke's Law

In 1678 Hooke published a short work entitled *Lectures de Potentia Restitutiva, or, Of Springs*,[1] in which he formally proposed the rule: 'The extension of any spring is proportional to the tension upon it.' This has become known as Hooke's Law, and is perhaps the most popularly recognised discovery of this remarkable polymath. He relates that in fact he had discovered the principle some eighteen years previously (1660), but had deferred publication as he had 'some particular applications' in mind. This absence of a formal claim obviously worried Hooke, for at the end of his *A Description of Helioscopes* (1676) he included the anagram 'ceiiinosssttuu'. In *Of Springs* he assembled this into 'Ut tensio sic vis', which he translated as 'The power of any spring is in the same proportion with the tension thereof'. That is, if one power will stretch or bend it one unit, two will bend it two units, and so on. Another way of expressing this is that the restoring force exerted by a spring is proportional to the displacement from the rest position.

Experimental tests

Hooke's rule appears to have (at least initially) been based entirely upon experimental observations.

Straight wires The simplest arrangement Hooke employed was to clamp a long straight wire of drawn iron, steel or brass at an unyielding elevated point, and allow it to hang vertically with a scale pan at the lower end. He could then measure the distance of the pan above the ground consequent upon the addition of various weights, and prove that the stretching of a given wire was proportional to the load upon it.

Helical springs An awkwardly long straight wire is required to show an obvious extension under load. It is far more convenient to wind the wire around a cylindrical former to bend it into a helix (Figure 8.1). A minute torsional displacement is then integrated around the turns to appear as a substantial change in the overall length of the helix. Hooke noted the position of a weighted pan against a fixed scale to show that a linear displacement with load was characteristic and repeatable. He realised that he had invented a conveniently portable 'philosophical scales' that, as the spring balance, is still in common use.

It will be realised that a helical spring formed with spaces between the turns can also be compressed, exhibiting analogous behaviour.

Spiral springs Hooke states that if a pre-curved watch spring be placed within a light pivoted drum, and have its ends secured at the

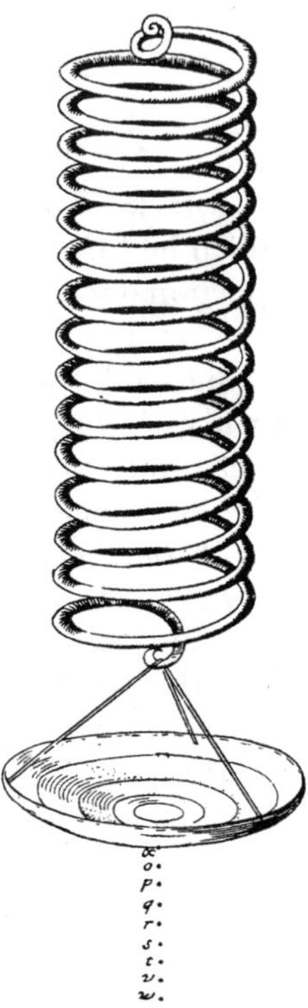

Figure 8.1. Investigation of a helical spring. (Hooke, *Of Springs*, 1678.)

axis and the periphery (Figure 8.2) then *provided no part of the spring touch any other part* (my italics) the rotation induced by a weight hanging from a thread wound around the outside of the drum is proportional to that weight. Calibration marks placed on the circumference of the drum and read against a fixed index would therefore produce another form of spring balance. However, such a device would have a limited range (<360°) since, besides confusion with the numbering, the linearity would fall off as portions of the spring came into contact with each other or with the case (see below).

Limitations of Hooke's Law

Elastic limit[2, 3] Hooke nowhere specifically states that there is a limit beyond which any stretched material no longer returns to its original dimensions. Instead, it takes up a permanent deformation or 'set' (see below). He was obviously aware of the phenomenon, as it is this property that enables wire to be coiled into a helical spring. The cylindrical

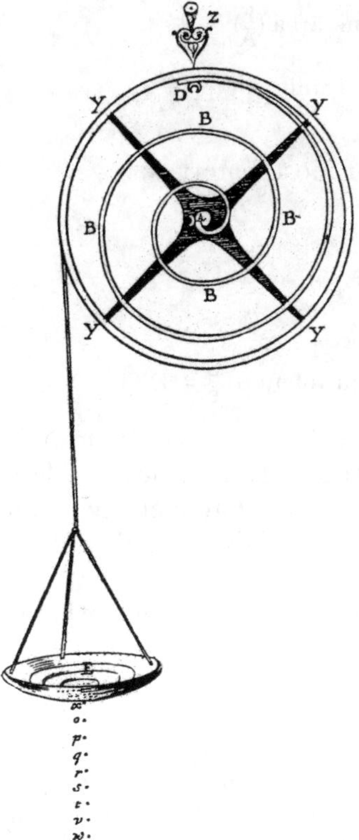

Fig. 8.2. Application of a spiral spring. (Hooke, *Of Springs*, 1678.)

former on which the helix is wound must be of lesser diameter than the intended internal diameter of the final spring.

Linearity The general usefulness of the spring balance and its derivatives shows that Hooke's Law is obeyed very closely, provided the load is not allowed to exceed a certain limit. Searle[4] claimed to have detected very tiny deviations from linearity – so small as to require special methods for their assessment – but it appears difficult to distinguish such small discrepancies from ordinary experimental error.

Young's Modulus

The quantitative relationship between tension and extension is specific to any given spring. Thomas Young[5] saw the need for a more general expression, but his wording is so convoluted that it can hardly be understood, even retrospectively. The present-day formulation is due to Thomson and Tait,[6] who first define:

Stress(σ) = Force per unit area $(\frac{F}{A})$

Strain(ε) = Extension per unit length $(\frac{\Delta l}{l})$

and then show that for most materials:

Stress α Strain

or

$$\frac{\text{Stress}}{\text{Strain}} \quad \text{constant (E), equivalent to } \frac{\sigma}{\varepsilon} = E$$

The constant of proportionality E is nevertheless known as Young's Modulus (of elasticity), and is a characteristic of a material in a defined (usually metallurgical) state. Again, it holds only below a certain limiting stress.

It may be shown that for a given spring working in the linear region:

$$k = \frac{EA}{l}$$

where *k* is the *spring constant* for that particular spring. It increases with the strength of the spring. It will be seen that increasing the cross-sectional area of its constituent wire, or decreasing its length, serves to strengthen a spring,

Graphical representation and definitions[7]

The changing length of a steel wire or helical spring in response to a varying applied force is most clearly illustrated by plotting stress against strain (Figure 8.3). For small values, when stress is proportional to strain, the graph is a straight line. This represents the linear (or Hooke) region for the material. Beyond the linear limit A the stress is no longer accurately proportional to the strain. However, up to the elastic limit or yield point B, the spring still returns to its original length when the applied force is removed. The deformation up to B is said to be elastic. If the force is further increased, the strain increases rapidly. In this region, if the applied force is removed the wire does not return completely to its original dimension, but retains a permanent deformation or set. Nevertheless, it can still behave linearly (dotted line), as shown by a helical spring wound in this way.

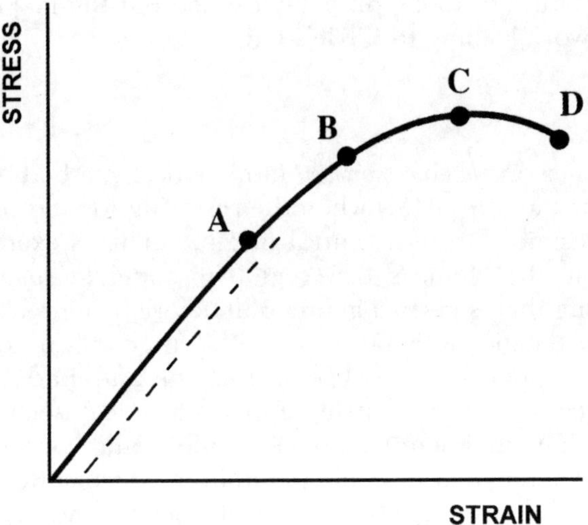

Fig. 8.3. Diagrammatic graph of stress *versus* strain for a typical spring steel wire.

The highest point C on the stress–strain graph is the ultimate tensile strength, or maximum endurable stress. Beyond this point, additional strain is produced even by a reduced applied force, and fracture occurs at point D. From B to D the material is said to undergo plastic deformation, and may 'neck down'. If C and D are close together the material is said to be brittle, and if they are comparatively far apart the material is ductile. In high-carbon steel these properties may be controlled by tempering. Spring steel wire (sometimes called 'piano wire') is treated to possess optimum spring-making properties.

A stress at an angle to the axis of a wire (a 'bending stress') will deform it into a curve, and some part of this curve will remain if the maximum stresses and strains (along the inside and outside of the curve) exceed the elastic limits of the material.

Other materials

Hooke's Law is generally associated with strong elastic solids such as steel and other metals, but also applies (within narrower limits) to materials like wood, horn, bone, tendon, and even masonry. Hooke himself, while working for Robert Boyle, found that 'the spring of the air' obeyed the analogous relationship:

Pressure x Volume = Constant

at constant temperature.[8] Hooke probably carried out the majority of the experimental work leading to Boyle's Law.[9]

Applications

Simple harmonic motion: the balance spring Mathematically, a body moves in simple harmonic motion (SHM) when the restoring force is proportional to its displacement from a central origin.[10] This is exactly the motion imparted in the Hooke's Law region to a weight suspended from a helical spring that is given a gentle pull before being released.

The vital characteristic of SHM is that the time taken for one complete oscillation ('period') is *independent* of the amplitude, so an oscillating weight controlled by a spring appears an ideal isochronous timekeeping element independent of excursion and orientation. Theoretically, it is better than a simple pendulum, which suffers from 'circular error'. Hooke was well aware of this property,[1] and his desire to apply it to portable timekeepers (and especially the longitude problem) was why he delayed publication of his relationship for so long. Two years earlier he had made a claim to this effect in *Helioscopes*, in a cryptic passage written in Wilkins' 'Real Character'. This passage has been translated by Andrade.[11] Wright[12] has suggested practical ways in which Hooke could have been experimenting with helical and other springs attached to a balance wheel. It was news of Huygens' essays into this field that forced Hooke to announce his ideas, and claim priority on a basis of informal private disclosures in the 1660s. It is uncertain whether Hooke utilised the very convenient flat spiral spring at this early date, but it seems very likely that he independently invented some form of balance spring.[13] The anchor escapement is more problematic.[14] The whole sorry story has been reviewed by Jardine.[15]

Subsequent developments[16] showed that other factors made the pendulum best for static, land-based installations; but the balance wheel fitted with a fine, widely spaced, spiral or helical spring proved pre-eminent for portable watches and chronometers for centuries. It was not replaced by the quartz crystal oscillator until the twentieth century.

Engineering and architectural construction Steel girders, wooden beams and thick masonry also – within limits – obey Hooke's Law in extension, compression and displacement. A vital part in the modern design of structures is calculation of stresses and movement, ensuring that these remain within safe limits even under extreme conditions. It is here that formulae based on Hooke's Law find major employment today.[17]

Non-linear springs

Hooke made it quite clear that his rule applied only to wires, springs or other elastic elements that hang completely free, and never come into contact with portions of themselves or some other component. If they do come into contact, then linearity may no longer be displayed. It is surprising how many springs in common use today do not obey Hooke's Law.

The mainspring

The traditional 'clockwork' clock, watch or toy obtains its power from a source of stored energy in the form of an initially more-or-less straight ribbon of steel wound into an enclosing drum.[10] One end is secured to the axle, and the other to the barrel. A ratchet on the axle enables the spring to be wound up into a tight coil tending to turn either component. The degree of bending exerted upon the fully-wound strip is usually sufficient to exceed its elastic limit, so that if subsequently released from the drum it assumes a loosely coiled spiral shape.

It is common knowledge that the moment ('power') exerted by the coiled spring decreases as it unwinds, and high-class clocks and watches would attempt to compensate for this by incorporating a tapered 'fusee'.[10] Practical clockmakers knew that due to friction and varying contact between the coils, the loss of power did not precisely follow a linear (Hooke) régime, so would experimentally machine the fusee to match a given spring-and-drum combination. This did not prevent more mathematically-minded horologists attempting to derive a theoretical section for the fusee.[10] Argument has continued until surprisingly recent times.[18]

Belleville washers

Perforated spring steel discs pressed into a concave dish shape are known as Belleville washers. Showing a strongly non-linear response to load,[19] they are occasionally placed beneath screw fastenings to give resistance to loosening as a result of vibration or thermal changes. A pile of Belleville washers placed alternately up and down along a stud provides a simple and powerful non-linear spring.

The constant-tension spring

Not for three centuries was it realised that the completely opposite situation to Hooke's – namely, a very highly deformed steel ribbon that remains tightly coiled in the 'resting' condition – possesses contrary properties that could be most valuable.

Wahl[19] claims that the principle was first enunciated by Axel Fornelius[20] in a U.S. patent dated 1934. A long ribbon of spring steel (nowadays, 18/8 stainless steel and various non-ferrous alloys complement carbon steel) is given a slight curvature across its width, and is then drawn by powerful machinery at an acute angle over a radiused edge. The yield point is exceeded on both top and bottom surfaces, the residual set then producing the desired resting form of a tightly-wound spiral. Further heat treatment may be given to ensure that this is a stable and reproducible condition (Figure 8.4(a)). (The phenomenon may be demonstrated by drawing a paper ribbon at a sharp angle across a finger nail or blunt knife.)

If the steel coil is then mounted so that it can rotate – say, by enclosing it in a cavity or pushing it upon a drum and axle – then its outer part may be extended by a force P (Figure 8.4(b)), the coil unwinding to suit. The magnitude of P is determined only by the work required to straighten the material in zone X from its coiled condition, and remains substantially the same throughout the uncoiling process. The force required to extend the ribbon is therefore nominally constant, producing a constant-tension (CT) spring.[21] The material in zone L is under stress, and the energy stored in it (proportional to its length) is available to exert a constant force or do work. It is possible to maintain the designed characteristics up to a length of some fifty times the diameter of the resting coil – a remarkable extension compared with conventional springs. Fornelius suggested the CT spring be employed to return the carriage in manual typewriters – and it was indeed used in this way. It will be apparent that if a smooth or stepwise variation in force is desired, then this may be achieved by appropriate adjustment of the width of the pre-coiled strip. However, such springs are unusual.

The above patent was assigned to Eastern Metals Research

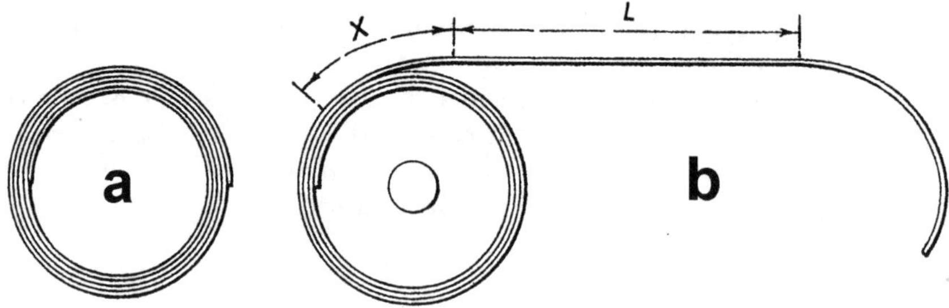

Fig. 8.4. The basic constant-tension spring: a, resting state; b, partially extended.

Corporation of the U.S.A., and was soon followed by a stream of others in this field. Manufacture was taken up by the Hunter Spring Company under the brand name 'Negator'. In the U.K., such springs were made and sold under the brand name 'Tensator'.[22] Manufacture has now passed to Spiroflex Ltd, of Milton Keynes.

Modern applications may be divided into unmounted, drum-mounted and motor springs.

Unmounted constant-tension springs

The action of a 'bare' CT spring is clearly visible in Figure 8.5, where it is acting as a simple book-end. A similar arrangement is used to maintain a constant pressure upon the brushes of electric motors.

Constant-force extension springs

If a CT spring is mounted upon a freely rotating drum, its free end provides a constant pull over a long distance in a more precise and controlled manner than the unmounted coil (Figure 8.6). It can therefore function as a counterbalance, but the assembly is much lighter and more compact than a weight suspended by a pulley and cord. An early application of this form of CT spring was therefore as a counterbalance for sash windows in railway carriages.[23, 24, 25] Remarkably, research has shown that exactly the same system – specifically claimed to provide a constant tension support for windows – was patented by Hiram Smith in the U.S.A. in 1871.[26] It is therefore surprising that the above patents were granted!

Constant-force retraction springs

Another family of drum-mounted CT springs serves to act as retraction springs. The inner end of the tightly coiled spiral is attached to a fixed stud, and the outer end to the inside of an enclosing co-axial rotatable drum (Figure 8.7). Motion of the latter is arranged to unwind the CT spring. A tape measure, flexible electrical cable, seat belt, dog lead or similar item stored on the outside of the drum may therefore be withdrawn under constant tension, and will rewind when a brake is released. Another application is the familiar 'Tensator' crowd-control barrier.

Constant-tension springs as motors

CT springs may be arranged in one of two ways to provide long-running constant torque spring motors. In both, the tightly wound

Fig. 8.5. The basic constant-tension spring used as a book-end.

Fig. 8.6. One of a range of constant-tension springs manufactured by
Spiroflex Ltd.

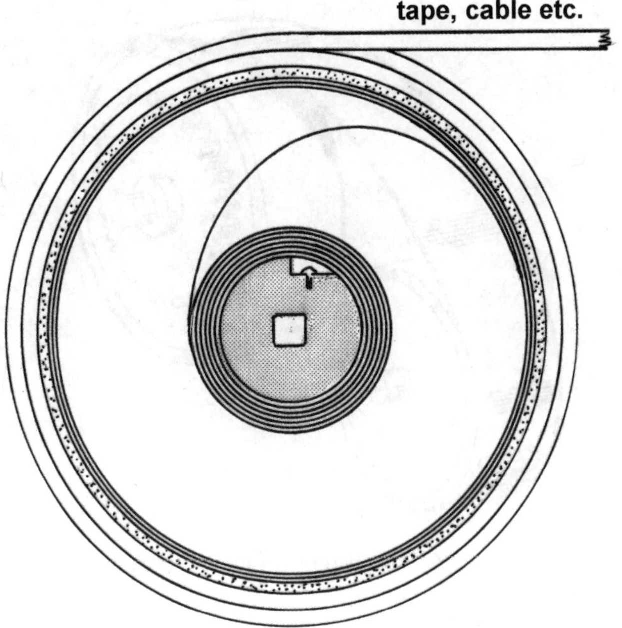

Fig. 8.7. Principle of the constant-force retraction spring.

spiral spring is mounted upon a small rotatable 'storage' drum, and the free end taken to a second, larger, 'torque' drum. It may then be wound in the same direction upon the latter, exerting a torque upon it to produce a Type A motor (Figure 8.8). If the direction of winding is reversed (Figure 8.9), the stress is increased and a greater torque exerted in the resulting Type B motor. It is achieved at a cost of diminished working life. Perhaps the best-known application of the Type B motor is in the 'wind-up' radio invented by Trevor Baylis.

Hooke's early experimental observations of elasticity in solids, gases and liquids constitute a remarkable contribution to technology. It was an accumulation of careful observations that led to Hooke's Law and to a succession of applications in ever more refined and sophisticated forms. Since the first discovery in the 1610s, there has been outstanding progress in the design and use of springs and in the understanding of the principles involved. The world will always be indebted to the most ingenious inventor Robert Hooke for his enduring contributions.

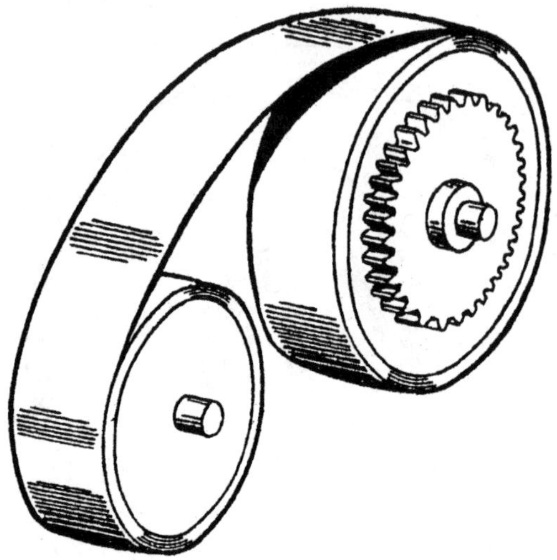

Fig. 8.8. Constant-tension motor, type A.

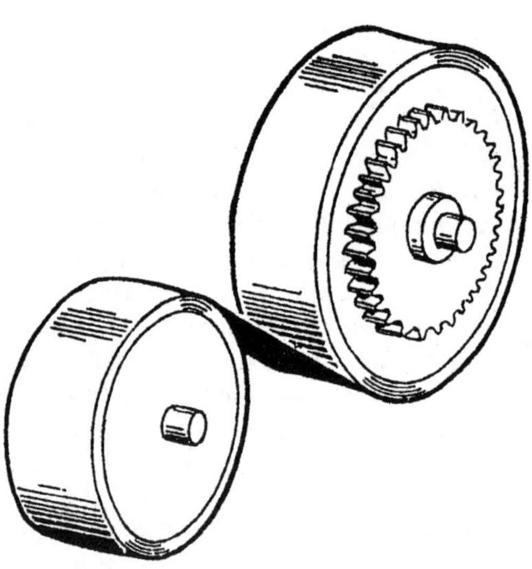

Fig. 8.9. Constant-tension motor, type B.

Notes and references

1 Robert Hooke, *Lectures de Potentia Restitutiva, or, Of Springs, Explaining the Power of Springing Bodies, to which are added Some Collections* (John Martyn, London, 1678); facsimile in Robert T. Gunther (ed.), 'The Cutlerian Lectures of Robert Hooke', *Early Science in Oxford*, **8** (Oxford, 1931).

2 E. Williams, 'Hooke's Law and the Concept of the Elastic Limit', *Annals of Science*, **12** (1956), 74–83.

3 B. Cotterell and J. Kamminga, *Mechanics of Pre-Industrial Technology* (Cambridge University Press, 1990).

4 G. F. C. Searle, *Experimental Elasticity* (Cambridge University Press, 1933).

5 Thomas Young, *A Course of Lectures on Natural Philosophy and the Mechanical Arts* (two volumes, London 1807).

6 W. Thomson and P. G. Tait, *Treatise on Natural Philosophy* (Oxford, 1867).

7 J. W. Kane and M. M. Sternheim, *Physics* (Wiley, 1984).

8 N. Mohler, 'The Spring and the Weight of the Air', *American Physics Teacher*, **7** (1939), 380–9.

9 F. F. Centore, *Robert Hooke's Contributions to Mechanics* (Nijhoff, The Hague, 1970).

10 A. L. Rawlings, *The Science of Clocks and Watches* (Pitman, London, 1948).

11 E. N. da C. Andrade, 'The Real Character of Bishop Wilkins', *Annals of Science*, **1** (1936), 1–12.

12 M. Wright, 'Robert Hooke's Longitude Timekeeper', in M. Hunter and S. Schaffer, *Robert Hooke: New Studies* (Boydell Press, Woodbridge, 1989), Chapter 3.

13 A. R. Hall, 'Robert Hooke and Horology', *Notes and Records of the Royal Society*, **8** (1951), 167–77.

14 E. N. da C. Andrade, 'Robert Hooke, 1635–1703', *Nature*, **171** (1953), 365–7.

15 L. Jardine, *Ingenious Pursuits* (Doubleday, 1999).

16 J. F. W. Bishop, 'Physics of Clocks and Watches', *Journal of Scientific Instruments*, **32** (1955), 289–93.

17 S. P. Timoshenko, *History of Strength of Materials, With a Brief Account of the History of Theory of Elasticity and Theory of Structures* (McGraw-Hill, 1953).

18 Various authors, 'Theory of the Fusee', *Horological Journal*, **137** (1995), 189, 232–5; **140** (1998), 122–3.

19 A. M. Wahl, *Mechanical Springs* (McGraw-Hill, 1963). The author succeeds in writing an entire text-book on springs without once mentioning Hooke's Law!

20 A. Fornelius, 'Spring Power Mechanism', U.S. Patent 1,977,546 of 16 October 1934.

21 F. A. Votta and P. A. Lansdale, 'Theory and Design of Long-Deflection Constant Force Spring Elements', *Transactions of the American Society of Mechanical Engineers*, **74** (1952), 439–50.

22 Anon., 'Constant Tension Spring', *The Engineer*, **202** (1956), 630.

23 B. Lermont and L. R. Birdsall, 'Window Actuating Mechanism', U.S. Patent 2,560,179 of 10 July 1951.

24 E. F. Foster, 'Spring Sash Counterbalance', U.S. Patent 2,609,193 of 2 September 1952.
25 C. Pernetta, 'Improvements in Controlling Mechanism for Windows, Doors, Panels and Like Sliding Elements', U.K. Patent 723,056 of 2 February 1955.
26 H. Smith, 'Improvement in Sash Balances', U.S. Patent 122,288 of 26 December 1871.

Chapter 9

The civic virtue of Robert Hooke

Michael A. R. Cooper

Although the importance and range of Hooke's scientific achievements are now generally recognised, details of his surveying, having been revealed only recently, are less well known.[1] The main purpose of this chapter is to show that his experience in science[2] led him to display civic virtue when working as London's City Surveyor in the aftermath of the Great Fire of September 1666. In order to see more clearly the significance of his surveying, some of his experimental science is discussed. A few other details of his life up to 1666 and a description of events in London around the time of the Fire are presented to explain why the City[3] chose him as a Surveyor. The chapter also contains evidence that Hooke made use of his early experience of surveying when writing his scheme for natural philosophy.

Experimental philosopher to surveyor

By appointing Hooke as one of the City Surveyors in the aftermath of the Great Fire, the wealthy merchants who ruled London departed from their traditional practice of appointing their surveyors from among London's master craftsmen. A seven-year apprenticeship as bricklayer, mason or carpenter, for example, followed by election to a livery company, admission to the freedom of the City, and years of successful practice designing, managing and supervising construction work, were prerequisites for appointment as City Surveyor. Such men were not simply craftsmen; their services to private and institutional clients resembled those now provided by 'design and build' companies. Robert Hooke's qualifications and experience, however, were very different.[4] Hooke was educated at Westminster School and later at Oxford, where he was a member of a group of outstanding scientists around John Wilkins (Figure 9.1) at Wadham College. In the late 1650s he moved to London with Robert Boyle, and on the foundation of the Royal Society in 1660 became its Curator of Experiments.

Hooke soon took on another prestigious appointment when in 1665, at the age of thirty, he was appointed Professor of Geometry at Gresham College. A little over a year later, in the immediate aftermath of the Great Fire, he was again 'head-hunted' – this time for the position of City Surveyor for New Buildings.

It is not immediately clear from Hooke's career up to that time why the City chose him for this important position. It placed him literally face-to-face with London's citizens in their desperation to rebuild their homes and businesses amid the rubble, civic confusion and rumours of insurrection which permeated the city after the Fire. There can be traced several influences on the development of Hooke's intellect and practical skills during his formative years at Westminster, Oxford and London which led the City to see in him the required qualities for their urgent task of rebuilding London.

Hooke's belief that practical mechanics had both moral and intellectual purpose probably began at Westminster School. When John Wilkins heard from Richard Busby, the Head Master, that the Westminster schoolboy Hooke had an exceptional mechanical talent, Wilkins presented Hooke with a copy of his little book on practical mechanics entitled *Mathematicall Magick* (Figure 9.2). The title seems surprising, given the empiricism and rationality of its contents, but it was deliberately chosen by Wilkins because:

> The art of such Mechanicall inventions as are here chiefly insisted upon, hath been formerly so styled; and in allusion to vulgar opinion, which doth commonly attribute all such strange operations unto the power of Magick.[5]

This volume is an early example of a science book marketed for general readership. Wilkins reminded the reader that when the followers of Heraclitus were ashamed to follow their teacher into a tradesman's shop, Heraclitus told them:

> The gods were as well conversant in such places as in others; Intimating that a divine power and wisdome might be discerned even in those common arts, which are so much despised; And though the manuall exercise and practise of them be esteemed ignoble, yet the study of their

Fig. 9.1. John Wilkins as Bishop of Chester. Engraving by Robert White. (Author's collection.)

general causes and principles, cannot bee prejudiciall to any other (though the most sacred) profession.[6]

A copy of *Mathematicall Magick*, published in 1648, was in Hooke's library at his death.[7] It is not too fanciful to think that it was the same copy given to him by Wilkins in 1648, or soon after, and that its contents determined Hooke's view of moral purpose in experimental philosophy, evident in his 'Preface' to *Micrographia*:

> By the addition of such artificial Instruments and methods, there may be in some manner, a reparation made for the mischiefs, and imperfection, mankind has drawn upon itself, by negligence and intemperance, and a wilful and superstitious deserting the Prescripts and Rules of Nature, whereby every man, both from a deriv'd corruption, innate and born with him, and from his breeding and converse with men, is very subject to slip into all sorts of errors.[8]

It should not be assumed, however, that moral purpose was the only or even the most important incentive to Hooke in his science. He also knew that power, wealth and fame could come to those who were the first inventors of useful mechanisms or the first to make use of new understanding of natural phenomena. Recognition that theoretical and applied mechanics were not only useful, but also intellectually and morally valuable, was not common in England at that time. The application of mechanics and mathematics was regarded with varying degrees of distaste, suspicion and hostility by many in positions of political or social power. The merchants and traders who ruled London in the seventeenth century showed no such niceties when, faced with the desolation and dangers of a ruined city and thousands of homeless citizens, they appointed Hooke as Surveyor for New Buildings.

Although Hooke's expertise in practical mechanics and his ability to understand and work with craftsmen were important to the City, his scientific use of that expertise was also valued. At Oxford, his first achievement in his work for Boyle was to accomplish what Ralph Greatorex – one of the best scientific instrument-makers in England – had failed to do: make a working air-pump for experiments on the properties of air.[9] Hooke later wrote:

> In 1658, or 9, I contriv'd and perfected the Air-pump for Mr Boyle, having first seen a Contrivance for that purpose made for the same honourable Person by Mr Gratorix, which was too gross to perform any great matter.[10]

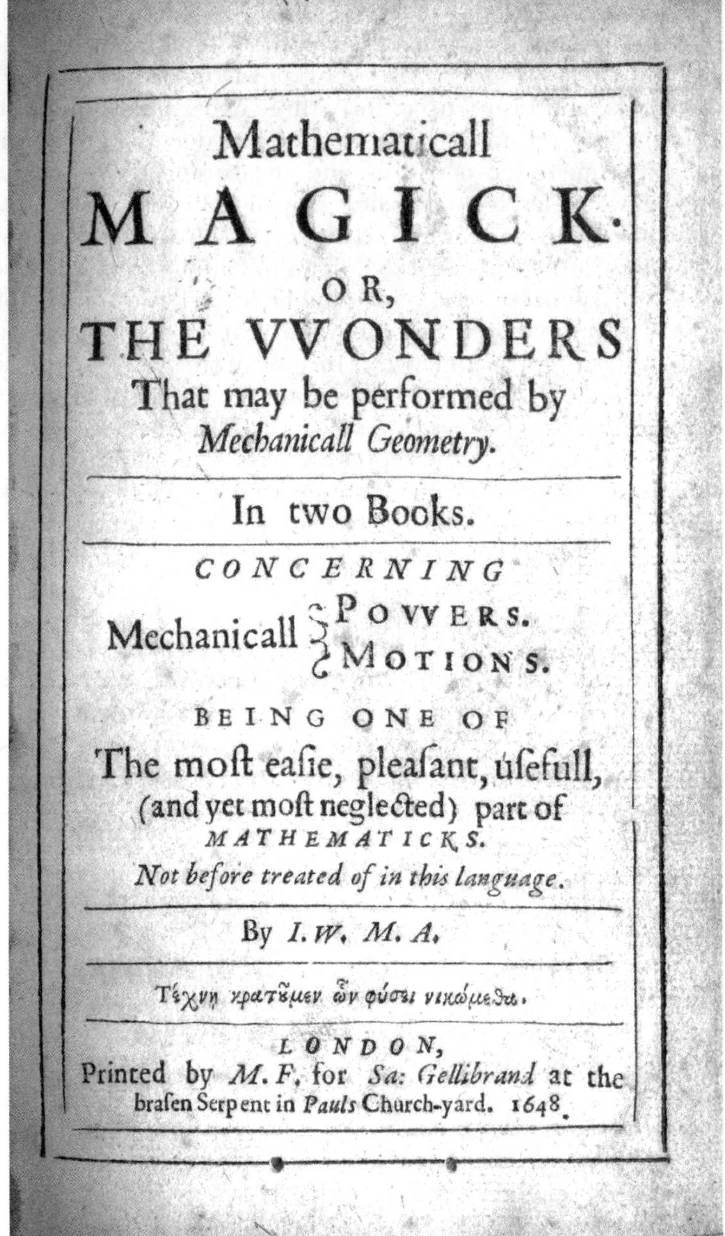

Fig. 9.2. The title-page of the first edition of John Wilkins' *Mathematicall Magic*, London, 1648. (Author's collection.)

Hooke understood why Greatorex's pump had failed and what should be done to rectify its defects, and by his redesign of the pump and choice of materials and workshop practices he ensured that a working pump was produced. Boyle acknowledged the contributions made by Hooke and his pump to forty-three experiments published in 1660,[11] but it was not until two years later that details were published of their experimental procedures and measurements (discussed in detail below) which led to what is now known as Boyle's Law.[12]

By the time of the Great Fire, Hooke was already well-known to leading figures in the City. In 1664 Sir John Cutler, a wealthy Grocer, endowed a salary for Hooke to give public lectures on the History of Trades in Cutler's name.[13] The following year Hooke was appointed Gresham Professor of Geometry.[14] Income from rents in the Royal Exchange (founded by the Tudor merchant Sir Thomas Gresham) was administered by the Trustees of Gresham's will to pay the salaries of seven professors appointed by representatives from the City and from the Mercers' Company. The committee which appointed Hooke as Gresham Professor was chaired by Sir John Lawrence – a well-respected City Whig who had courageously remained in London when he was Lord Mayor in the plague year of 1665. The immediate popularity of *Micrographia* – the first best-selling book of popular science, published by Hooke in 1665 – brought him wider fame. Soon after the Fire had died down, the City had further reason to be impressed – this time by Hooke's plan for the city's rapid recovery from disaster.

In the three weeks following the Fire, several layout plans for rebuilding a new city were produced by various men, including three leading members of the Royal Society: Christopher Wren, John Evelyn and Robert Hooke. The complex detail and careful draughtsmanship in some of these plans suggest that they could not have been produced from scratch within such a short time. The need to modernise London had been discussed at Court and in the City even before the Fire, and there can be little doubt that Wren, Evelyn, Hooke and others had been thinking and talking of what a new London should look like. The Fire now made major rebuilding both necessary and urgent. Hooke presented his layout plan first to the City in the person of Sir John Lawrence, who quickly showed it to the Royal Society, saying that the City had adopted Hooke's plan in preference to the plan devised by the present City Surveyor, the master bricklayer Peter Mills. The Royal Society, pleased at the news, affirmed that Hooke would be available to assist the City in its important work of rebuilding.

More than 80% of the city was destroyed by the Great Fire of September 1666. In only five days, thousands of citizens lost their houses and their livelihoods, the daily life of the crowded and bustling city was ruined, and lawlessness was imminent. The prisons, the courts of law and the administrative centre of Guildhall were made useless, the Royal Exchange and most of the livery company halls – the centres of the city's mercantile activities and trades – were destroyed, and more than a hundred parish churches were damaged beyond use. The desolation can be judged by contemporary reports that it was possible to see east–west from one side of the city to the other, and that the Thames was visible from Cornhill. The ground was covered by a layer of smoking debris – all that remained of timber-framed houses and shops. Surrounded by lath and plaster walls, generations of citizens had lived, sold their goods and worked at their trades. Here and there the remains of church spires stood above the rubble, as reminders of where the lost streets and houses had once been. Above all loomed the ruined gothic mass of St Paul's cathedral – a stark reminder of the extensive damage and the enormity of the task of restoration facing the rulers of the city.

Although most members of the City's Court of Aldermen had lost their houses and businesses and had much to attend to on their own accounts, they showed an admirable sense of civic duty. On 6 September 1666, while the city was still smouldering, they met, and acted quickly to stop riot and profiteering by showing that despite the ruinous state of the city and rumours that the Fire had been started deliberately, the restoration of order and normal commerce had begun. The King played his part by placing the army, under the command of the Duke of York, in the city, and tents for the homeless were erected in Moorfields. Relations between Court and City had to remain harmonious if further calamities were to be avoided.

At a meeting with the Privy Council in early October 1666, representatives of the City were told that the King had already appointed Hugh May, Roger Pratt and Christopher Wren as his Commissioners for Rebuilding, to work with three men to be nominated by the City. May and Pratt were experienced architects and administrators of large building works, but Wren was by far the youngest and least experienced of the three. The City responded by nominating two experienced master craftsmen – the carpenter Edward Jerman, and the City Surveyor, the bricklayer Peter Mills. Between them, May, Pratt, Jerman and Mills had decades of experience in the finance, management, design and construction of buildings. But the rebuilding now necessary was unprecedented in its extent and urgency. If not begun quickly, London's mercantile and business life might well be re-established elsewhere, probably to the east of the city wall, and the old City of London would cease to exist as a major financial and trading centre. Due to the unprecedented magnitude and urgency of building, and the desire to create a more beautiful city, it was highly probable that it would be necessary to devise new methods of organising and managing materials and workmen to construct new kinds of buildings. Men whose reputations had been made in the past would perhaps alone not ensure success in the future.

The King showed foresight in appointing Christopher Wren – a clever and ambitious young man – as his third Commissioner. Wren was already well known to the City, having, in 1657, been appointed Gresham Professor of Astronomy at the age of twenty-five.[15] The City had to respond with a nominee who had intellectual abilities and ambitions similar to Wren's and who could work harmoniously with him. They knew that Hooke and Wren – distant cousins, and friends for many years – were successfully working together in experimental science. Hooke's *Micrographia* had begun as a cooperative venture with Wren, and when he acknowledged Wren's contribution he said of him: 'I must affirm, that, since the time of Archimedes, there scarce ever met in one man, in so great a perfection, such a Mechanical Hand, and so Philosophical a Mind.'[16]

It was this combination of exceptional practical and intellectual abilities, possessed by both Wren and Hooke (although Wren became the senior partner), which would be needed if the rebuilding was to be successful. At a time when many thousands had suddenly become homeless and the complex social and economic life of a great city had collapsed, the City might have been accused of taking an undue risk in nominating Hooke as their third Surveyor of New Buildings. But it was a wise choice.

Science and surveying

Although measurements were characteristic of Hooke's science and of his surveying, they served different purposes in each case. In the experiments that led to Boyle's Law, Hooke's measurements were crucial, and his mechanical ingenuity and the procedures he devised for making and analysing measurements were ideal complements to the aristocratic Boyle's moral and social rectitude.

In the stairwell of Boyle's residence in Oxford they set up a cylindrical glass tube more than 9 feet (about 3 metres) long and bent into the shape of the letter J, the shorter arm being about 1 foot (0.3 metre) in height (Figure 9.3). With both ends of the J-tube open, a little mercury was poured in and allowed to settle to the same level in each arm. The end of the shorter arm was then sealed, trapping the air inside at the atmospheric pressure P_0. Successive quantities of mercury were poured

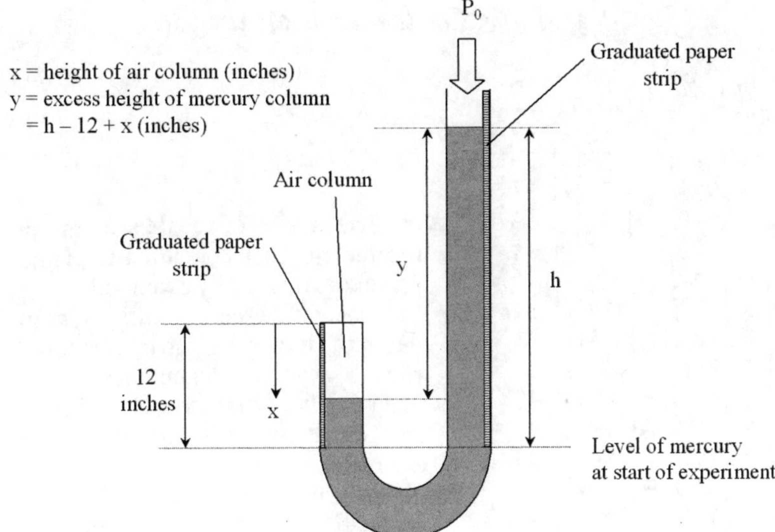

Fig. 9.3. Measurements made by Boyle and Hooke of levels of mercury inside a glass J-tube, which led to Boyle's Law.

into the longer arm and allowed to settle each time before readings were taken of the levels of the surface of the mercury in each arm against the adjacent graduated scale. The reading shown as x is proportional to the volume of the air trapped in the shorter arm,[17] while the pressure on the trapped air is the sum of y and the atmospheric pressure P_0 (in inches of mercury). Boyle's Law can be briefly stated as follows: the pressure and volume of a given mass of air at constant temperature are in inverse proportion; that is, $x(y + P_0)$ is a constant.

The numerical results of the experiment were published in tabulated form (Figure 9.4).[18] The first two columns (AA) show measured values of x in quarter-inches and in inches; the third column (B) shows the corresponding measured values of y, the excess height of the mercury in the long arm; the fourth column (C) shows the atmospheric pressure P_0 in inches of mercury; the fifth column (D) shows the pressures on the air in the shorter arm, determined by adding P_0 to each value of y; and the sixth column (E) shows what the pressures should be if the hypothesis that pressure and volume are in reciprocal proportion is true.[19] Boyle and Hooke described the experiment in great detail, but invited the reader to decide whether or not to accept the hypothesis, and urged others to perform experiments and publish details of their own procedures and measurements. In this way, acceptance or rejec-

A Table of the Condensation of the Air.

A	A	B	C (Added to $29\frac{1}{8}$ makes)	D	E
48	12	00		$29\frac{2}{16}$	$29\frac{2}{16}$
46	$11\frac{1}{2}$	$01\frac{7}{16}$		$30\frac{9}{16}$	$30\frac{6}{16}$
44	11	$02\frac{11}{16}$		$31\frac{15}{16}$	$31\frac{12}{16}$
42	$10\frac{1}{2}$	$04\frac{6}{16}$		$33\frac{8}{16}$	$33\frac{1}{7}$
40	10	$06\frac{3}{16}$		$35\frac{5}{16}$	$35\,\text{--}$
38	$9\frac{1}{2}$	$07\frac{14}{16}$		$37\,\text{--}$	$36\frac{15}{19}$
36	9	$10\frac{2}{16}$		$39\frac{1}{16}$	$38\frac{7}{8}$
34	$8\frac{1}{2}$	$12\frac{8}{16}$		$41\frac{10}{16}$	$41\frac{2}{17}$
32	8	$15\frac{1}{16}$		$44\frac{2}{16}$	$43\frac{11}{16}$
30	$7\frac{1}{2}$	$17\frac{15}{16}$		$47\frac{1}{16}$	$46\frac{3}{5}$
28	7	$21\frac{3}{16}$		$50\frac{5}{16}$	$50\,\text{--}$
26	$6\frac{1}{2}$	$25\frac{3}{16}$		$54\frac{5}{16}$	$53\frac{10}{13}$
24	6	$29\frac{11}{16}$		$58\frac{13}{16}$	$58\frac{2}{8}$
23	$5\frac{3}{4}$	$32\frac{2}{16}$		$61\frac{5}{16}$	$60\frac{18}{23}$
22	$5\frac{1}{2}$	$34\frac{15}{16}$		$64\frac{1}{16}$	$63\frac{6}{11}$
21	$5\frac{1}{4}$	$37\frac{15}{16}$		$67\frac{1}{16}$	$66\frac{4}{7}$
20	5	$41\frac{9}{16}$		$70\frac{11}{16}$	$70\,\text{--}$
19	$4\frac{3}{4}$	$45\,\text{--}$		$74\frac{2}{16}$	$73\frac{11}{19}$
18	$4\frac{1}{2}$	$48\frac{12}{16}$		$77\frac{14}{16}$	$77\frac{2}{3}$
17	$4\frac{1}{4}$	$53\frac{11}{16}$		$82\frac{12}{16}$	$82\frac{4}{17}$
16	4	$58\frac{2}{16}$		$87\frac{14}{16}$	$87\frac{3}{8}$
15	$3\frac{3}{4}$	$63\frac{15}{16}$		$93\frac{1}{16}$	$93\frac{1}{5}$
14	$3\frac{1}{2}$	$71\frac{5}{16}$		$100\frac{7}{16}$	$99\frac{6}{7}$
13	$3\frac{1}{4}$	$78\frac{11}{16}$		$107\frac{11}{16}$	$107\frac{7}{13}$
12	3	$88\frac{2}{16}$		$117\frac{9}{16}$	$116\frac{4}{8}$

AA. The number of equal spaces in the shorter leg, that contained the same parcel of Air diversly extended.
B. The height of the Mercurial Cylinder in the longer leg, that compress'd the Air into those dimensions.
C. The height of a Mercurial Cylinder that counterbalanc'd the pressure of the Atmosphere.
D. The Aggregate of the two last Columns *B* and *C*, exhibiting the pressure sustained by the included Air.
E. What that pressure should be according to the *Hypothesis*, that supposes the pressures and expansions to be in reciprocal proportion.

Fig. 9.4. Published data from the J-tube experiments which led to Boyle's Law. (Robert Boyle, *A Defence Of the Doctrine touching the Spring and Weight Of the Air* (London, 1662), p. 60. Royal Society.)

tion of the hypothesis would come through general agreement based on accumulating evidence, and not through the authority or reputation of an individual. Here we see the first publication of experimental data in a form which is now commonplace in science, in which measured values are presented alongside the predicted values in order to show whether or not a particular hypothesis is acceptable. The closer the measured values are to the predicted values, the more confident we can be in accepting the hypothesis.

A recent statistical analysis of the measurements published by Boyle and Hooke has shown how well they demonstrate the validity of the hypothesis.[20] The standard deviation of the measurements is ±1.6 mm

– a surprisingly high precision, even though we know Boyle and Hooke used magnifying glasses to read the positions of the mercury meniscus against the scales. The measurement residuals (which can be regarded as 'corrections' to the measurements which will make them conform to the hypothesis 'pv is constant') are all less than the value of the standard deviation, and give no indication that significant systematic errors are present in the measurements. The statistics lead to the conclusions that the J-tube was very well made and that painstaking and cooperative observational procedures were followed. It is probable that the published results are not the outcome of just one experiment, but are average values taken from many repetitions. Boyle's Law can be regarded as much Hooke's as it is Boyle's. Hooke went on independently to perform and report similarly in other experiments, but Boyle's work thereafter was different. Hooke's scientific observations and measurements were characterised by high measurement accuracies, patience in making and using apparatus, and wary publication of reports; but he abandoned such characteristics when he came to make measurements in surveying.

Although the King and the City wanted to build a grand, completely new city to demonstrate to the world that national and civic power and pride had not been diminished, it soon became clear that the idea was impracticable. The cost and time necessary to purchase thousands of land parcels from citizens to provide space for a new layout of streets and public places, and to then return new land parcels to private owners, would be unacceptable to London's inhabitants. Rebuilding would therefore take place mainly on the old foundations. Regulations had to be devised which would lead to significant improvements in the appearance and convenience of the city. Hooke's first surveying task took place during the exceptionally cold winter of 1666–67, when he represented the City in drafting the building regulations for the parliamentary rebuilding acts.

Members of the Royal Society had scientific evidence of the importance of light and air to life, and it is probable that Wren and Hooke ensured that the draft legislation would allow fresh air and light to enter more freely into the hitherto cramped and enclosed spaces between the houses. Other members of the Royal Society (John Evelyn and Sir Robert Moray, for example) supported the draft proposals at Court and in Parliament. The Rebuilding Acts[21] went as far as was feasible to ensure that the new city would be a healthier and more pleasant place in which to live. The Acts classified new buildings according to their locations, and specified the form and maximum height of each class. All walls were to be made of brick or stone, and were to be built vertically from the ground up. The old timber-framed buildings with upper stories jetting out above crooked, narrow lanes leading only into small enclosed yards were all forbidden, and noxious trades such as soap-making, distilling and metal-working were to be confined to specific locations. The Acts provided for some existing streets to be widened or straightened and their gradients eased, and a few new streets were defined. The old street markets were to be relocated in open spaces, new sewers and water supplies would be laid and covered by paving, and places were set aside for laystalls[22] and houses of common ease-ment.[23] Fleet Ditch would be canalised and made navigable as far as Holborn Bridge, with broad new wharves along each side, and a new broad quay alongside the Thames from the bridge to Temple Gardens – an idea much favoured by the King – was also included in the Acts. To pay for these unprecedented public works, a new tax on coal was levied. All the improvements drafted by the King's Commissioners and City Surveyors were realised – except the Thames quay, as the money and the will to finish it had been exhausted by the other improvements.

The Rebuilding Acts set up Fire Courts specifically to deal with disputes about tenancies, leases, rents and disagreements about who should pay the costs of private rebuilding. Although under the Acts the City had the authority and obligation to carry out public works, admin-ister the new building regulations and settle disputes arising from rebuilding (other than those dealt with by the Fire Courts), they dele-gated to the Surveyors the responsibility and obligation to do what was necessary. More often than not, Hooke was involved, and from the outset he took on the leading role. The City had nominated Mills, Hooke and Jerman as Surveyors, but Jerman preferred to work for private clients, and Mills was ill; and when Mills died soon after rebuilding had begun, the City appointed the glazier John Oliver in his place. Hooke was the only City Surveyor who worked throughout the rebuilding programme. He did as much routine surveying in private rebuilding as Mills and Oliver together, and took on nearly all the surveying for public rebuilding.[24]

In March 1667 Hooke and Mills had begun to stake out new and widened streets – a task which took only seven weeks. The double lines of timber stakes driven into the rubble revealed the skeleton of the new street alignments, and everyone could see where and how much private ground was being lost, and by whom. The speed with which the staking-out was completed, and the small number of complaints that arose, are evidence that the Surveyors' actions were accepted by the great majority of the citizens. As Mills and Hooke measured with their rods and scales, and aligned stakes by eye, those watching could see for themselves that one side of a street being widened was not favoured at the expense of the other, and that the work was being carried out fairly, in accordance with the Rebuilding Acts and the City's published documents.[25]

The amount of compensation for ground taken away depended on its area and location. The dimensions of each area of lost ground were measured by a Surveyor, who calculated the area and gave to the claimant a certificate giving the location of the site, its dimensions and its area. The claimant then presented the certificate to the City Chamber, where a clerk calculated the amount of compensation, usually at the rate of 5 shillings per square foot.[26] An order was then written and given to the claimant for payment six months later. Hooke issued more than three hundred certificates of lost ground – about half the total. There can be no doubt that he knew that Surveyors' measurements of lost ground were generally insufficient to calculate areas. The procedure was to multiply the length of the frontage to the street by the average of the depths of ground lost at each side. It was correct only if the shape of each parcel of lost ground was trapezoidal, rectangular or square, but such regularity was unusual in the mediaeval streets and buildings, and ground was being taken to remove irregularities from the street alignments. A more accurate procedure would have been to define each shape more rigorously by taking additional measurements such as the length of a diagonal or the angles between adjacent sides; but it would have added considerably to the time spent taking measurements and calculating areas, and would have made only a small difference to the amount of compensation payable. The high accuracy which Hooke sought so assiduously in scientific measurements was not appropriate when performing his civic duties, and he therefore traded high accuracy for expediency.

One of Hooke's area certificates[27] (Figure 9.5) records his measurements of a piece of ground taken from 'a foundation belonging to Mr. Eaglesfeild formerly now in the possession of Coll. Clegat' for the widening of Little East Cheap. The dimensions are 21 feet 8 inches along the frontage, 7 feet 8 inches at the west end, and 7 feet 5 inches at the east end, and his calculation of the area is written in the left-hand margin. He writes the frontage as $21\frac{2}{3}$ feet and the average depth as $7\frac{1}{2}$ feet (7 feet $6\frac{1}{2}$ inches is the accurate value), and multiplies $\frac{2}{3}$ foot by 7 feet and writes 5 square feet ($4\frac{2}{3}$ square feet is the accurate value). He then multiplies $\frac{1}{2}$ foot by 21 feet to give $10\frac{1}{2}$ square feet, and 7 feet by 21 feet to give 147 square feet, but does not bother to evaluate $\frac{2}{3}$ feet by $\frac{1}{2}$ foot ($\frac{1}{3}$ square foot). The sum of these three products is $162\frac{1}{2}$ square feet – the approximate area of a parcel of ground roughly trapezoidal in shape. The speed with which the measurements and calculations were carried out justified the inaccuracies. The manuscript also shows a clerk's calculation, by means of a

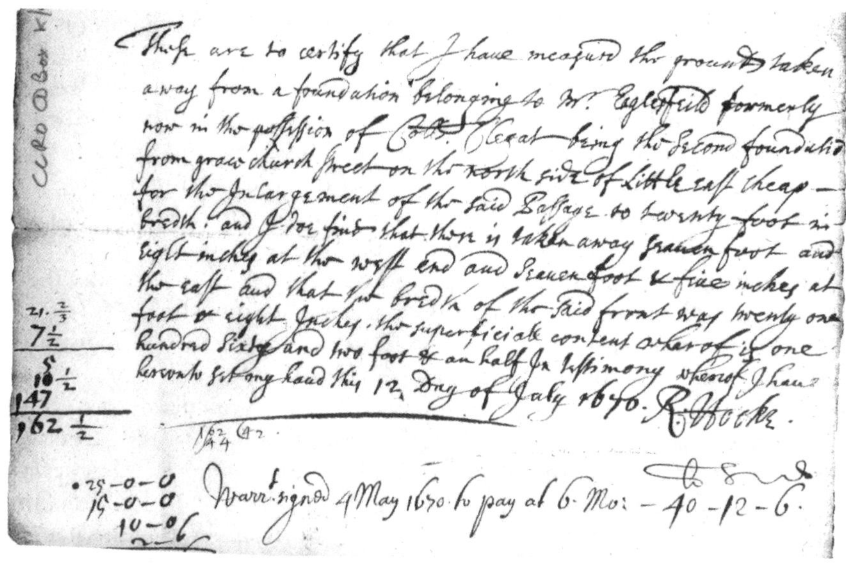

Fig. 9.5. One of Hooke's certificates for ground compulsorily purchased for widening streets. (Corporation of London Records Office Comptroller's Deeds Box K/C/21. Corporation of London.)

ready-reckoner, of the compensation payable at a rate of 5 shillings per square foot (£40 12s 6d). In this certificate Hooke uses decimal fractions, but more often he used duodecimal fractions in his mental arithmetic.

No private rebuilding could begin until a foundation was staked out, measured and certified by a Surveyor. The certificate included information such as the place and date of the survey, the dimensions of each foundation staked out, and names of the recipient of the certificate and of the neighbours. Demands for this service were heavy, and sometimes as many as twenty requests for staking out foundations were made in a day. The sum of 6s 8d (a third of a pound) for each foundation was paid to the City Chamberlain's office by the person responsible for rebuilding. This money – known as the Foundation Cash – was used by the City to pay the Surveyors' annual salaries of £150. Hooke certified more than 3,000 of the 8,000 foundations.

Although primary records of nearly all these foundation surveys are now lost, transcriptions of Mills' and Oliver's survey books, produced by the City in the eighteenth century, were later published in facsimile.[28] Hooke, however, refused to hand in his survey books to the City. They were therefore not transcribed, and after his death they may have been considered as having no importance, and were probably destroyed. From the secondary records it has been possible to find measurements of the sides of a few contiguous foundations and to fit them together numerically, as in a mosaic. Statistical analyses of the measurements of the sides and of the small gaps and overlaps that arise when the foundations are fitted together show that the measurements were made with standard deviations of about $\pm 3\frac{1}{2}$ inches (± 10 cm), which is less accurate than was possible at that time using surveyors' bands, rods and chains.[29] Here again we see high accuracy abandoned for civic necessity.

When private rebuilding began, complaints inevitably arose between neighbours. Allegations were made of infringements of rights to light, or drainage, or access. Party walls were a common source of complaint. The cost of rebuilding a party wall had to be paid initially by the person rebuilding first, but finally had to be shared equally. Sometimes the second neighbour refused to pay because no holes had been left in the brickwork for his joists. In many cases the new vertical party walls resulted in all or part of an upper room which formerly extended over a neighbour's lower room being lost to the advantage of the neighbour. These intermixtures of interest had to be investigated and settled by payment of appropriate compensation by one neighbour to the other. There were frequent allegations of encroachments into a passageway or onto a neighbour's ground, and dangerous encroachment sometimes took place below ground level when a neighbour extended a cellar below the foundations of the party wall into space beneath the neighbour's building. Other complaints were brought to the City alleging infringements of the Rebuilding Acts involving use of illegal materials, excessive building heights, frontages projecting over the streets, poor workmanship, prohibited workshops, and illegal garrets. All of these complaints had to be investigated by the Surveyors, who reported in writing to the City the evidence that they had found and what settlement they had arranged, subject to the City's approval. The complexity of the allegations and counter-allegations, and the general intransigence of the parties involved, made views (reports) far more demanding on the Surveyors' time and patience than certifying lost ground and new foundations, but in fewer than 1% of about a thousand views did the matter go beyond the jurisdiction of the City, acting on the Surveyors' recommendations. Hooke produced at least 550 views on infringements.

In his work as City Surveyor, Hooke came face-to-face with literally thousands of individual Londoners when he certified their lost ground, staked out their foundations, and took views of their complaints and allegations. The citizens, eager to resume normal domestic and business life, demanded a speedy and efficient service from the City and from its Surveyors in particular. Hooke's services to private citizens were in most demand throughout the seven years from mid-1667, during which period he spent most of his mornings (except Sundays) on his duties as Surveyor. He kept his own careful record of places, people and measurements, so that even after an interval of more than ten years he could find all the information necessary to write a repeat certificate to replace one that had been lost. Much of his time during those mornings was spent either in the city's streets taking measurements, looking for evidence of earlier foundations in the rubble, taking note of oral and written evidence in a dispute, or in coffee houses and inns, writing his reports. His movements around the city were public knowledge. He was readily available to anyone who needed his services; and if anyone wanted to find him, they could do so.

In addition to their annual salaries of £150, the Surveyors received negotiable fees from their clients for certifying areas of lost ground, issuing foundation certificates, and taking views. Varying from a few shillings to a few guineas, but generally not more than a guinea (£1 1s), these fees brought considerable wealth to the Surveyors – particularly Hooke, who undertook more work than either Mills or Oliver. It has been estimated that in the eight years immediately after the Fire, Hooke was paid more than £1,600 by the citizens of London for his services as Surveyor – a measure of the value of his work to his clients.[30] In contemporary records of his thousands of private transactions, no evidence has yet been found that he was anything other than scrupulously fair and astonishingly efficient.

As private rebuilding began to slow down, so the rate of the City's own rebuilding programme increased. The City relied on Hooke to decide on all administrative and technical matters relating to new works, and he found little respite from his civic duties.. He drew up designs, recommended which contractors should be employed and approved wage rates for their workmen, made frequent inspections of construction work in progress, and wrote many lengthy reports to the City on the quality of materials, workmanship, and contractors' bills of quantity. He also attended the regular meetings of the City Lands Committee, which gave him the responsibility of seeing that its decisions were implemented quickly, efficiently and economically. He had to overcome exceptional difficulties in the two most important rebuilding schemes: the canalisation of Fleet Ditch, and the construction of a broad new quay along the north bank of the Thames. The first brought unexpected technical problems which were overcome by cooperation between himself and Wren, and his relationship with Sir John Lawrence – 'my one true friend'[31] – enabled the three men to persuade the City to fund a succession of increases in the cost of the work. The

Thames quay scheme, on the other hand, ultimately proved impossible to complete, due to political and social disputes which might have been overcome if more finance had been raised; but the City had exhausted its money and its will to raise more by the efforts to complete the canalisation of Fleet Ditch.

The close cooperation between Hooke and Wren can also be seen in the rebuilding of St Paul's cathedral and the parish churches. They worked in close partnership, and transformed the way in which large construction works were designed and managed.[32] From 1671 to 1693 Wren authorised payments amounting to £2,820 to be paid to Hooke from the fund for rebuilding churches.[33] Such a large sum (about half the cost of rebuilding a large London church) is evidence of the major contribution Hooke made to the rebuilding of London's parish churches. During his frequent visits to the construction sites, confident of Wren's trust in him, he was able to decide on the quality of workmanship and of materials, and authorise alterations to the design as the need arose. He relieved Wren of much detailed, onerous, but essential work, and ensured that the churches were rebuilt as quickly as possible. The cooperation between the two friends and scientific colleagues can also be seen in the construction of the Monument in Fish Street Hill, which they intended to be a zenith telescope as well as a memorial to the recovery from the disastrous Fire. Wren obtained the King's approval of Hooke's design and subtly deflected the City from its intention to surmount the column with a gilded statue of Charles II, which would have prevented its use as a telescope.[34]

Hooke's most comprehensive statement of what he thought should be the grounds of natural philosophy was found, undated, among his papers after his death, and was published posthumously by Waller in 1704.[35] Hooke titled his statement: 'A General Scheme, or Idea, of the Present State of Natural Philosophy, and how its Defects may be Remedied by a Methodical Proceeding in the Making Experiments and Collecting Observations Whereby to Compile a Natural History as the Solid Basis for the Superstructure of True Philosophy.' The use of analogies from building practice to explain his ideas, evident in the title, was taken much further by Hooke in the early part of the work when he wrote about collecting a 'Philosophical History',

> ... which shall be as the Repository of Materials, out of which a new and sound body of Philosophy may be raised ... and indeed until this Repository be pretty well stored with choice and sound Materials, the Work of raising new Axiomes or Theories is not to be attempted, lest beginning without Materials, the whole Design be given over in the middle, for out of this are to be taken the Foundation Stones, on which the whole Structure should be raised, and those ought to be propor-

tioned according to the rest of the Materials; for otherwise there may follow great Inconveniences, in prosecuting of it, here therefore there ought to be laid up the more substantial Parts: But as for the most curious and precious things which may serve for the finishing, or compleating this grand Structure, they are to be sought for as occasion shall require and prompt. For as in any great building, none can be so perspicacious as to forsee every particular thing he shall need, for the compleating of it, but leaves the Care of providing them till occasions call for them, as being then best able to judge which of that kind of Material which is wanting will be most fitting for his purpose ... and so from time to time furnishes himself with those more choice things, as the Occasions require ... thereby his Work would be carried on the more compleatly and uniformly, without Necessity of pulling down, or altering, or piecing, or transforming any part, or staying or interrupting.

The Case is much the same in providing a proper History for the perfecting of a new Body of Philosophy, the Intellect should first like a skilful Architect understand what it designs to do, and then consider as near as can be, what things are requisite to be provided in order to this Design, then those Materials are to be sought for and collected, and safely laid up in so convenient an Order, that they may not be far to seek when they are wanting, nor hard to come by when they are found: In the choice of which, Care ought to be taken that they are found and good, and cleans'd and freed from all those things which are superfluous and insignificant to the great Design; for those do nothing else but help to fill the Repository, and to incumber and perplex the User, yet notwithstanding, Brevity is not so much to be studied, as to omit many little Circumstances which may be considerable in the use of it, for as in the laying up of Timber, the keeping on a branching part does make it serviceable for many Designs which it would be wholly unfit for, if it had been squared off, so it will be in the fitting and preparing the Particulars for a Philosophical History.[36]

Although 'A General Scheme ...' is undated, the forgoing extract, full of references to architecture and building, is a strong indication that Hooke wrote it at a time when he had already thought about planning the rebuilding of London – possibly as early as November 1666, when he took on his first building survey. He was asked by the Gresham Trustees to examine the ruins of the Royal Exchange and advise them on its rebuilding. He reported that by cleaning and reusing many damaged materials, the Royal Exchange could be rebuilt for the modest sum of about £4,000. His advice was rejected. The Gresham Trustees favoured a grand new building which would show the world that London had emerged from disaster richer and more powerful than before. The extravagant decision cost twelve times as much as the rebuilding proposed by Hooke. More than forty years later, when the

Gresham Trustees were beset by debt, Hooke successfully fought against their petition to Parliament for permission to sell Gresham College.[37]

As the rebuilding of London neared completion, the City decided that a new map of the city was necessary as an aid for administration and for planning new public works. Hooke was given the task of directing the surveying and cartography. The map would have to be geometrically accurate and at a commensurate scale. It would have to show physical details such as buildings, streets, lanes, courtyards, docks and wharves, and other information such as ward and parish boundaries and the types of buildings depicted. A method would also have to be devised for identifying on the map the major buildings and all thoroughfares, markets, and other important locations. It would be unlike any other map of London that had been produced. But the City had no money to finance the enterprise. Hooke therefore brought in John Ogilby,[38] an entrepreneurial map publisher, in a sort of public–private partnership with the City. Hooke managed the project, dealing with William Leybourne for the surveying and Wenceslaus Hollar for the engraving and printing.

Accuracy was now paramount. Hooke knew that traditional methods of field surveying – with plane table, chain, circumferentor and magnetic needle – would not work well for large-scale mapping of an urban environment. In their place he devised a network of interconnected polygons running through the streets (Figure 9.6), with sides and internal angles which could be measured and subsequently plotted using scale ruler and protractor. Features adjacent to the sides of each polygon could be located by measuring and plotting chainages along the lines and perpendicular offsets from them. The main consideration for deciding on the map scale was the accuracy of manual plotting. It was impossible to plot by unaided eye to an accuracy better than 0.01 inch (0.25 mm), but at the convenient scale of 1/1,200 (1 inch to 100 feet) the plotting accuracy is equivalent to 1 foot on the ground. Conventional rods and chains would therefore be adequate for linear measurements. For angular measurements, 1 foot on the ground is equivalent to an accuracy of $\frac{1}{2}°$ over a distance of 120 feet, although most distances were less than this, so existing angle-measurement instruments reading to $\frac{1}{2}°$ (Figure 9.7) would therefore be adequate. If the map scale were smaller, its accuracy and usefulness would decrease. If it were larger, the costs would increase through the need for more accurate instruments and procedures, and more map sheets. Although Hooke was the most ingenious designer of scientific instruments of his time, he made no instrumental innovations for large-scale urban mapping, because there was no need to do so.

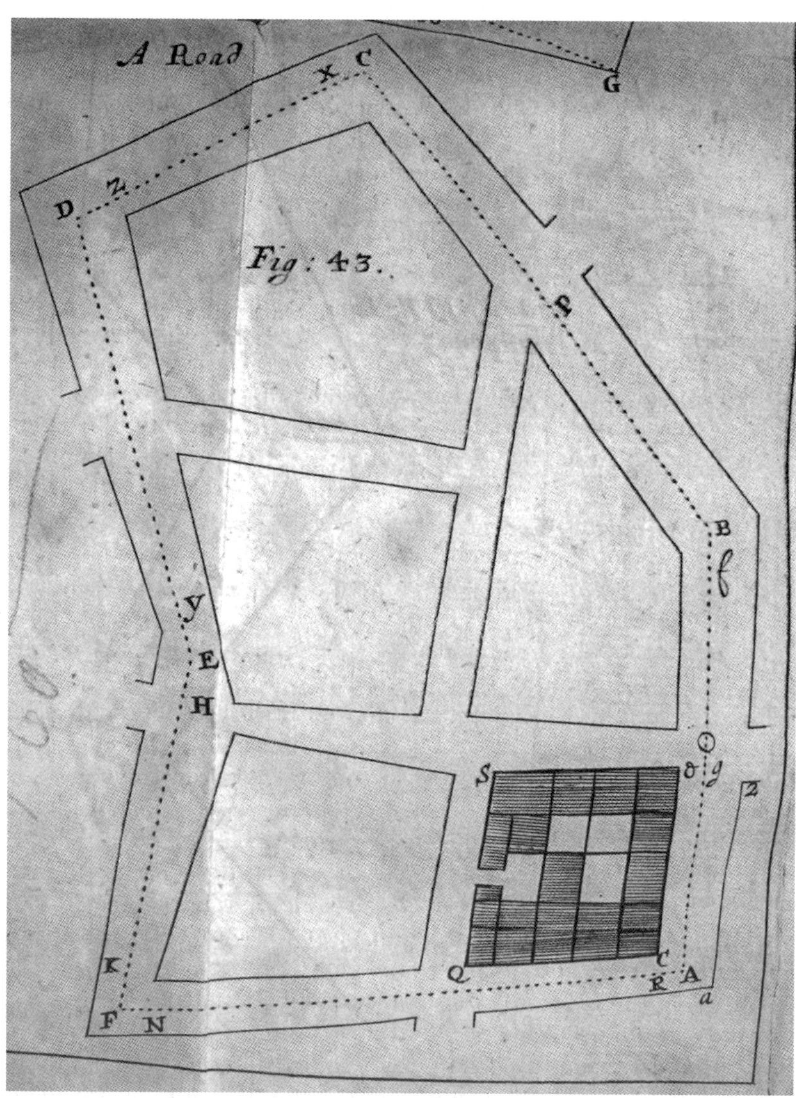

Fig. 9.6. The polygonal layout of survey lines used for mapping the rebuilt City of London. John Holwell, *A Sure Guide to the Practical Surveyor in Two Parts*, London, 1678, fig. 53. (Graves 124.c.2. University College London Library Services.)

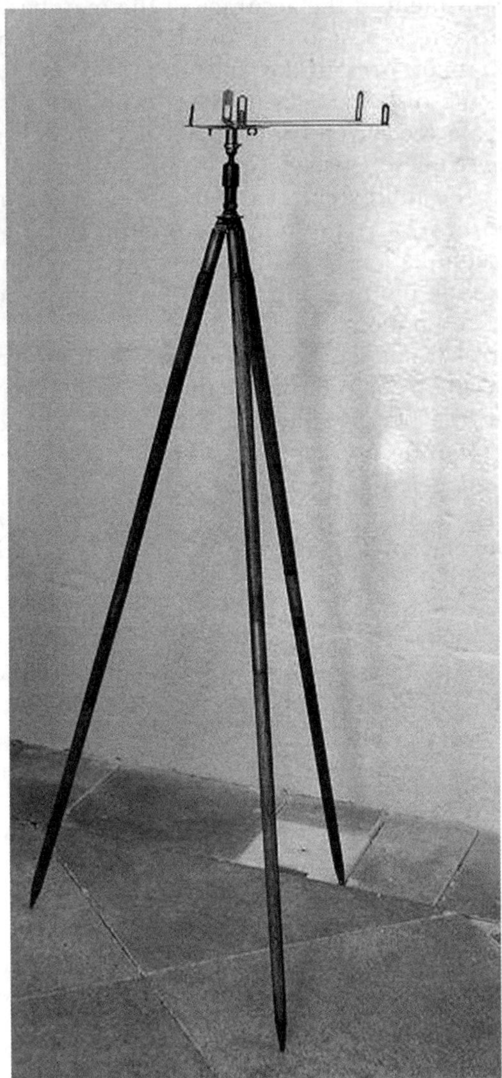

Fig. 9.7. An English semicircle and tripod of the type used for measuring the angles in the polygons illustrated in Figure 9.6. (Inv. no. 17420, Museum of the History of Science, Oxford.)

A statistical assessment of the accuracy of the map has recently been made by comparing the positions on it of corners of buildings still in existence, with their present-day positions on Ordnance Survey maps.[39] Locally, the discrepancies in relative positions are no greater than would be expected, given the probable distortions of a number of successive paper copies between the original plot and the modern version.[40] Across the full extent of the map (about 3 km east to west) the discrepancies in relative positions are up to about 5 metres, probably due to the accumulation of errors as successive polygons were fitted together by manual plotting methods. Discrepancies of this order would not have been noticeable at the time.

Although Hooke found no need to make innovations in surveying instruments, he made significant changes to the management of surveying and to the cartography of urban areas. A land surveyor in England at that time was an independent practitioner whose measurements were not subjected to the regular scrutiny of his peers, but were justified by his particular experience, skills and reputation. Hooke changed that convention. A small team of surveyors would be required, and he divided up the city and allocated each area to a particular surveyor. It was essential that each surveyor's plotted polygons fitted together not only within his own area, but also with the polygons in adjacent areas. Hooke ensured that the inevitable discrepancies were resolved by agreement through rational debate and cooperative remeasurement – a typically scientific practice. A surveyor's age, social status, previous reputation or wealth could no longer determine the outcome of a disagreement over measurements.

Hooke's cartographic design was equally innovative. Hitherto, large-scale maps and plans of London were in the form of 'bird's-eye' views, at uncertain and variable scales. Hooke's mapping of the rebuilt city was mathematically rigorous: an orthogonal projection onto a horizontal plane at a defined scale. Although orthogonal projection was frequently used for plotted surveys of particular buildings, Hooke was able to extend the method across London by maintaining accuracy through the framework of polygons, as triangulation was impractical in London's streets. The number of individual map sheets and the boundaries between them had to be decided. Hooke had always shown an inclination for frugal use of engraved plates – as evident in some of his multiple illustrations in *Micrographia* – and he settled on a scheme for twenty individual map sheets to cover the city, without undue wastage of space on any plate. He designed various symbols and shading to depict administrative boundaries and different classes of building (Figure 9.8), and also devised a system for finding particular places on the map from a catalogue of place names and a coordinate

Fig. 9.8. Detail of Ogilby and Morgan's 1676 map of the rebuilt City of London, reproduced at reduced scale. The original scale is 1/1,200. (Guildhall Library, Corporation of London.)

reference system. The map was published by Ogilby's step-grandson William Morgan in 1677, shortly after Ogilby's death. Now known as 'Ogilby and Morgan's map of London', a copy of the sheets, mounted and framed, hangs on a wall in Guildhall. It is an impressive sight, about $1\frac{1}{2}$ metres high and nearly 3 metres wide – a silent tribute to Hooke's scientific outlook and management skills.

Conclusion

Overall, it has been shown that Hooke's experimental science was characterised by innovative design and meticulous use of instruments, high accuracy in measurement, painstaking procedures, and wary publication of results. His surveying, however, was often routine, accurate enough for the particular purpose, and immediately reported. Only when he judged that traditional methods of surveying were inadequate did he introduce new practices and direct others to carry them out efficiently. He brought an intense and organised energy to his work, and during the first few years after the Fire spent six mornings a week on his surveying. Despite meeting the individual demands of thousands of his fellow citizens, desperate to rebuild their homes and livelihoods, no evidence has been found that he was anything other than impartial in his judgments and astonishingly efficient in performing and recording his work. He had the trust of the City and of his fellow citizens. He showed civic virtue by applying to his surveying the Baconian principles of cooperative observation and rational thought, by helping to draft for Parliament and then apply the civil law, and by his work in creating a healthier and more pleasant city.

Notes and references

1 Michael A. R. Cooper, 'Robert Hooke's work as Surveyor for the City of London in the aftermath of the Great Fire', *Notes and Records of the Royal Society*, **51** (1997), 161–74; **52** (1998), 25–38, 205–20.

2 The terms 'natural philosophy' and 'natural philosopher' were commonly used in the seventeenth century for what we would now refer to as 'science' and 'scientist' respectively – words which came into use in the nineteenth century. Here they are used interchangeably, with the addition of 'experimental philosopher' as someone who seeks truth about the natural world, particularly by performing experiments.

3 'City' is used here to mean the officers and members of the various committees and courts who ruled London; 'city' is used to refer to the geographical city and liberties of London.

4 Recent publications on Hooke's life and work include: Stephen Inwood,

The Man Who Knew Too Much (Macmillan, London, 2002); J. A. Bennett, M. A. R. Cooper, M. Hunter and L. Jardine, *London's Leonardo: The Life and Work of Robert Hooke* (Oxford University Press, 2003); Michael A. R. Cooper, *'A More Beautiful City'. Robert Hooke and the Rebuilding of London after the Great Fire* (Sutton, Stroud, 2003); and L. Jardine, *The Curious Life of Robert Hooke: The Man Who Measured London* (Harper Collins, London, 2003).

5 John Wilkins, *Mathematicall Magick* (London, 1648), sig. A4v-5r.

6 Ref. 5, sig. A4r.

7 Leona Rostenberg, *The Library of Robert Hooke* (Modoc Press Inc., Santa Monica, California, 1989), p. 197.

8 Robert Hooke, *Micrographia, or Some Physiological Descriptions of Minute Bodies Made by Magnifying Glasses with Observations and Inquiries Thereupon* (London, 1665), sig. a1r.

9 J. A. Bennett, *The Mathematical Science of Christopher Wren* (Cambridge University Press, 1982), pp. 17, 40, 74.

10 Richard Waller (ed.), *The Posthumous Works of Robert Hooke, M.D., F.R.S.* (London, 1705), p. iii.

11 Robert Boyle, *New Experiments Physico-Mathematicall, Touching the Spring of Air and its Effects* (Oxford, 1660).

12 Robert Boyle, *A Defence Of the Doctrine touching the Spring and Weight of the Air* (London, 1662).

13 Michael A. R. Cooper, in J. A. Bennett *et al.*, *London's Leonardo* … (ref. 4), pp. 11–13.

14 Michael A. R. Cooper, in J. A. Bennett *et al.*, *London's Leonardo* … (ref. 4), pp. 23–6.

15 Wren had resigned in 1661 when he was appointed Savilian Professor of Astronomy at Oxford.

16 Hooke, *Micrographia* (ref. 8), sig. g2r&v.

17 Assuming the cross-sectional area is constant throughout the range.

18 Boyle, *A Defence* … (ref. 12), p. 60.

19 It can be deduced that Boyle and Hooke calculated the constant k from pv = k using the initial pair of values for p and v, and then used this value for k to calculate subsequent values of p from p = k/v.

20 Michael A. R. Cooper and Marek Zeibart, 'Twenty-first-century analysis of seventeenth-century measurements', paper presented at Internationales Wissenschaftshistorisches Symposium Anlässlich des 400. Geburstages Otto von Guericke, Otto-von-Guericke-Museum, Magdeburg, 28 November 2002.

21 18/19 Charles II, c.8 of 8 February 1667; and 22 Charles II, c.11 of 11 April 1670.

22 Places where rubbish could be piled up awaiting collection.

23 Public latrines.

24 Cooper, *'A More Beautiful City'* (ref. 4), pp. 95–220, discusses details of Hooke's surveying.

25 For example, two hundred copies of the City's Act of Common Council, setting out details of the new street alignments, were printed by James

Flesher, the City's Printer: Corporation of London Records Office Printed Document 10.54(L).

26 About £2.70 per square metre.

27 Hooke's area certificate: Corporation of London Records Office Comptroller's Deeds Box K/C/21.

28 *The Survey of Building Sites in the City of London after the Great Fire of 1666* (London Topographical Society, London), **3** (1962 (a)), **4** (1962 (b)), **5** (1962 (c)), **2** (1964), **1** (1967).

29 James Brennan, *As-Burnt Surveys* (unpublished M.Sc. project report, Department of Geomatic Engineering, University College London, 1998).

30 Cooper, *'A More Beautiful City'* (ref. 4), pp. 41–2.

31 Henry W. Robinson and Walter Adams (eds.), *The Diary of Robert Hooke, M.A., M.D., F.R.S., 1672–80 (transcribed from the original … in Guildhall Library)* (Taylor and Francis, London, 1935, reprinted 1968), p. 125, 7 October 1674.

32 Jacques Heyman, 'Hooke and Bedlam', paper presented at the Hooke conference at the Royal Society, 6–10 July 2003 (Royal Academy of Engineering).

33 Guildhall Library, MS 25,548, pp. 17–19.

34 Cooper, *'A More Beautiful City'* … (ref. 4), pp. 198–205.

35 *Posthumous Works* (ref. 10), pp. 1–70.

36 *Posthumous Works* (ref. 10), p. 18.

37 Cooper, *'A More Beautiful City'* … (ref. 4), pp. 120–5.

38 Katherine S. Van Eerde, *John Ogilby* (Dawson, Folkestone, 1976).

39 Caroline Mayo, *Is the 'A to Z of Restoration London' Accurate?* (unpublished M.Sc. project report, Department of Geomatic Engineering, University College London, 2001).

40 London Topographical Society, *The A to Z of Restoration London*, introduction by Ralph Hyde (London Topographical Society, London, 1992).

Index

Adams, George, 137, 138, 139, 140, 143
Adams, Walter, 31
air pump, 2, 54, 61, 75, 97, 164, 166
Akers, W.A., 38
All Souls College, 6, 54, 57
Allstree, Richard, 42, 49, 58
anatomy, 51, 60
architecture, 75, 116, 152, 178
area certificates, 173, 174
Aske, Alderman, 24
Aston, Francis, 70
astronomy, 53, 67, 75, 95
atherosclerosis, 30
Aubrey, John, 1, 9, 11, 12, 24, 29, 34
Auzout, Adrien, 103, 119

Bacon, Francis, 15, 18, 35, 49, 67, 134
Bacon, Nicholas, 67
Baker, Henry, 135, 136, 137, 143
Ball, Peter, 65, 120
Ball, William, 120
Banks, Joseph, 53
barometer, 75, 97
Bathurst, George, 57, 63
Baylis, Trevor, 157
Bethlehem Royal Hospital, 3
Bion, Nicholas, 31
Bloodworth, Thomas, 36
Bodleian Library, 43
Boyle, Robert, 1, 2, 14, 16, 19, 20, 21, 29, 39, 49, 51, 53, 54, 55, 56, 60, 61, 62, 64, 65, 67, 68, 71, 128, 162, 166, 168, 169, 170, 171

Boyle's Law, 2, 89, 166, 168, 169, 170, 171
Brahe, Tycho, 15, 66, 96
British Museum, 6
Brouncker, Viscount, 21, 57, 65, 69, 71, 114
Bruce, David, 65
Bruno, Giordano, 67
Burlington, Lord, 3
Burnet, Bishop, 80
Busby, Richard, 2, 12, 34, 46, 47, 162
Button, R., 58

Campani, Giuseppe, 97, 99, 106
Canterbury College, 44
Cassini, G.D., 98, 100, 103, 106, 109, 116, 118, 120, 122
cell biology, 1, 6
Charles I, King, 12, 39, 40, 43, 52, 53, 67
Charles II, King, 3, 4, 24, 36, 41, 61, 67, 84, 89, 128, 131, 167, 171, 172, 177
Charles Louis, Prince, 52
chemistry, 49, 57, 60, 75
Christ Church, 2, 11, 13, 19, 31, 32, 38, 41, 44, 45, 58, 59, 60, 65
City of London, 14, 20, 24, 116, 161
City University, 7
Civil War, 39, 40, 67
Clarendon, Lord, 14
Clayton, Thomas, 52, 53
clocks/watches, 1, 2, 16, 54, 75, 89, 97, 114, 152, 153
Cock, Christopher, 127

188   *Robert Hooke and the English Renaissance*

coffee houses, 20, 25, 29, 41, 67, 68
combustion, 1, 3, 49, 89
comets, 4, 16, 89, 108, 122
Commonwealth, 40
continental drift, 85, 86, 87, 91
Conway, Lord, 3
Copernicus, Nicholas, 15, 95, 96
Cornish, H., 58
Covenant, 40
Creed, William, 58
Crew, Nathaniel, 57
Cromwell, Henry, 53
Cromwell, Oliver, 13, 39, 40, 43, 52, 53, 57, 58, 67, 70
Cromwell, Richard, 58, 60
Cromwell, Robina, 57, 70
crystals, 1, 2, 16
Cutler, John, 68, 73, 89, 166

Darwin, Charles, 4
Deijl, Harmanus van, 125
Descartes, René, 15, 16
diabetes mellitus, 49
diseases, 54
Divini, Eustachio, 97, 106
Dolben, John, 42, 49, 58
Dollond, John, 125
Donné, Alfred, 143
Drake, Francis, 15, 18
Duncan, Robert, 88
Durham cathedral, 41
Durham College, 57, 58, 60

earthquakes, 4, 80, 93
eclipses, 114
Elizabeth I, Queen, 47, 67
Espinasse, Margaret, 31
Evelyn, John, 2, 20, 44, 70, 71, 120, 166, 171
evolution, 1, 4
Exeter College, 53

Fairfax, Thomas, 44
Fell, John, 42, 49, 57, 58, 59
Fell, Samuel, 13, 41, 42, 45, 63
flames, 111, 112
Flamsteed, John, 113
flight, 52, 54, 121
Fontana, Francisco, 104

Fornelius, Axel, 154
fossils, 4, 10, 80, 81, 90
Foucault, J.B.L., 143
Fox Talbot, Henry, 143
Fox, George, 58
French Academy, 143

Gale, Thomas, 70, 73
Galilei, Galileo, 15, 18, 66, 95, 97, 99, 104, 113, 115, 120
Galler, Johannes C., 115
Gardiner, Richard, 44, 58
Gascoigne, William, 119
gases, 1, 2
Gaudy Oration, 31, 38
gears, 1
geology, 6, 75, 89, 91
Gilbert, William, 15
Giles, Ann, 11
Glorious Revolution, 84
Goddard, Jonathan, 53, 65, 118, 121
Goodman, Cardell, 11, 13, 33, 63
Goodman, Mr, 47
gravity, 16, 17, 23, 77, 89, 111, 122
Great Fire, 1, 3, 20, 72, 89, 161, 162, 166
Greatorex, Ralph, 164, 166
Gresham College, 2, 4, 6, 7, 14, 21, 22, 23, 29, 30, 31, 35, 38, 57, 61, 62, 66, 69, 90, 93, 98, 116, 162, 179
Gresham, Thomas, 166
Grew, Nehemiah, 70, 71, 73
Guildhall Library, 31
Gunther, Robert T., 31

Halley, Edmond, 82, 84, 89
Harris, John, 128
Hartsoeker, Nicolaas, 128
Harvey, William, 15, 18, 52, 63, 64, 66, 127
health, 27
heliocentric theory, 95, 96
Henry VIII, King, 67
Henshaw, Thomas, 70
Hevelius, Johannes, 98, 108, 122
Hill, Abraham, 65, 70, 71
Hobbes, Thomas, 60
Hollar, Wenceslaus, 179

Holmes, Mary, 22
Holmes, Robert, 22
Hooke, Cecillie, 8, 9, 11
Hooke, Grace, 22, 23, 25
Hooke, John (brother), 11, 22, 23, 29, 33
Hooke, John (father), 8, 9, 11, 12, 29, 30, 33, 40
Hooke's Law, 146, 147, 148, 149, 152, 157
Hoskins, John, 71
Hoskyns, John, 9, 12
Hunt, Harry, 116
Hunton, Philip, 57
Hutton, James, 75, 76, 85, 89
Huygens, Christiaan, 2, 54, 89, 97, 98, 99, 100, 104, 115, 116, 120, 122

Inwood, Stephen, 73, 74
iris, 1, 75

James I, King, 67
James II, King, 36, 84
Jerman, Edward, 167, 172
Jones, Richard, 70
Jones, William, 3
Jupiter, 99, 110, 116, 119

Kelsall, Frank, 37
Kepler, Johannes, 18, 96
King, Bishop, 44
King, Henry, 44
Kneller, Godfrey, 19
kyphosis, 28

Lawrence, John, 20, 29, 35, 166, 176
Ledermüller, Martin, 137, 141
Leeuwenhoek, Antoni van, 124, 127, 128
Lely, Peter, 2, 12, 40
Lester, John, 37
Leybourne, William, 179
Lichfield, Peter, 59
light, 1, 2, 17, 89, 111, 134
Lincoln College, 57
Lister, J.J., 143
Locke, John, 39, 46, 47, 51, 53, 57, 60, 63

Longley, H., 58
Lord, Doll, 22
Lower, Richard, 51, 57, 60

magnetism, 15, 97, 111
Malpighi, Marcello, 124, 128
Mars, 96, 99, 102, 104, 116, 121, 122
Marshall, John, 127, 128
Maunder, E. Walter, 114
May, Hugh, 167
Mayne, Jasper, 58
Mayow, John, 51, 89
Mears, Monica, 22
Mercers' Company, 14, 166
Mercury, 114
Merton College, 52, 53
meteorology, 75
microscopy, 1, 2, 3, 60, 95, 124
Milles, John, 58
Millington, Thomas, 51
Mills, Peter, 166, 172, 174, 176
milometer, 1
Montague, Lord, 3
Monument, 6, 89, 177
Moon, 95, 96, 106, 114, 115, 119, 134
Moore, Jonas, 114
morals, 23
Moray, Robert, 65, 68, 171
Morgan, William, 183, 184
Morley, George, 58
Morris, Tony, 119, 121

Nachet, A., 143
Neile, Paul, 65, 118, 121
Newham, Thomas, 14
Newton, Isaac, 6, 19, 20, 23, 31, 53, 60, 71, 76, 77, 78, 79, 80, 81, 88, 89, 90, 91, 96

octant, 1, 4
Ogilby, John, 179, 183, 184
Oldenburg, Heinrich, 70
Oldenburg, Henry, 19, 70, 71, 72, 73, 77, 120
Oliver, John, 172, 174, 176
Olley, William, 143
Orchard, Bette, 22

Owen, John, 41, 49, 60, 61, 63
Oxford Philosophical Society, 82
Oxford University, 40, 41

Paynter, J., 58
Pembroke College, 52, 53
Penn, William, 60, 61
Pepys, Samuel, 1, 8, 20, 68, 69, 71
Petty, William, 53, 65
plate tectonics, 86, 88
Pleiades, 104, 115
Pocock, Edward, 58
polar wander, 79, 81, 82, 85, 86, 87, 88, 91
Pott, Perceval, 28
Potter, John, 37
Pott's Disease, 28, 37
Pratt, Roger, 167
Ptolemy, Claudius, 15, 95, 96

Ragley Hall, 3
Ramsbury Manor, 3
Ranelagh, Lady, 21, 62, 70
Raspé, Erich R., 85
Rebuilding Acts, 171, 172, 173, 175
Reeves, Richard, 104, 121, 127
religion, 23
respiration, 1, 3
Restoration, 58
Reynolds, Edward, 41, 45, 58, 60
Rhea, 116
Richer, Jean, 81
Robinson, Henry W., 31
Rogers, Christopher, 58
Rogers, T., 38
Rooke, Lawrence, 65
Royal College of Physicians, 3
Royal Exchange, 166, 167, 178
Royal Institution, 6
Royal Microscopical Society, 143
Royal Observatory, Greenwich, 4
Royal Society, 1, 2, 6, 8, 10, 14, 15, 19, 20, 23, 25, 30, 31, 32, 38, 53, 57, 60, 61, 62, 65, 76, 79, 89, 90, 93, 98, 106, 109, 113, 116, 118, 120, 127, 128, 131, 134, 137, 144, 162, 166, 171

Sanderson, Robert, 58
Saturn, 96, 99, 102, 103, 108, 120, 122
Saye and Sele, Lord, 52
Scheiner, Christoph, 113
scoliosis, 28
sextant, 75
Shaftesbury, Earl of, 51
Sheldonian Theatre, 59
Short, T.V., 38
Smith, Hiram, 155
Smith, Sebastian, 58
spirit level, 1
Spratt, Thomas, 39, 62
springs, 1, 17, 54, 89, 114, 146
St Helen's church, 26, 30, 90
St Paul's cathedral, 3, 4, 5, 26, 89, 167, 177
St Peter's church, 26
Stahl, Peter, 57
stars, 96, 97, 115, 134
Stenonis, Nicolaus, 75, 89, 92
Stone, Edmond, 31
Stubbe, Henry, 46
Sun, 95, 96, 97, 99, 113
surveying, 161, 162, 168, 179, 180
Sydenham, Thomas, 54

Taylor, Bridget, 21
telescopes, 96, 97, 98, 99, 113, 115, 118, 119, 124, 125, 134, 177
Test Acts, 25, 27, 36
thermometer, 75
Tillotson, Elizabeth, 21
Tillotson, John, 26
Titan, 99
Tompion, Thomas, 2, 21, 35
Townley, Richard, 26, 119
Trapezium, 104, 115
Trinity College, 53
tuberculosis, 28

University press, 59

Venus, 96, 104, 115, 116

Wadham College, 39, 42, 47, 51, 57, 60, 61, 65, 97, 108, 128, 162

Wall, John, 41, 58
Waller, Richard, 9, 11, 19, 20, 27, 28, 30, 31, 98, 109, 177
Wallis, John, 39, 53, 57, 71, 82, 83, 84, 85
Ward, John, 6
Ward, Seth, 14, 39, 53, 62, 98, 118
waves, 17, 111
way-wiser, 53
Wegener, Alfred, 76, 85, 87
Westfall, Richard, 78
Westminster School, 2, 12, 13, 19, 46, 47, 65, 162
Whiston, William, 130
Whitrow, G.J., 38
Whittington, Richard, 37
Wilkins, John, 2, 14, 15, 26, 39, 43, 51, 54, 57, 60, 61, 62, 65, 68, 70, 97, 98, 108, 117, 152, 162, 163, 164, 165
Wilkinson, H., 58
Willen, 47

William of Orange, 84
Williams, Abigail, 21
Williamson, Joseph, 57, 71
Willis, Thomas, 14, 19, 25, 39, 42, 47, 48, 49, 51, 59, 60, 62
Wilson, James, 128
wind gauge, 53, 75
Wood, Anthony, 49, 51, 57
Wood, J.G., 142
Wood, Robert, 57
Wren, Christopher, 1, 2, 3, 4, 6, 14, 20, 25, 29, 31, 39, 46, 47, 51, 54, 57, 60, 65, 71, 89, 98, 108, 117, 118, 120, 121, 128, 166, 167, 168, 171, 176, 177

Yarwell, John, 127, 128
Young, Nell, 21, 22, 35
Young, Thomas, 6, 149

Zollman, Philip, 66